Inequality and Prosperity

A volume in the series

Cornell Studies in Political Economy

EDITED BY PETER J. KATZENSTEIN

Inequality and Prosperity

SOCIAL EUROPE VS. LIBERAL AMERICA

JONAS PONTUSSON

A Century Foundation Book

Cornell University Press

ITHACA AND LONDON

First published 2005 by Cornell University Press
First printing, Cornell Paperbacks, 2005

Printed in the United States of America

Library of Congress Cataloging-in-Publication Data
Pontusson, Jonas.
    Inequality and prosperity : social Eruope vs. liberal America / Jonas Pontusson.
        p. cm. – (Cornell studies in political economy)
    Includes bibliographical references and index.
    ISBN-13: 978-0-8014-4351-0 (cloth : alk. paper)
    ISBN-10: 0-8014-4351-2 (cloth : alk. paper)
    ISBN-13: 978-0-8014-8970-9 (pbk. : alk. paper)
    ISBN-10: 0-8014-8970-9 (pbk. : alk. paper)
        1. Income distribution–Europe, Western.   2. Income distribution—United States.
3. Capitalism–Europe, Western.   4. Capitalism–United States.   5. Welfare state–Europe, Western.   6. Welfare state–United States.   7. Europe, Western–Economic conditions–1945–
8. United States–Economic conditions–1945–   I. Title.   II. Series.
    HC240.9.I5P66 2005
    339.2′0982′1–dc22   2005015045

Cornell University Press strives to use environmentally responsible suppliers and materials to the fullest extent possible in the publishing of its books. Such materials include vegetable-based, low-VOC inks and acid-free papers that are recycled, totally chlorine-free, or partly composed of nonwood fibers. For further information, visit our website at www.cornellpress.cornell.edu.

Cloth printing   10   9   8   7   6   5   4   3   2   1
Paperback printing   10   9   8   7   6   5   4   3   2   1

For Alexander

Contents

Foreword by Richard C. Leone   ix

Acknowledgments   xiii

1. Rethinking the Trade-off between Growth and Equality   1
2. Varieties of Capitalism   15
3. Income Distribution and Labor Markets   32
4. Employment Performance   67
5. Macro-Economic Management and Wage Bargaining   95
6. Participation, Security, Mobility, and Skills   114
7. Welfare States, Redistribution, and Economic Growth   142
8. Welfare States in Retrenchment   182
9. Directions for Progressive Reform   204

   Notes   221
   Index   235

Foreword

Americans often seem to view the experience of other nations as scarcely relevant to that of the United States. On economic matters, this self-absorption is especially acute. One might oversimplify the national "folk wisdom" on this topic as follows: We are the richest, we grow the fastest, and the world would be a better place if all other nations adopted something closer to the form of capitalism that has developed in the United States. This high sense of self-regard even has deep roots in the academic world, with much of mainstream economics convinced that only America and a few other nations are roughly at the right place on the spectrum between unfettered capitalism and various mixes of regulation and free markets. Obviously, this conclusion is related to the preference among many economists for very limited government interference in markets. These beliefs and conclusions often are justified by reference to the assertion that American economic performance is consistently better than that of Western Europe and Japan, particularly over the past twenty-five years.

Readers of this volume by Jonas Pontusson, professor of politics at Princeton University, will find that the facts about national economic performance and personal income require more nuanced international comparisons. And that is what Pontusson provides, breaking significant new ground and offering multidimensional insights into the ways that different clusters of modern economies are adapting to changes in demographics, workforce competition, and politics. Pontusson offers evidence, for example, that general levels of growth and income in countries that have relatively large welfare systems have been comparable in virtually every way to those with smaller public sectors and less government intervention.

The issues he addresses are those that have been at the heart of the work of The Century Foundation over the past decade, resulting in such books as *Created Unequal* by James Galbraith, *Securing Prosperity* by Paul Osterman, *Growing Prosperity* by Barry Bluestone and Bennett Harrison, *Top Heavy* by Edward Wolff, *Why Economies Grow* by Jeff Madrick, *The New Ruthless Economy* by Simon Head, *Making Capitalism Work* by Leonard Silk et al., and numerous studies of America's social insurance systems, especially *Beyond the Basics: Social Security Reform*, edited by Richard C. Leone and Greg Anrig. Our work in this critical area is continuing with support for studies such as Edward Wolff's forthcoming book on skill, work, and inequality, as well as Amy Dean's new look at unions and Timothy Smeeding's examination of the costs and consequences of economic inequality in America.

In this volume, Pontusson traces the rise since the 1970s of conservative political parties with strongly fundamentalist attitudes in favor of capital markets. He shows how workers in many countries have seen an erosion of safety nets and have experienced some degree of income stagnation, although the United States stands out in this regard. Nevertheless, Pontusson argues that closer examination indicates that welfare states and worker support of public safety nets have been surprisingly resilient. Even in Britain after Thatcher, he finds, for example, that social spending has continued to increase.

As populations age somewhat and the number of workers in retirement increases in relation to those in the workforce, there is likely to be continuing political pressure for still more spending on such programs as retirement income support. In addition, while the United States stands out in terms of the high costs of its health care, all countries with aging populations are likely to experience pressures in the provision of health services. And since an even larger percentage of those services are paid for by governments in other democracies, there seems little likelihood that their overall spending for social programs will decrease.

It appears that economic realities have had a sobering effect on governments on ideological binges. Americans, and to a lesser extent the British, may salute individualism and personal responsibility, but they depend on social insurance systems just as do the more "collectivist" continental Europeans. This similarity may be merely an expression of the fact that a relatively large number of people support such programs, and after all, these are democracies in which, however crudely, public opinion is reflected in at least major aspects of governmental priorities.

Of course, it is important to acknowledge that while the Germans and the French, for example, may sing the praises of their health and public pensions systems, their citizens too would like to find a less costly way to meet social needs. In other words, political circumstances are not quite as dramatically different among these countries as superficial analysis would lead one to believe. In the end, the part of politics that is tough and real on both sides of the North Atlantic is the expectation that government will provide citizens with what they are willing to pay for and that it will do a reasonable job both in setting up systems to deliver services fairly and efficiently and in finding equitable ways to pay for them. Pontusson allows us to grapple with these issues constructively rather than ideologically, assembling a rich collection of data, examining studies from scholars across the political spectrum, and drawing his conclusions with a restraint founded in the evidence rather than his own predispositions.

In the end, the rich, well-educated adults who vote in Europe and North America must choose governments that deliver the services they want with relative cost effectiveness. After the posturing and the search for costless panaceas have fizzled, all the remedies involving clearing up fraud, waste, and abuse have been tried, and all the promises of supply side economics are exhausted, people would be wise to look into volumes like this one. It belongs on a small shelf of invaluable studies that leaders can consult to learn how these basic problems are met in sister economies. In the United States, those leaders might have to do so furtively, with a flashlight under the blanket, but they will nonetheless discover things that will be useful in the American context. Pontusson shows how much there is to learn from comparative policy studies. It is now up to the voters to choose governments that are willing to read, learn, and listen.

On behalf of the Trustees of The Century Foundation, I thank him for this contribution to our understanding of economic affairs.

Richard C. Leone, President
The Century Foundation

Acknowledgments

This book was commissioned by the Twentieth Century Fund, now The Century Foundation, in 1996. I am most grateful to The Century Foundation for its support. In particular, I want to thank Richard C. Leone, Greg Anrig, and Bernard Wasow for their encouragement, critical feedback, and, above all, their patience. I completed the final manuscript as a visiting scholar at the Russell Sage Foundation in the fall of 2004, and I am also most grateful to this foundation for its support.

Over the last twenty years or so, the comparative study of advanced capitalist political economies and welfare states has generated a rich and vibrant literature. While advancing my own perspective, this book tries to synthesize the ideas and findings of this literature and to present them in a way that is accessible to a broader readership. Thus I draw extensively on ideas and research by other scholars. The book also contains a lot of data which I have drawn from many different sources, mostly OECD publications. I have tried to be meticulous in documenting my data sources. As for the sources of my ideas, I have tried to keep such citations to a minimum, in order to make the book more readable. Quite a few people may feel that I have appropriated their ideas and arguments without adequate acknowledgment. I take this opportunity to acknowledge that my intellectual debts to the scholars cited in the notes are far more extensive than my citations of their work might suggest—and I invite others to recycle these ideas without necessarily acknowledging my book (or, if so, then at most only once or twice!). At the risk of offending those I have omitted, I wish to acknowledge, in particular, my deep and diffuse intellectual debts to Geoffrey Garrett, Peter Hall, Torben Iversen, Peter Katzenstein, and David Soskice. The work of these five scholars has profoundly shaped the way I think about comparative political economy.

I owe a special debt to Lane Kenworthy. Halfway through this project, Lane and I started working on a joint paper on changes in income distribution and redistribution in OECD countries, drawing data from the Luxembourg Income Study. Most of the LIS data presented below were generated by Lane, as part of our joint project. Lane also read an early version of this manuscript. For comments on the entire manuscript, I am grateful to Harry Katz, David Rueda, Mary O'Sullivan, and Kathleen Thelen as well. Further, I would like to acknowledge the research assistance of Yuriko Takahashi and the critical but always constructive feedback of Mary O'Sullivan during the final stage of revisions. My friend and two-time editor Roger Haydon at the Cornell University Press also deserves special thanks, for his keen editorial comments as well as his interest in my project.

Over the last four or five years, I presented parts of this project at various workshops and seminars and used draft chapters in my teaching. I received many useful comments from my students as well as from workshop and seminar participants. In particular, I wish to acknowledge the input of Daniel Kinderman, Hyeok Yong Kwon, Johannes Lindvall, and Yuriko Takahashi, and a special debt to Bruno Palier: he convinced me that my initial inclination to argue for means testing as part of a progressive reform package for European welfare states was wrong-headed.

Finally, as I am about to leave Cornell after twenty years, I must acknowledge that this project has benefited tremendously, in many ways, from the stimulating intellectual environment of the government department at Cornell and the support of my friends and colleagues there. I am particularly grateful to Valerie Bunce, Ron Herring, Peter and Mary Katzenstein, Sidney Tarrow, and Christopher Way for their support.

I would be truly ashamed that it has taken me so long to complete this book if it were not for the fact that I accomplished a great many other things while working on it. If I were to list those accomplishments, the list would prominently include some very challenging hikes, the names of rock and ice climbing routes that pushed me to my limits and the summits of several pretty big mountains. This book is dedicated to my guide and companion in all of those endeavors.

J. P.

New York City

CHAPTER 1

Rethinking the Trade-off between Growth and Equality

Across the advanced capitalist countries, economic growth has been quite sluggish over the last twenty-five years, at least by the standards of the golden postwar era. At the same time, income disparities have increased. In the United States, low-income families experienced a steady decline in real income from the late 1970s through the first half of the 1990s. This decline came to an end as employment growth accelerated in the course of the 1990s, but inequality remains an enduring legacy of the last quarter century. In some European countries, labor market institutions have constrained inegalitarian market forces and welfare states have to a greater extent compensated low-income families, but these achievements seem to have been accompanied by more sluggish employment growth. Are we caught in a situation in which governments can no longer do much to improve the economic prospects of low-income workers and their families?

This book explores public policy issues related to economic growth, employment, and income distribution by means of cross-national comparison. For all the talk of globalization in recent years, it remains meaningful and quite instructive, I believe, to analyze national economies and to compare them. Such an exercise strikes me as particularly appropriate in view of the current disengagement in the "war of the models."[1] In Europe, Margaret Thatcher became the figurehead of radical pro-market forces in the 1980s, advocating an embrace of the American model. Politically, this movement ran out of steam in the early 1990s, paving the way for a more pragmatic and incremental approach to economic reform. On the other hand, foreign models seem to have disappeared almost entirely from American public debate as Germany and Japan have been overcome by economic and political difficulties. To hail either of these countries as a model for America, as many did in the 1980s, would today seem quite ridiculous. Are there no longer any alternative models to be admired and perhaps emulated? I shall try to make the case that there is still a viable European model of welfare capitalism, but this model is different from the German model of the 1980s.

The complex of issues that I explore in this book revolves around the relationship between, on the one hand, equality, redistribution, and social protection and, on the other hand, economic efficiency, growth, and employment. The theme of equality and efficiency, whether and how they might be reconciled, lies at the core of democratic politics in capitalist societies, always lurking behind the narrower issues that we contest in elections and legislative battles. While capitalism generates inequality, democracy is a source of egalitarian pressure.

The rich have many more resources to influence the political process than the poor do, but democracy still entails formal equality among citizens: each person has one vote, and elections do matter. The distribution of power in the polity is more equal than the distribution of power in the economy. And even in the most egalitarian of today's capitalist societies, the distribution of income is skewed toward the rich in the sense that the distance between the incomes of households in the top decile of the income distribution and the median household income is invariably larger—typically much larger—than the distance between the incomes of households in the bottom decile and the median household. Put differently, the median household income is less than the mean household income. This means that a majority of households stands to gain from progressive taxation and redistributive spending.[2] At the same time, however, all citizens who are motivated by material concerns, even those at the very bottom of the income distribution, must worry about the average standard of living in their society. For the majority, a more egalitarian society is preferable to a less egalitarian society, but a rich society is also preferable to a poor society. Democratic capitalist politics is about distributive conflict tempered by a common interest in economic growth.

The egalitarian logic of democracy manifests itself in the industrial sphere as well as in the political sphere. A very substantial body of research demonstrates that collective bargaining between employers and unions typically produces a more egalitarian distribution of wages than that which results when wages are set by contracting between employers and individual employees. In the United States, wages in unionized sectors of the economy tend to be more compressed than wages in non-union sectors, and a significant part of the increase in wage inequality since the 1970s can be attributed to de-unionization. On a cross-national basis, we also observe a consistent association between unionization and wage compression. Unions are not necessarily paragons of democratic virtue, but their internal decision-making usually involves voting, based on the "one person, one vote" principle and some approximation of majority rule. Whenever the mean wage exceeds the median wage, we might expect a majority of union members to favor redistributive wage demands, with some portion of wage increases perhaps being specified in dollars rather than as a percentage of current wages. Again, however, there is an important caveat for this expectation: the majority of union members can be expected to support redistributive wage demands only so long as such demands do not negatively affect their employment situation.

For a host of historical reasons, the egalitarian thrust of democratic politics has been more pronounced in Western Europe than in the United States.[3] While the United States lagged behind Western Europe in the development of comprehensive social welfare provisions during the postwar era, in Western Europe the Scandinavian countries led the way. Among the large European countries, West Germany developed the most comprehensive system of social protection, coordinated wage bargaining, and industrial citizenship. Borrowing a term coined by German Christian Democrats in the 1950s, I here refer to Germany and its immediate neighbors—Austria and Switzerland to the south; Belgium and the Netherlands to the west; and Denmark, Sweden, Norway, and Finland to the north— as "social market economies" or, for short, SMEs. Throughout the book, I contrast the institutional arrangements of this set of countries to those of the United States and other "liberal market economies"—LMEs—and compare the two groups of countries in terms of various aspects of egalitarianism and economic performance.[4]

I stress at the outset that the "Social Europe" to which the title of this book refers is not the same thing as the European Union. Three social market economies—Germany, Belgium, and the Netherlands—were part of the original European Economic Community. Denmark joined in 1975, and Austria, Finland, and Sweden followed suit in 1995. Still, two of the social market economies, Norway and Switzerland, remain outside the EU and another two, Denmark and Sweden, have yet to join the single currency. On the other hand, the European Union encompasses two countries that fit the liberal market model quite well, Ireland and the United Kingdom, and several southern European countries that do not neatly fit either model. This said, it is impossible to discuss the experience of the social market economies over the last two decades without some discussion of the process of European economic and political integration. Decisions by the European Union influence the social market economies in powerful ways. It is also the case that the political debate surrounding the future of the social market model in Germany and elsewhere matters greatly to the evolution of the European Union.

The "Europe vs. America" Debate Revisited

It is commonplace for economists, not to mention business reporters, to posit a trade-off between efficiency and equality. A famous essay by Arthur Okun refers to this as "the big trade-off." Observing that "the market creates inequality and efficiency jointly," Okun flatly asserts that "we can't have our cake of market efficiency and share it equally." It is noteworthy that Okun quickly qualifies this statement by noting that "the presence of a trade-off between efficiency and equality does not mean that everything that is good for one is necessarily bad for the other . . . techniques that improve the productivity and earnings potential of unskilled workers might benefit the society with greater efficiency *and* greater equality."[5] For Okun, inequality of opportunity is a source of inefficiency as it implies a misallocation of natural talent, but inequality of rewards boost efficiency by providing individuals with incentives to invest, to innovate, and to work hard.

According to the economic orthodoxy of our times, which I shall refer to as the "market-liberal view," governments may create a more equal distribution of income and consumption through taxation, transfer payments, and the provision of services, but in so doing they inevitably distort market forces and undermine efficiency, which in turn leads to slower growth, less employment, and lower average standards of living.[6] In the debate about whether or not the minimum wage should be increased, we are often told that this type of government intervention in the labor market is counterproductive, creating a disincentive for employers to hire low-skilled workers. The same logic applies to union efforts to raise the relative wages of the low-paid through collective bargaining. The market-liberal view holds that redistributive policies not only have negative consequences for average incomes; worse still, they especially hurt the people they are supposed to benefit.

The implication of the market-liberal view is that countries in which wages are more equally distributed should have lower living standards and/or slower rates of economic growth than countries in which wages are less equally distributed. Similarly, redistributive taxes and social programs should be associated with worse economic performance on a cross-national basis. Is this in fact so? Table 1.1 presents some very basic economic data that bear on this question. Let me immediately make clear that the purpose of presenting these data here is not to settle the matter, but rather to frame the treatment of more specific questions and more detailed evidence in the chapters that follow.

Table 1.1 includes data for eighteen OECD countries, that is, long-time member states of the Organization for Economic Cooperation and Development (OECD).[7] The first column presents the most recent observations

Table 1.1 Selected indicators of economic performance

	Most recent Gini coefficients for disposable household income	GDP/capita in US$ at PPPs, 2002	Annual real GDP/capita growth, 1960–80	Annual real GDP/capita growth, 1980–2000	Exports in percent of GDP, 2000	Average unemployment rates, 2000–03	Annual employment growth, 1990–2002
	(1)	(2)	(3)	(4)	(5)	(6)	(7)
SMEs	**.257**	**28,883**	**3.1%**	**1.9%**	**48.2**	**5.5%**	**0.5%**
Austria	.266	28,872	3.7	2.0	50.1	4.0	0.9
Belgium	.250	27,716	3.6	2.0	86.3	7.3	0.5
Denmark	.236	29,328	2.7	1.7	43.8	4.8	0.2
Finland	.247	26,478	3.7	2.4	42.9	9.3	-0.4
Germany	.264	25,917	3.1	1.6	33.7	8.4	-0.2
Netherlands	.248	29,009	2.9	1.9	67.2	3.0	2.0
Norway	.251	35,482	3.7	2.5	46.6	3.9	1.1
Sweden	.252	27,209	2.7	1.6	47.2	5.3	-0.5
Switzerland	.307	29,940	2.1	1.0	46.4	3.2	0.7
LMEs	**.330**	**29,483**	**2.5**	**2.3**	**40.0**	**5.6**	**1.7**
Australia	.311	28,068	2.5	1.9	22.9	6.4	1.5
Canada	.302	30,303	3.2	1.5	45.9	7.3	1.4
Ireland	.325	32,646	3.5	4.7	94.9	4.3	3.5
New Zealand		21,783	1.4	1.3	36.7	5.3	2.0
United Kingdom	.345	27,976	2.0	2.0	28.1	5.1	0.5
United States	.368	36,121	2.1	2.1	11.2	5.1	1.2
France	.288	27,217	3.5	1.6	28.7	9.0	0.6
Italy	.333	25,568	4.0	1.8	28.4	9.4	0.6
Japan		26,954	6.0	2.3	10.8	5.1	0.3

Sources: (1) Luxembourg Income Study: www.lisproject.org/kevfigures/ineqtable.htm, November 2004. (2) OECD, Main Economic Indicators, May 2004, 252–55. (3) OECD, National Accounts, 2000, vol. 1. (4) OECD, Historical Statistics, 2001, 48. (5) OECD, Historical Statistics, 2001, 71. (6) OECD, Employment Outlook, 2004, 293. (7) OECD, Historical Statistics, 2001, 31, and Main Economic Indicators, September 2004, 17.

Note: Gini coefficients refer to 1997–2000 except for Denmark (1992), Switzerland (1992), Australia (1994) and France (1994).

of Gini coefficients for disposable household income available from the Luxembourg Income Study. The Gini coefficient is a commonly used measure of income inequality, the meaning of which will be discussed at some length in chapter 3. Suffice it to say for now that higher numbers signify greater inequality. Among the nine countries that I classify as "social market economies," Switzerland stands out as the least egalitarian country by this measure, with a Gini coefficient of .307. The other eight SMEs fall in a fairly narrow range, with Gini coefficients between .236 (Denmark) and .266 (Austria). By contrast, Gini coefficients for the "liberal market economies" range between .302 (Canada) and .366 (U.S.). The distinction between SMEs and LMEs appears to correspond to a major divide among advanced capitalist countries with respect to income distribution.[8] To put these figures in perspective, it might be noted that the Gini coefficient for the United States, as measured by the Luxembourg Income Study, increased from .301 in 1979 to .372 in 1997 (and then fell slightly from 1997 to 2000). Most observers would agree that inequality among American households increased dramatically over this period. In absolute terms, the difference between the average Gini coefficient of SMEs (.257) and the average Gini coefficient for LMEs (.330) in the 1990s is of just about the same magnitude as the difference between the U.S. Gini coefficients for 1979 and 1997.

The second column of table 1.1 provides 2002 figures on GDP per capita, expressed in U.S. dollars. "GDP per capita" is the value of all goods and services produced by an economy divided by the total population. The conversion into U.S. dollars was done at "purchasing power parities," which is to say that these figures take into account cross-national differences in the cost of living. The figures in the second column thus provide a measure of average living standards that can be compared, at least roughly, across countries. With a GDP per capita of $36,121, the United States stands out as the richest of all the rich countries. It is noteworthy, however, that the poorest of all the countries included in table 1.1, New Zealand, is also a liberal market economy, and that the second-richest country, Norway, is a social market economy. Generalizing across all LMEs and SMEs, average living standards in these two sets of countries appear to be more or less the same.

Needless to say, resource endowments and a host of other factors that have little or nothing to do with politics or political-economic institutions must be taken into account to explain why some countries are richer than others. The unique characteristics of the continental American economy hardly need to be belabored. While oil revenues are the key to Norway's relative prosperity, New Zealand's unique combination of small size and geographic isolation (the latter restricting its ability to reap the benefits of international trade) obviously puts it at a disadvantage.

Arguably, economic growth rates provide a better standard for assessing the relative merits of social and liberal market economies as models of economic governance than (cumulative) levels of economic development. The third and fourth columns of table 1.1 report average annual growth rates of GDP per capita from 1960 to 1980 and from 1980 to 2000, respectively. Despite higher taxes and a more egalitarian distribution of income, the social market economies of northern and central Europe generally achieved higher rates of economic growth than the liberal market economies over the 1960s and 1970s. Looking at the figures in column 4, it is immediately apparent that New Zealand's anemic performance drags down the average growth rate for the LMEs, but even without New Zealand the LME average is considerably lower than the SME average (2.7 percent as compared to 3.1 percent). Crucially, the apparent success of social market economies in achieving more rapid growth under more egalitarian auspices in this period was not based on insulation against the competitive pressures of world markets. To the contrary, the social market economies of northern and central Europe have long been more dependent on international trade than most liberal market economies. As background information, the fifth column of table 1.1 provides figures on the value of exports relative to GDP in 2000.[9]

In all but three of the OECD countries, average annual growth rates from 1980 to 2000 were lower than the corresponding figures for the previous two decades. Unchanged, the comparatively low growth rates of the United States and the United Kingdom in the 1960s and 1970s became standard growth rates in the 1980s and 1990s. As indicated by the fourth column of table 1.1, the deceleration of economic growth was much more pronounced for SMEs than for LMEs. On average, LMEs performed better than SMEs over the last two decades of the twentieth century, but this difference is largely, if not entirely, attributable to Ireland's "economic miracle." Excluding the fastest-growing country in each group (Norway and Ireland), the average growth rates of LMEs and SMEs turn out to be exactly the same from 1980 to 2000: 1.8 percent per year. To be sure, the determinants of economic growth are complex, and we ought to control for a number of other factors in order to assess the impact of income distribution, political-economic institutions, and government policy. For now, suffice it to say that simple comparisons of growth rates over extended periods of time do not yield any unambiguous support for the proposition that liberal market economies are inherently superior to social market economies.

Many authors invoke the postwar experience of the social market economies not only to question the idea of a necessary trade-off between equality and efficiency, but also to suggest that egalitarianism and big government may be good for economic growth, competitiveness, and efficiency. We can distinguish four basic arguments to this effect. First, proponents of the social market model commonly argue that the economy-wide collective bargaining characteristic of northern and central Europe facilitates the exercise of wage restraint and possibly enables these countries to achieve a better trade-off between inflation and unemployment. A second line of argument holds that low wages should be regarded as a subsidy to inefficient companies and that wage compression serves a productive function, putting pressure on companies to rationalize their use of labor. Third, some observers argue that the "big government" characteristic of the social market economies encompasses a strong commitment to public education and worker training and that many social welfare programs should also be seen as an investment in human capital. The final argument focuses on the willingness of individuals and organized interests to accept economic adjustments dictated by world markets. By socializing the costs involved, so this argument goes, the welfare state facilitates the process of adjustment and preempts political pressures for tariffs on imports and other forms of protectionist trade policy. In a similar vein, it might be argued that the worker participation schemes characteristic of the social market economies serve to overcome worker resistance to change and contribute to productivity enhancement at the level of firms.

As recently as the 1980s, hardly anyone would have contested the claim that social market arrangements were working well for the countries that had them. Most of the debate about Europe in the United States instead focused on normative and cultural issues, as critics of the idea that Sweden or Germany might be seen as a model for American policy essentially argued that social market arrangements entail a loss of individual freedom or that they presuppose a degree of cultural homogeneity that simply does not exist in the United States. In the course of the 1990s, however, it became increasingly common for European as well as American observers to question the viability of the social market model and to paint a picture of "Social Europe" as unable to compete in world markets because of excessively high taxes and excessively rigid labor markets. To escape this quagmire, the social market economies of continental Europe would have to engage in radical reform, cutting taxes and deregulating both labor markets and product markets.

As indicated already, the data on aggregate economic growth hardly justify the ascendancy of the American side of the "America vs. Europe" debate of the 1990s. Rather, it seems to be comparative employment performance that has provided the proponents of the liberal market model with wind in their sails. Propagated most prominently by the *Economist,* the standard version of the new orthodoxy contrasts the unemployment trajectories of liberal America and social Europe in the 1990s. With

"Social Europe" being equated with the European Union, the basic facts are compelling. In the United States, the rate of unemployment rose from 5.6 percent in 1990 to 7.5 percent in 1992, and then fell for eight consecutive years until it reached 4 percent in 2000. In the economic arena encompassed by the European Union, the rate of unemployment was somewhat higher to begin with, 8.4 percent in 1990, and rose more sharply during the recession in the early 1990s, peaking at 11.1 percent in 1994. For the EU, moreover, the subsequent economic recovery did not translate into as much improvement on the unemployment front as it did for the United States. In 2000, the EU rate of unemployment was still 7.8 percent, not much lower than the 1990 figure. The U.S. rate of unemployment increased more sharply than the EU rate in the early 2000s, but it still remained significantly lower than the EU rate in 2003: 6.0 percent as compared to 8.1 percent.[10]

The conventional comparison of unemployment rates is flawed in that it treats the European Union as a proxy for "Social Europe." Over the three years 2000–03, the rate of unemployment in the EU as a whole averaged 7.7 percent. As shown in the sixth column of table 1.1, however, national rates of unemployment were lower than the EU rate in seven of the nine countries that I designate as SMEs. Austria, Denmark, the Netherlands, Norway, and Switzerland not only outperformed the EU, but also outperformed the United States with respect to unemployment in the early 2000s. Despite the high rate of unemployment in Belgium, Finland, and Germany, the average rate of unemployment for SMEs was nearly identical to the average rate for LMEs over 2000–03.[11] The commonly drawn contrast between unemployment rates in the United States and the EU hides the huge variation among EU member states. As Stephen Nickell puts it, "While it is sometimes convenient to lump all the countries of western Europe together in order to provide a suitable contrast to North America, most of the time it is a rather silly thing to do."[12]

The EU's unemployment problem turns out to be primarily the problem of four large member states: France, Italy, Germany, and Spain. From this list, the German case is most relevant to the concerns of the present inquiry, which does not directly address the question of what explains the high rates of unemployment in southern Europe.[13] Among European countries, strong unions and large redistributive welfare states certainly do not distinguish France, Italy, and Spain. As for Germany, the exceptional circumstances of German unification must be taken into account. With the newly incorporated eastern territories accounting for roughly one-fifth of the total labor force at the time of unification and featuring virtually no viable businesses, it is hardly surprising that mass unemployment has been a persistent problem for Germany over the last fifteen years. Germany's current difficulties, its apparent political impasse

9

as well as its persistent employment crisis, have undoubtedly weakened the ability of the social market economies of northern and central Europe to assert their interests within the European Union and to project themselves as a model for Europe as a whole and, specifically, as a model for new East European member states. However, if our objective is to assess the relative strengths and weaknesses of the social market model judiciously, we should guard against generalizing from the German experience of the 1990s. By the same token, a judicious assessment of the relative strengths and weaknesses of the liberal market model ought to draw on the experiences of all the liberal market economies, not just the experience of the United States. This is not simply a matter of "fairness": from a methodological point of view, the variation among SMEs and LMEs is critically important because it provides the leverage we need to test specific hypotheses about the determinants of employment performance (and other outcomes as well).

The seventh column of table 1.1, finally, presents figures on the average annual growth of civilian employment, measured in terms of the number of people in employment, over the period from 1990 to 2002. More than any of the other evidence presented in table 1.1, these figures do support the claims of the proponents of the liberal market model, pointing to a potential trade-off between equality and employment growth. The only social market economies that managed to achieve annual employment growth rates above 1 percent over this period were the Netherlands and Norway, and Norway just barely did so. By contrast, employment growth exceeded 1 percent per year in all the liberal market economies except for the United Kingdom. The difference between SME and LME averages is quite striking.

These observations raise two puzzles. To begin with, the liberal market economies have tended to generate more new jobs than the social market economies over the last fifteen years, but their superior performance in terms of employment growth does not appear to have translated into lower rates of unemployment. The second puzzle is that the superior employment growth performance of the liberal market economies also has not translated into more rapid growth of average living standards, as measured by GDP per capita. The first of these puzzles reflects the fact that the labor force has tended to grow more rapidly in LMEs than SMEs. As I shall document below (chapter 4), several factors have been at work here: larger youth cohorts entering the labor force, higher rates of immigration of working-age adults, larger increases in female labor-force participation rates, and smaller decreases in male labor-force participation rates.

The second puzzle introduces the question of whether employment growth is necessarily a good thing. Hypothetically, suppose that we have two economies that are growing at the same rate, but one achieves this growth by means of productivity improvements while the other achieves it by employing more people. Is one of these scenarios preferable to the other? On the assumption that the former scenario would entail higher wages and more stimulating jobs, the answer would seem to depend largely on two considerations: whether unemployment is a temporary or semi-permanent condition, and what the societal provisions for transferring income from the employed to the unemployed are. One of the difficulties we confront in seeking to evaluate the employment performance of SMEs relative to LMEs is that these considerations cut in opposite directions. On the one hand, the loss of income associated with unemployment is considerably smaller in the SMEs than in the LMEs. On the other hand, the duration of unemployment tends to be much longer in the SMEs than in the LMEs.

The American "jobs miracle" of the 1990s entailed not only a major increase of the number of employed people but also a major increase of the number of hours worked by employed people. According to one OECD estimate, the average employed American put in fifty-eight more hours of work per year in 2000 than in 1990. By the end of the decade, the United States had surpassed Japan to become, of the eighteen OECD countries covered in this analysis, the leader in average annual hours of work.[14] The improvement of America's relative standing in the GDP per capita league appears to have entailed a loss of leisure and increase in stress. Indeed, the question arises whether our high level of GDP per capita has to do with the American economy being particularly efficient or with a greater willingness to work on the part of Americans.

Arguably, if our objective is to compare the efficiency of different institutional arrangements, GDP should be measured per hour worked rather than per capita. The OECD data on average annual hours worked are fraught with definitional issues that render cross-national comparisons problematic. Keeping this in mind, table 1.2 presents the results that we obtain if we divide GDP in 2002, expressed in U.S. dollars at purchasing power parities, by the product of multiplying average annual hours worked and the total number of employed people. In contrast to the GDP per capita figures presented in table 1.1, the United States no longer stands out as a particularly strong or successful economy in table 1.2. According to these estimates, each hour worked yields a significantly larger amount of output in Belgium, Norway, and Ireland than in the United States and roughly the same amount of output in France and Italy.[15] And even if we leave out the exceptional case of New Zealand, the average GDP per hour worked for LMEs falls short of the average for SMEs by nearly two dollars.

Table 1.2 GPD per hour worked in US$ at purchasing power parities, 2002

	GDP per hour
SMEs	**37.15**
Belgium	41.11
Denmark	36.77
Finland	31.08
Germany	37.33
Netherlands	32.18
Norway	50.51
Sweden	34.37
Switzerland	33.82
LMEs	**33.32**
Australia	30.55
Canada	31.97
Ireland	41.87
New Zealand	23.99
United Kingdom	32.38
United States	39.17
France	39.72
Italy	38.11
Japan	28.28

Sources: Author's calculations based on GDP figures from OECD, *Main Economic Indicators*, May 2004, 252–55; total number of employed people from OECD, *Labor Force Statistics*, 2003, 13, and average annual hours worked per employee from OECD, *Employment Outlook*, 2004, 312.

AGENDA

Europe's social market economies should indeed be concerned about the sluggishness of their employment growth over the last two decades. Even if the comparison of unemployment rates is not particularly unfavorable to the SMEs, high levels of unemployment, and especially long-term employment, do pose a serious problem for these countries. Moreover, achieving higher levels of employment growth is necessary in order to maintain the levels of public spending on social transfers and services to which citizens of these countries have become accustomed. The question arises whether the anemic rate of job growth in most social market economies derives from intrinsic features of the social market model, as the market-liberal view would have it, or should rather be seen as a result of exogenous shocks and possibly also misguided macroeconomic policies. To the extent that current employment problems have to do with the social market model, two additional questions arise. What

is it about present-day economic conditions that has made it more difficult to reconcile efficiency and equality? And exactly what features of the
social market model represent obstacles to employment growth?

In what follows, I shall argue that external shocks and macro-economic
management account for a great of deal of the SMEs' weak employment
performance in the 1990s. Micro-economic considerations must also be
taken into account, and the SMEs do need to undertake structural reforms, but the reorientation of macro-economic policy is an essential part
of any strategy to stimulate employment growth. I do not believe that economic globalization by itself poses a serious threat to Europe's social
market economies. Again, the institutional arrangements characteristic of
these economies developed precisely in order to cope with the consequences of trade dependence. Cross-national capital mobility and foreign
ownership of major firms in these countries represent new developments,
but it is far from clear why these developments should render the social
market model unworkable.

I will put forward two main ideas for reforming social market
economies that address the problem of employment growth. First, the
social market economies should reduce employment protection, allowing
employers greater flexibility while maintaining, indeed reinforcing,
public support for the unemployed as well as retraining and other programs designed to promote the employability of the unemployed.
Second, the social market economies should seek to shift the tax burden
from payroll taxes to income taxes. Such a shift would stimulate demand
for less skilled labor and, at the same time, offset some of the inegalitarian effects of contemporary labor market dynamics.

While advocating reform of the social market model, this book also
argues that the experience of Europe's social market economies is more
relevant to public policy debate in liberal market economies than is commonly supposed. Social market institutions cannot readily be transferred
to countries like the United States or the United Kingdom. However, the
social market economies—in particular, the Nordic countries—exemplify
policies that do seem to mitigate the trade-off between equality and efficiency. Further, these policies do not necessarily presuppose social market
institutions.

The empirical chapters address discrete elements of the broad picture
sketched above. While chapter 3 explores trends in the distribution of
wages and household income across the OECD countries over the last two
decades, chapter 4 compares these countries in terms of various indicators of employment performance. Chapter 5 discusses the macro-
economic implications of different labor market institutions. Focusing
more on micro-economic issues, chapter 6 addresses the implications of
workplace industrial relations, employment security, and active labor

market policies as well as education and vocational training. Chapter 7 explores the consequences of the size and organization of welfare states for income distribution, growth, and employment. Very briefly, chapter 8 addresses the origins and implications of recent changes in the public provision of social welfare. Before delving into these topics, the next chapter elaborates on the distinction between liberal and social economies and situates my approach in relation to the existing literature on varieties of capitalism.

CHAPTER 2

Varieties of Capitalism

The analytical perspective of this book draws on the tradition of comparative political economy within political science and sociology. The term "political economy" signals an interest in how politics and economics relate to each other, while "comparative" implies an interest in cross-national variation. More sharply, the analytical approach of comparative political economy is distinguished from that of economics by the importance that it assigns to institutions. It is only a slight caricature to say that economists theorize about the behavior of economic actors—firms, workers, and consumers—based on an abstract, ahistorical conception of markets, and that their theories are supposed to apply anywhere and everywhere. By contrast, political economists emphasize that market behavior is embedded in societal institutions; indeed, markets are themselves institutions, which can be configured in different ways.

While all capitalist economies share certain basic characteristics, their institutional arrangements differ markedly, and these differences shape the choices that economic actors make. The institutional configuration of "actually existing capitalisms" must be taken into account to explain economic as well as political outcomes. Moreover, collective political action, as distinct from the market behavior of individuals, occupies a central role in the process whereby these different institutional configurations are formed and re-formed.

The perspective of comparative political economy invites us to explore how the relationship between equality and efficiency is affected by domestic institutional arrangements as well as changing global economic conditions. Arguably, the changing dynamics of the world economy have rendered these objectives less complementary—or less readily reconcilable—than they were during the "golden era" of postwar growth. More to the point, it may be that certain institutional arrangements render equality and efficiency more complementary or, at least, mitigate the trade-off between them. Consider, for instance, the effects of increasing the minimum wage on the demand for unskilled labor. As I shall document later, the literacy skills of unskilled American workers are exceptionally poor by comparative standards. Under these conditions, it is reasonable to expect that increases in the minimum wage would translate into less demand for unskilled labor, but the effect might be quite different in a country like Sweden, with a more compressed distribution of cognitive abilities and better absolute standards at the lower end of the distribution.

Put differently, the perspective of comparative political economy implies that the question of whether or not there is a trade-off between equality and efficiency cannot be answered in the abstract. Furthermore, the observation that a trade-off exists in any one instance—or many instances—leaves open what is surely the crucial issue from the point of view of politics and public policy: What is the slope of the trade-off? How much efficiency must be sacrificed to achieve a certain level of equality? The answer to this question is likely to vary across countries. The perspective of comparative political economy also invites us to explore how countries negotiate whatever trade-off between efficiency and equality they may face. If we find that some other country has achieved a better trade-off between equality and efficiency than the United States or perhaps has escaped the dilemma of choosing between these objectives altogether, Americans should surely strive to emulate that country. The observation that other countries value equality more than the United States does not carry the same public policy implications, but it does shed light on the politics of inequality.

A central feature of the comparative political economy tradition is the idea of "varieties of capitalism" or, in other words, the idea that the advanced capitalist countries cluster around a limited number of more or less coherent models of economic governance. A number of different typologies are proposed in the existing literature. For example, Peter Katzenstein distinguishes between "liberal," "statist," and "corporatist" political economies.[1] This typology focuses on the organization of interest groups and the degree to which state bureaucrats play an important autonomous role in the policy-making process. Focusing instead on how the public provision of social welfare relates to the market economy, Gøsta Esping-Andersen's well-known typology distinguishes between "liberal," "social democratic," and "conservative" welfare states.[2] More recently, the distinction between "liberal market economies" and "coordinated market economies," originally proposed by David Soskice, has become very popular, focusing our attention on the capacity of firms and other economic actors to coordinate their behavior.[3] To a large extent, these classificatory schemes overlap with each other and the differences among them have to do with the particular outcomes of interest to different authors. In my view, we should not think of typologies as being right or wrong. Rather, we should think of them as heuristic devices—ways of organizing information—that may be more or less useful. The usefulness of any particular typology depends on what it is that we want to explain.

Drawing on the work of Katzenstein, Esping-Andersen, and Soskice, my own approach to grouping the OECD countries hinges on the distinction between social market economies (SMEs) and liberal market economies (LMEs). As the introductory chapter illustrates, this distinction captures important differences between two groups of countries: on the one hand, Germany, Austria, Switzerland, Belgium, the Netherlands, Denmark, Sweden, Norway, and Finland and, on the other hand, the United States, Canada, the United Kingdom, Ireland, Australia, and New Zealand. From an institutional point of view, three core features distinguish the former set of countries from the latter. First, the SMEs are distinguished by densely organized business communities or, to use Soskice's terminology, coordinated business. Second, they are distinguished by strong unions and by highly institutionalized collective bargaining systems. Third, the social market economies are distinguished by extensive public provision of social welfare and employment protection.

In the following discussion, I will elaborate on these three features of the social market model and explain why Japan, France, and Italy fit neither the social market model nor the liberal market model. In the course of this discussion I will also introduce an important secondary distinction (anticipated in the introductory chapter) between two different types of social market economies, which I will refer to as the "Nordic" variant and the "continental" variant. (I speak of "Nordic" rather than "Scandinavian" SMEs because the group includes Finland as well as Denmark, Norway, and Sweden.)

SOCIAL MARKET ECONOMIES and COORDINATED MARKET ECONOMIES

Let me begin by articulating how my approach to varieties of capitalism relates to that of David Soskice and his collaborators, who often refer to themselves as the "Varieties of Capitalism School" of comparative political economy.[4] For these "VofC scholars," the problem of mapping varieties of capitalism comes down to a single overriding question: do firms and other political-economic actors have the capacity to coordinate among themselves to overcome collective action problems and engage in mutually beneficial cooperation? To illustrate, skill formation can be seen as a collective goods problem from the point of view of business. As a group, all companies benefit from having a skilled workforce, but individual companies have little assurance that they will be able to reap the benefits of investing in worker training under free market rules. Other companies are likely to engage in poaching, offering better wages and benefits to the workers that the company has trained. In this situation, companies will only invest in narrow (firm-specific) skills that are of little or no value to other companies, resulting in a situation wherein the productive potential of the economy as a whole might be held back by a shortage of workers with generally useful skills. According to the conventional wisdom, Japanese employers resolved this problem in the postwar era by recruiting their core workers straight out of high school, paying large wage premiums based on seniority and, in effect, agreeing among themselves not to hire workers away from each other. Involving cooperation among unions, employer associations, and the government, the German system of apprenticeship-based vocational training represents another coordinated response to the problem of skill formation (see chapter 6).

Primarily concerned with the ability of business to coordinate, Soskice and his collaborators argue persuasively that coordinating capacities depend on institutional arrangements and that there exists strong institutional complementarities across different spheres of the political economy. In Japan and Germany alike, companies coordinate among themselves to set wages, spread technological innovations, and train workers. Also, relations between big Japanese or German companies and their suppliers go beyond short-term market transactions, involving long-term commitments and, as a result, extensive information-sharing. Based on such observations, VofC scholars divide the capitalist world into two camps. One camp consists of economies in which coordination and long-term, trust-based relations play a prominent role, designated as "coordinated market economies" (CMEs). The other camp consists of economies in which market transactions largely define relations among companies as well as relations involving companies, unions, and other relevant actors, designated as "liberal market economies" (LMEs). It should be noted that VofC scholars recognize that markets serve to coordinate economic activities: what distinguishes CMEs is not coordination per se but rather the prevalence of "non-market modes of coordination" or, in a slightly different formulation, "strategic coordination."

The countries that I designate as LMEs are the same countries that VofC scholars designate as LMEs. In terms of country coverage, the main difference between my classificatory schema and Soskice's is that my category "social market economies" does not include Japan.[5] To my mind, treating Japan as exemplifying the same variety of capitalism as Germany and Sweden obscures as much as it reveals. Comparing Japan to the social market economies of northern and central Europe, the role of organized labor in the political economy is strikingly different. Though unions play an important role inside many Japanese companies, by European standards the rate of unionization is low. At the same time, political parties representing the interests of organized labor (or the "class interests" of workers) have traditionally been and remain effectively marginalized in Japan. Over the last several decades, unions have come to play a more prominent role in lobbying government, but from a European perspective the Japanese political economy remains distinguished by the absence of an institutionalized system of economy-wide bargaining among unions, employers, and government officials and the concomitant absence of direct linkages between wages and government-provided social benefits.[6] Closely related to this, Japan ranks at the bottom of the OECD league in terms of the share of GDP dedicated to public social expenditures.

With respect to wage formation, Soskice argues that the key issue is the ability of employers to coordinate their behavior so as to avoid competitive bidding, which tends to push wages to levels that undercut international competitiveness, and that Japanese employers are just as able to do this as German or Swedish employers are.[7] This argument may serve to explain developments in aggregate wage levels, but whether or not unions participate in managing the wage-setting process seems to matter a great deal for the distribution of wages. Similarly, lifetime employment and corporate welfare provide certain categories of Japanese workers with considerably more "social protection" than American workers enjoy, but the distributive implications and political dynamics of these arrangements are fundamentally different from those of European welfare states. To continue in the same vein, it is true that employers in Japan and Germany alike have solved the training problem by engaging in nonmarket coordination, but their solutions are very different from the perspective of workers and their relationship to their employers. Whereas the Japanese solution involves workers' careers being tied to particular firms, externally validated occupational credentials are an important feature of the German apprenticeship system.[8] The cooperative and participatory nature of workplace industrial relations in both Japan and Germany might well be contrasted to the "adversarial" cast of industrial relations in the United States and the United Kingdom, yet the organization and dynamics of workplace industrial relations are nonetheless quite different. In the social market economies, worker participation in management decision-making is prescribed by law and involves industrial unions constituted outside the company.

In my conceptualization, coordinated business constitutes an important feature of social market economies, but it is not the only feature that distinguishes social market economies from liberal market economies. Equally important, social market economies are distinguished from liberal market economies by economy-wide collective bargaining, by some form of legal provisions for labor to have a voice in corporate affairs, and by high levels of social protection provided by the government. Whereas the distinction between CMEs and LMEs proposed by Soskice focuses almost exclusively on the institutional conditions for solving coordination problems, to the benefit of workers as well as of companies, my distinction between SMEs and LMEs takes into account the institutional legacies of conflicts between labor and business and the enduring importance of the exercise of political power.[9]

Institutional Underpinnings of Business Coordination

As the preceding discussion implies, coordination is an outcome rather than an institutional structure. What then are the institutional conditions that make it possible for firms in social market economies to behave in a more coordinated fashion than firms in liberal market economies? To frame my analysis of labor market institutions and welfare states properly, it is necessary to dwell briefly on this question.

One strand of comparative political economy points to business associations as mechanisms whereby firms coordinate economic as well as political activities. I am not aware of any comprehensive measure of business associational density across countries, but all available evidence indicates that business communities in Japan, Scandinavia, and continental Europe are much better organized than business communities in the Anglo-Saxon countries. In northern and central Europe, virtually all large and medium-sized firms belong to an employer association that bargains with unions on their behalf. Most firms also belong to one or several trade associations that lobby governments and provide various services to their respective members. Chambers of commerce represent another organizational network that ties firms to each other.

The main tradition in comparative political economy treats the role of business associations as a secondary issue and instead looks to the historical role of markets for corporate equity or, more broadly, the institutional complex of corporate finance and governance as the primary source of differential business capacities to coordinate. The distinction that VofC scholars draw between liberal and coordinated market economies closely resembles the distinction that John Zysman, among others, has drawn between "marked-based" and "bank-based" systems of corporate finance as well as the distinction that Will Hutton, among others, has drawn between "shareholder capitalism" and "stakeholder capitalism."[10] Though scholars use different labels and diverge in many other respects, there is a strong consensus in this literature around the proposition that the prominence of markets for corporate equity distinguishes the historical experience of Anglo-Saxon capitalism. On the European continent, and also in Scandinavia and Japan, bank credit played a more important role than stock markets in financing industrialization. Banks with long-term claims on industrial firms are forced to monitor corporate management and, in effect, become agents of coordination among firms as well as corporate consolidation. Alongside this argument about the role of bank credit in financing industry, it is commonplace to point out that ownership of firms tends to be more concentrated in more coordinated market economies and, again, to link differences in the structure of ownership to the development of equity markets. With limited exit options, owners of large equity stakes can be expected to behave quite differently from portfolio investors or small shareholders operating in highly liquid markets. The conventional wisdom of the comparative political economy literature holds that "strategic investors" provide management with the luxury of pursuing more "long-termist" strategies or, in other words, to operate with a longer investment horizon. Along the same lines, many observers of corporate affairs suggest that cross-shareholding among firms and overlapping directorships have protected Japanese and European companies from the vagaries of stock markets and have also facilitated the exchange of information and cooperation among companies.

The first column of table 2.1 reports on the relative importance of stock markets and banking in the eighteen countries covered by this book during the 1980–95 period. The figures reported here were obtained by dividing the current value of publicly listed equities by the value of bank credits to the private sector (averaged over the 1980–95 period). Any ratio of less than one means that the total value of outstanding bank credit exceeds the total value of tradable corporate equity. By this measure, the liberal market economies clearly stand out as far more equity-oriented than other OECD economies. With a equity-to-credit ratio of .89, the United States is the least equity-oriented of the LMEs, but only one of the nonliberal economies, Sweden, comes even close to a equity-to-credit ratio of this magnitude. While the liberal market economies form a remarkably cohesive group, the variation in equity-to-credit ratios among the social market economies is huge. Belgium, the Netherlands, and Denmark had, along with Sweden, credit-to-equity ratios greater than .5

Table 2.1 Selected measures of corporate finance, ownership, and governance, 1990s

	Equity relative to bank credit[a]	Widely held firms in percent of total[b]		Anti-director shareholder rights[c]
		Large firms	Medium firms	
Nordic SMEs	.49	31	20	3.0
Denmark	.52	40	30	2
Finland	.27	35	20	3
Norway	.31	25	20	4
Sweden	.86	25	10	3
Continental SMEs	.41	30	18	1.8
Austria	.08	5	0	2
Belgium	.70	5	20	0
Germany	.22	50	10	1
Netherlands	.55	30	10	2
Switzerland	.49	60	50	2
LMEs	.98	67	60	4.5
Australia	.98	65	30	4
Canada	.98	60	60	5
Ireland	1.00	65	63	4
New Zealand	.98	30	57	4
United Kingdom	1.03	100	60	5
United States	.89	80	90	5
France	.24	60	0	3
Italy	.24	20	0	1
Japan	.70	90	30	4

Definitions and sources:
 [a] Average value of domestic equities traded on domestic exchanges (in percent of GDP) divided by the average value of outstanding bank credits to the private sector (in percent of GDP), 1980–95. Ross Levine, "Bank-based and Market-based Financial Systems," Carlson School of Management, University of Minnesota, January 2000.
 [b] Percentage of publicly traded firms without an "ultimate owner" (individual or family) who controls at least 20% of shareholder votes. The figures are based on tracing ownership to its ultimate source when shares are owned by institutions or other corporations. Large firms are defined as the 20 largest firms in each country, based on market capitalization at the end of 1995. Medium-sized firms are defined as the 10 smallest firms with a market capitalization of at least $500 million at the end of 1995. Rafael La Porta, Florencio Lopez-de-Silanes, and Andrei Shleifer, "Corporate Ownership Around the World," *Journal of Finance* 54 (1999), 492–95.
 [c] Index of shareholder rights vis-à-vis boards of directors, 1990s. Rafael La Porta, Andrei Shleifer, Robert W. Vishny, and Florencio Lopez-de-Silanes, "Law and Finance," *Journal of Political Economy* 106, no. 6 (1998), 1130–31.

in this period, but Austria's ratio was a puny .08. (If one removes Austria from the continental SME group, the average for continental SMEs becomes .49.)

Stock markets in the social market economies boomed in the 1990s, but so did stock markets in the liberal market economies. It is by no means obvious that recent developments have significantly changed country rankings with respect to equity-to-credit ratios. Leaving the implications of the rise of stock markets for Europe's social market economies aside for the time being, two important limitations of the equity-to-credit ratio as a measure of the differences between national systems of corporate finance deserve to be noted. First, this measure does not take into account the role of bonds as a source of corporate finance. Because American firms have relied heavily on bond markets as a source of finance, introducing bonds into the picture would make the American system of corporate finance look more market-based in comparison to other LMEs as well as the SMEs. The second limitation is that the size of the stock market does not tell us about the extent to which firms actually rely on the stock market as a source of finance. In the United States, new stock issues played an important role in corporate finance prior to the stock market crash of 1929 and again in the last two decades of the twentieth century, but for most of the twentieth century large firms relied overwhelmingly on retained earnings and, to a lesser extent, on bonds to finance their expansion.[11] Arguably, the stock market remained an important force shaping the behavior of American business because share prices determined the costs of raising capital in the bond market. Suffice to say that this topic has not been thoroughly explored in the comparative political economy literature.

It should also be noted that a number of recent comparative studies of corporate finance do not support the conventional view that German firms rely more on bank credit as a source of finance than American and British firms. In the postwar era, high profits enabled German firms to finance investment through retained earnings and to reduce their liabilities to the banks. In terms of net financial flows, German firms actually borrowed less money from the banking sector than either American or British firms over the 1970–94 period.[12] This does not necessarily call into question the notion that banks play an important coordinating role in the German economy. As Reinhard Schmidt and Marcel Tyrell argue, the role of banks does indeed distinguish German capitalism from Anglo-American capitalism, but the distinction has more to do with the ownership structure of German firms and corporate governance arrangements than with corporate reliance on bank loans to finance new investment.[13]

In contrast to the United States, German law allows deposit-taking commercial banks to own corporate equity, and the big commercial banks have traditionally held substantial equity stakes in many companies with whom they have long-term banking relationships. In addition, it is common for small individual shareholders in Germany to transfer their voting rights to their bank. According to one estimate, shareholder proxies gave banks, on average, 61 percent of the voting rights present at shareholder meetings of Germany's twenty-four largest joint stock companies in 1992.[14] As Richard Deeg emphasizes, it is rare that any one bank dominates shareholder meetings. Large firms have close relations with several banks and may be able to play their bankers off against each other. The relationship between banks and firms is a complex one, and it does not seem very useful to generalize about the power of banks vis-à-vis firms. The important point is that the banks are an integral part of the German system of corporate governance.[15]

Family ownership and cross-shareholding among nonfinancial firms constitute other important sources of ownership concentration and stability in Germany. While proxy voting by banks is a uniquely German practice, the other social market economies of northern Europe are also characterized by concentrated ownership and what is commonly termed "insider systems" of corporate governance. In some of these countries, notably Sweden and the Netherlands, preferential shares provide some owners with disproportionately large voting rights relative to their share of equity capital. The second and third columns of table 2.1 illustrate the differences between liberal and social market economies in this respect. Taken from a recent article by Rafael La Porta, Florencio Lopez-de-Silanes, and Andrei Shleifer, the figures refer to the percentage of publicly traded firms that are widely held. Being "widely held" is here defined as the absence of any owner that controls more than 20 percent of the shareholder votes in the firm in question. By this criterion, the top twenty U.K. corporations, ranked by market capitalization, are all widely held, while eighteen of the top twenty U.S. corporations are widely held. Disregarding the outlying case of New Zealand, more than 60 percent of the largest twenty firms are widely held in every one of the liberal market economies. Even including New Zealand, the average for LMEs is twice the average for either the Nordic SMEs or the continental SMEs. The contrast between LMEs and SMEs in ownership concentration is even more pronounced for medium-sized firms.

Finally, the last column of table 2.1 reports the scores that each of our eighteen countries receives on an index of shareholder rights developed by La Porta, Lopez-de-Silanes, Shleifer, and Robert Vishny. Ranging between zero and five, this index measures the legal standing of shareholders vis-à-vis directors and, in particular, the legal protections of minority shareholders who are not represented on the board. Higher scores on this index indicate that "insiders" represented on boards of directors—management, large shareholders, and banks with long-term stakes—are more constrained by "outsiders," that is, by shareholders without any special relationship to the company in question. Setting aside Japan's surprisingly high score, the figures in the last column of table 2.1 confirm the conventional view that the corporate governance provisions of liberal market economies are particularly favorable to outsider interests.

In contrast to the tables presented in the introductory chapter, table 2.1 distinguishes between Nordic and continental SMEs. In the first instance, I have organized table 2.1 in this manner to make it compatible with the table about labor market institutions and welfare states in the next section. While ownership is equally concentrated in these two groups of countries, there is at least some indication that corporate finance tends to be more market-based and that "insider governance" is less prominent in the Nordic SMEs than in the continental SMEs. It is at least certain that the opposite is not the case. This suggests that we should be wary of arguments that attribute bank dominance, ownership concentration, or insider governance to strong labor movements and the political dominance of labor-affiliated parties.[16]

LABOR MARKET INSTITUTIONS AND WELFARE STATES

Since much of this book focuses on labor market institutions and welfare states, a very brief introduction to these topics will suffice. To begin with, the first column of table 2.2 presents the most recent data we have on union density in OECD countries. Along with France, the United States stands out as having an exceptionally weak labor movement. Whereas union members account for 14 percent of the employed labor force in the United States, the figure for Sweden, the most unionized OECD country, is 79 percent. As a group, the Nordic countries clearly stand out as highly unionized. The average unionization rate for the continental SMEs exceeds that of the LMEs by six percentage points, but this difference is entirely attributable to Belgium's exceptionally high unionization rate. Setting the Belgian case aside, unionization does not appear to be a feature that distinguishes continental SMEs from LMEs. As the OECD estimates reported in the second column of table 2.2 indicate, however, collective agreements negotiated by unions and employers typically cover almost the same percentage of the labor force in the continental SMEs as in the Nordic SMEs, and the average for either group of SMEs is much higher than the average for LMEs. Leaving aside Switzerland, collective bargaining coverage in SMEs ranges between 68 percent (Germany) and 95 percent (Austria). In LMEs, by contrast, collective bargaining coverage ranges between 18 percent (U.S.) and 32 percent (U.K.) if we leave out the highly exceptional case of Australia.

Relative to both the Nordic SMEs and the LMEs, the continental SMEs are distinguished by the "disconnect" between unionization rates and collective bargaining coverage rates. In these countries, employers are better organized than workers, and collective agreements typically stipulate that their terms apply to all employees of firms that are party to the

Table 2.2 Selected measures of labor market institutions and welfare states, early 2000s

	Labor		Social protection	
	Union density, 2000[a]	Collective bargaining coverage, 2000[b]	Public social spending, 2001[c]	Employment protection, 2003[d]
Nordic SMEs	**71%**	**83%**	**25.6%**	**2.3**
Denmark	74	80	27.7	1.8
Finland	76	90	23.9	2.1
Norway	54	70	23.1	2.6
Sweden	79	90	27.5	2.6
Continental SMEs	**32**	**75**	**24.8**	**2.2**
Austria	37	95	25.5	2.2
Belgium	56	90	25.9	2.5
Germany	25	68	26.3	2.5
Netherlands	23	80	20.3	2.3
Switzerland	18	40	25.9	1.6
LMEs	**26**	**36**	**17.0**	**1.2**
Australia	25	80	17.6	1.5
Canada	28	32	17.4	1.1
Ireland	38		13.1	1.3
New Zealand	23	25	18.0	1.3
United Kingdom	31	30	21.5	1.1
United States	13	14	14.6	0.7
France	10	90	27.2	2.9
Italy	35	80	23.9	2.4
Japan	22	15	16.6	1.8

Definitions and sources:

[a] For most countries, the figures refer to employed union members in percent of the employed labor force ("net union density"); for some, the figures include the unemployed in the numerator as well as the denominator. Retired persons who retain union membership are generally not included. OECD, *Employment Outlook*, 2004, 145.

[b] Percentage of the employed labor force covered by collective bargaining agreements. Ibid., 145.

[c] Total social expenditures, not including active labor market programs, in percent of GDP. OECD, Social Expenditure Database, http://www.oecd.org/els/social/expenditure, November 2004.

[d] Composite index of legal restrictions on the ability of employers to lay off or fire regular employees. OECD, *Employment Outlook*, 2004, 117.

agreement. In some instances, government legislation also provides for the extension of collective bargaining agreements to employers who are not parties to the contract.

Collective bargaining constrains the ability of individual employers to set wages and other terms of employment in the social market economies to a greater extent than it does in other capitalist economies. In this sense, we can speak of institutionalized economy-wide bargaining between unions and employers as a distinctive feature of the social market economies. I hasten to clarify that economy-wide bargaining does not necessarily imply a single wage settlement for the entire economy. The actual bargaining may well occur at the sectoral level and may also be regionalized, as in Germany (see chapter 5 for further discussion). The important point is that each set of bargaining agents—say, unions and employers in a particular sector—can readily anticipate and must take into account how their behavior affects the behavior of other sets of bargaining agents.

As noted earlier, "social protection" constitutes another key element of the distinction between social and liberal market economies. Social protection takes the form of government spending on transfer payments (social assistance, unemployment insurance, family allowances, and pensions) and social services, but also government regulation of employment contracts, defining the terms on which workers can be laid off or fired as well as holiday entitlements, working hours, and so on. As the third column of table 2.2 shows, total social spending as a percentage of GDP tends to be much higher in SMEs than LMEs. By this measure, the British welfare state is larger than the Dutch and Belgian welfare states, but the United Kingdom is the only LME that falls within the SME range. The last column of table 2.2 reports country scores on an index devised by the OECD to measure institutional constraints on the ability of employers to fire workers. Switzerland represents the lower end of the SME spectrum, but Switzerland still provides more employment protection than any of the LMEs.

On average, the Nordic SMEs spend only marginally more of their GDP on social welfare than the continental SMEs do. Nonetheless, it is precisely in the area of social welfare provisions that the distinction between Nordic and continental SMEs is most relevant. My threefold typology of political economies corresponds closely to the three types of welfare states identified by Esping-Andersen. It is not primarily the level of social spending but rather the way in which welfare benefits are dispersed that distinguishes the Nordic (social democratic) welfare states from their continental (conservative) counterparts. In the continental SMEs, contributory social insurance schemes account for the vast bulk of social spending, and these schemes are commonly organized (stratified) on an occupational basis. In the Nordic SMEs, the public provision of social welfare is based to a much greater extent on the principle of "social citizenship," which is to say that all citizens (or residents) enjoy the same entitlements. Related to this, social services provided directly by public authorities constitute a much larger component of total social spending in the Nordic SMEs than in the continental SMEs. Furthermore, the Nordic welfare states are distinguished by their commitment to gender equality and the promotion of female labor force participation. In a slightly different vein, it should also be noted that Finland, Norway, and Sweden, while distinguished by high levels of public investment in education, do

27

not have German-style systems of vocational training. (These observations will be documented in chapters 6 and 7.)

Table 2.2 brings out important differences among liberal market economies. Australia is comparable to the social market economies in terms of the extent of its collective bargaining coverage—at least, this was the case until the late 1990s, when the Australian system of setting wages through industrial tribunals was partly dismantled. Even after the Thatcher era, the level of social spending in the United Kingdom is comparable to that of the several continental SMEs. However, the data in tables 2.1 and 2.2 do not suggest any obvious distinction between LME subtypes. In a sense, each liberal market economy is different in its own way.

Judging by the quantitative indicators listed in tables 2.1 and 2.2, France seems to satisfy virtually all the criteria for being considered a social market economy. Compared to the average social market economy, banks are more important, collective bargaining coverage is higher, the welfare state is larger, and employment protection is stricter. On the other hand, French unions organize a smaller percentage of the labor force than their counterparts in any other OECD country. Also, French employers have traditionally been very poorly organized.[17] Despite some similarities, the weakness of its unions and the fragmented and adversarial nature of relations between unions and employers make me reluctant to categorize France as a social market economy. In terms of its labor market arrangements, Italy fits the social market model better than France. In this case, the lack of fit primarily pertains to the public provision of social welfare. Not only is the Italian welfare state relatively small by SME standards: it is also uniquely ineffective in redistributing income (see chapter 7).

France and Italy might be considered examples of a distinct southern European type of capitalism, encompassing Spain, Portugal, and Greece as well, but I find it difficult to articulate exactly what would be the defining features of such a "southern European model." It is easier to make the case for an East Asian model, typified by Japan, South Korea, and Taiwan. However, careful consideration of the East Asian experience would divert attention from the analytical questions at issue here. Instead of introducing additional types of capitalism into the mix, I will treat France, Italy, and Japan as individual cases of intrinsic interest.

METHODS OF CROSS-NATIONAL COMPARISON

Throughout this book are many tables organized like tables 2.1 and 2.2, with three county groupings and averages for each group, and there are also many scatterplots. These two ways of presenting empirical evidence correspond to two different explanatory approaches. Let me briefly elaborate on this point.

As the preceding discussion illustrates, the tables are designed to address the question of differences between groups of countries. For instance, we are interested in ascertaining whether inegalitarian labor market trends have been more pronounced in liberal market economies than in social market economies and also whether or not there are significant differences between Nordic and continental SMEs with respect to trends in the distribution of income from employment. In addressing such questions, it is not sufficient simply to compare group averages; we must also attend to the range of variation within the groups that we are comparing. To illustrate, tables 2.1 and 2.2 show that the range of variation among LMEs with respect to corporate finance (the ratio of equity to bank credit) is much smaller that the range of variation among LMEs with respect to collective bargaining coverage. Based on these data, one should feel more confident generalizing about corporate finance than collective bargaining in liberal market economies. However, the range of variation among SMEs with respect to corporate finance is quite large, which makes generalizing about the differences between LMEs and SMEs more precarious. In the language of statistics, comparing group averages is only meaningful if "between-group variance" is greater than "within-group variance."

I do not propose to test formally for the statistical significance of group averages. With such a small number of countries in play, it makes more sense to eyeball the individual country data used to calculate averages. In so doing, we must be attentive to the presence of outliers, or individual countries that do not conform to the pattern of the group as a whole. As we have already seen, dropping obvious outliers within one or both groups that are being compared can sometimes alter the comparison between groups in important ways. This approach invites us to probe what it is about the outliers that make them different from the rest of the group. When within-group variance is particularly large and not attributable to any obvious outlier, I will refrain from reporting group averages in the tables that follow.

To the extent that we can establish that SMEs differ from LMEs—or that Nordic SMEs differ from continental SMEs—with respect to some particular outcome, such as levels or changes in wage inequality, the question becomes, what is it about the institutional differences between SMEs and LMEs that explain the divergence in outcomes? Answering this question necessarily involves qualitative discussion, adjudicating between alternative explanatory arguments. For now, suffice it to say that framing the question in terms of differences between or among groups implies a bias in favor of arguments that emphasize institutional complementarities or, in other words, the idea that these groups of advanced capitalist political economies constitute two distinct "systems," operating according to fundamentally different principles.

The scatterplots presented here imply a more variable-oriented approach to cross-national comparison and explanation.[18] In scatterplots, each country represents a data point in a space defined by two discrete variables. When we look at scatterplots, we are interested in ascertaining whether or not the two variables are associated with each other and thus in testing claims that posit a causal relationship between two variables—for instance, the claim that high social spending reduces the rate of economic growth. In this setup, the typology of political economies set out above tends to disappear or, at least, takes on a secondary role. SMEs are distinguished from LMEs in that these countries, as a group, have higher levels of social spending, but it is social spending, not "SME-ness," that is supposed to be the explanation for different rates of economic growth. To the extent that scatterplots show consistent patterns of association between variables, we might conclude that the causal mechanisms at work in SMEs and LMEs are the same.

The obvious limitation of scatterplots is that they involve only two variables. Arguably, we must control for other variables, such as the level of economic development, in order to observe the true association between social spending and economic growth. By this reasoning, quantitatively inclined students of comparative political economy commonly resort to more or less sophisticated forms of multiple regression analysis. I will refer to some of this work and will on occasion report regression results of my own. However, I will try to keep my regression models as simple as possible, and for the most part I will stick with scatterplots. I like scatterplots because they are graphical and easy to interpret. Crucially, it should be noted that my scatterplots contain more information than simply that conveyed by the variables on the two axes. The data points have proper names, they represent countries about which we know a great deal. Looking at scatterplots with labeled data points thus facilitates a qualitative discussion of causal dynamics. When we observe that one country, or perhaps a group of countries, displays a different association between the two variables that define the space of the scatterplot, we want to probe why this is so. The reasons may be idiosyncratic, but scatterplots also stimulate us to think about "missing variables," that is to say, variables that must be taken into account to observe the true association between the two variables that define the space of the scatterplot.

To the extent that SMEs and LMEs operate according to different logics, as distinct from taking on different values on any particular causal variable, we should be able to see some evidence of this in the way that the countries line up in the scatterplot. Many students of comparative political economy choose to adopt either a typological approach or a variable-oriented approach. This book resists making that choice and instead seeks to draw insights from both ways of looking at the empirical evidence. As we shall see, the types of political economies that I have identified do indeed appear to be fundamentally different in some respects, but they also have much in common.

SUMMARY

To reiterate, three core features define the social market model and distinguish social market economies from liberal market economies. The first feature is "organized business." The structure of corporate finance and governance as well as business associations make SME firms (and Japanese firms) more capable of solving coordination problems and engaging in collective action vis-à-vis governments and unions. The second feature of the social market model is institutionalized, economy-wide collective bargaining between unions and employers. The third feature is extensive public provision of social welfare and employment protection. The preceding discussion also distinguishes two variants of the social market model. Relative to the continental SMEs, the Nordic SMEs are distinguished by higher levels of union density, more universalistic welfare states, and greater reliance on the public sector (services) in the provision of social welfare.

Let me emphasize again that these distinctions are essentially heuristic, providing a way to organize data and to think about the role of institutions. It is not my intention to argue that the threefold typology introduced in this chapter by itself provides anything like an adequate explanation of social and economic outcomes. As we have already seen, some social market economies have had much better employment performance than others, and the same goes for liberal market economies. This points to the need for a more fine-grained institutional analysis, but it also suggests that policy choices matter—and that policy choices do not follow directly from institutional arrangements.

Chapter 3

Income Distribution and Labor Markets

Rising income inequality represents a conspicuous feature of the "new economy" of the 1980s and 1990s. Focusing on wage differentials, a number of scholars as well as more casual observers have suggested that the American experience is quite exceptional in this respect and that other OECD countries have, for better or worse, followed a different trajectory, holding inequality at bay. In a somewhat different vein, some contributors to the varieties of capitalism literature argue that rising wage inequality is a distinctive characteristic of the way liberal market economies have adjusted to the intensification of international competition.[1] I argue in this chapter that rising inequality is a more pervasive phenomenon. The extent to which inequality has grown varies a great deal across OECD countries, but there is a common trend, and the American experience is not as exceptional as we often suppose.

I begin by looking at aggregate data on the distribution of disposable household income and then hone in on the distribution of gross earnings among working-age households. As we shall see, gross earnings became more unevenly distributed in all but one of the OECD countries for which we have time series data for the 1980s and 1990s (the Netherlands being the only exception), and the growth of earnings inequality provides a very strong predictor of the growth of disposable income inequality on a cross-national basis. To some extent, taxation and social spending have offset increases in earnings inequality, but redistribution by governments has failed to keep up with inegalitarian market forces. More tentatively, I shall argue that labor market dynamics are key to the general tendency for inequality to grow or, in other words, that changes in the distribution of wealth and financial market dynamics are of secondary importance.

To explain patterns of earnings inequality growth among working-age households, we must attend not only to changes in the distribution of wages among employed workers but also to changes in the distribution of employment across households. We observe in the United States and some other countries large increases in wage inequality over the 1980s and 1990s, but the effects of these increases for the distribution of household earnings were partly offset by increased employment among low-income households. In other countries, wage differentials remained more or less stable, but low-income households lost employment relative to high-income households. Access to employment thus emerges as a crucial source of inequality in the following analysis. Leaving the question of explaining comparative employment performance for subsequent chapters, I will explore the reasons why wage inequality has increased more in some countries than in others, emphasizing the role of political-institutional factors, and briefly address the relationship between wage inequality and productivity in the final sections of this chapter.

THE DISTRIBUTION OF HOUSEHOLD INCOME

Taken directly from *The State of Working America 2002/2003*, a comprehensive report by Lawrence Mishel, Jared Bernstein, and Heather Boushey, figure 3.1 illustrates the growth of inequality in the United States since the mid-1970s and the sharp departure that this trajectory represents relative to the 1950s and 1960s. With American families ranked according to income and then divided into quintiles, the top panel shows the cumulative growth of real gross family income—that is to say, inflation-adjusted income before taxes—for each quintile from 1947 to 1973. The bottom panel shows the corresponding figures for the period from 1973 to 2000. According to the data presented in figure 3.1, the gross income of the average American family nearly doubled in real terms (increasing by 99.4 percent) over the twenty-six years from 1947 to 1973 but increased by less than one-third (29 percent) over the twenty-seven years from 1973 to 2000. Equally striking, the latter period is distinguished from the former by a very different pattern of income growth across the income distribution.

Over the period from 1947 to 1973, the income of families in the bottom fifth of the income distribution (conventionally designated as the first quintile) grew more rapidly than the income of families in any of the other quintiles, while the incomes of families in the top fifth of the distribution (the fifth quintile) grew more slowly than the incomes of fam-

33

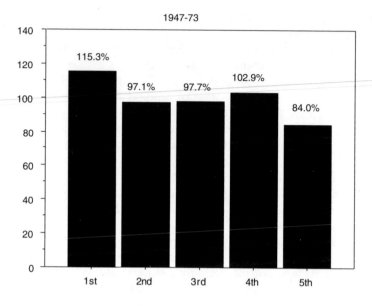

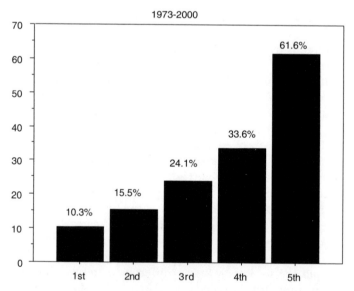

Source: Lawrence Mishel, Jared Bernstein, and Heather Boushey, *The State of Working America 2002/2003* (Ithaca: Cornell University Press, 2003), 57.

Figure 3.1 Growth of family income by quintile in the United States, 1947–2000

Table 3.1 Distribution of U.S. household income by quintile, 1947–2001

	1947	1979	2001
Top fifth	43.0%	41.1%	47.7%
Fourth fifth	23.1	24.0	22.9
Middle fifth	17.0	17.5	15.5
Second fifth	11.9	11.9	9.7
Bottom fifth	5.0	5.5	4.2
Top 5 percent	17.5	15.5	21.0

Source: Lawrence Mishel, Jared Bernstein, and Heather Boushey, *The State of Working America 2002/2003* (Ithaca: Cornell University Press. 2003), 54.

ilies in any of the other quintiles. In other words, the tide of postwar growth not only lifted all boats, it also boosted the relative position of low-income families. The 1970s mark the beginning of a sharp reversal of this pattern. As we move from the bottom to the top of the income distribution for the period from 1973 to 2000, each successive quintile fared better than the preceding quintile. In real terms, the incomes of the bottom fifth of families increased by only 10.3 percent over this period, while the incomes of the top fifth increased by 61.6 percent. As Mishel, Bernstein, and Boushey show, virtually all of the income growth at the bottom end of the income distribution occurred in the second half of the 1990s. Again adjusting for inflation, from 1979 to 1997 the income of families in the first quintile actually declined and the income of families in the second quintile did not change at all.[2]

Table 3.1 shows the cumulative effects of these differential rates of income growth for the distribution of family income by quintile. From an all-time high of 5.5 percent in 1979, the share of total income earned by the bottom fifth of families had fallen to 4.2 percent by 2001. More spectacularly, the top fifth's share of total income increased from 41.1 percent to 47.7 percent over the same period. As table 3.1 also indicates, the income share of the top 5 percent of families increased even more sharply.

Based on the Luxembourg Income Study (LIS), an ongoing project to pool individual-level data from national surveys and to organize these data in such a way that they are comparable across countries, table 3.2 puts the American experience in comparative perspective. Whereas the figures for the United States presented above refer to "family income," the LIS-based figures in table 3.2 refer to "household income." (The United States Census Bureau defines "families" as two or more related persons

Table 3.2 Distribution of disposable household income, as measured by Gini coefficient, 1979–2000

	Earliest	Lowest	Most recent	Average annual change since earliest	Average annual change since lowest
Nordic SMEs	**22.1**		**25.2**		
Denmark (1987–97)	25.4		25.7	.03	
Finland (1987–00)	20.9		24.7	.29	
Norway (1979–00)	22.3		25.1	.13	
Sweden (1981–00)	19.7		25.2	.29	
Continental SMEs	**25.3**		**26.7**		
Austria (1987–97)	22.7		26.6	.39	
Belgium (1985–00)	22.7		27.7	.33	
Germany (1981–00)	24.4		26.4	.11	
Netherlands (1983–99)	26.0		24.8	−.08	
Switzerland (1982–92)	30.9		30.7	−.02	
LMEs	**29.3**		**33.0**		
Australia (1981–94)	28.1		31.1	.23	
Canada (1981–00)	28.4	28.1 (1991)	30.2	.09	.23
Ireland (1987–00)	32.8		32.3	−.04	
United Kingdom (1979–99)	27.0		34.5	.38	
United States (1979–00)	30.1		36.8	.32	
France (1979–94)	29.3	28.7 (1989)	28.8	−.03	.02
Italy (1986–00)	30.6	29.0 (1991)	33.3	.19	.48

Source: Luxembourg Income Study, http://www.lisproject.org/keyfigures/ineqtable.htm, October 2004. Most recent Danish observation calculated by Lane Kenworthy from raw LIS data.
Note: The figures refer to disposable household income adjusted for household size (see note 3).

living together; the LIS definition of "households" includes persons living alone.) More important, the LIS data refer to disposable income rather than gross income and thus take into account the redistributive effects of taxation. Like the U.S. data presented above, the LIS data encompass cash payments received from the government and income from financial assets (rent, interest, and dividends) as well as income from self-employment and income from dependent employment (wages and bonuses) and also adjust for household size.[3]

The measure of income distribution presented in table 3.2 is the Gini coefficient. This is a very common measure of inequality, but a few words about the meaning of Gini coefficients might be in order before we look at table 3.2. As illustrated by figure 3.2, the Gini coefficient is obtained by arranging all units of observation—in this case, households—in ascending order from the unit with the lowest income to the unit with the highest income and then plotting the cumulative income share of

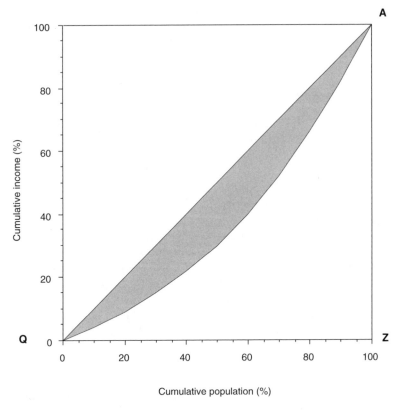

Source: Adapted from Deborah Mitchell, *Income Transfers in Ten Welfare States*. (Aldershot: Avebury, 1991), 106.

Figure 3.2 Illustration of the Gini measure of income inequality

these units against their cumulative population share. If all households had the same income, the result of this exercise would be a straight diagonal line from point Q to point A. Across countries and over time, actual income distribution will look more like the curve below the "line of perfect equality" in figure 3.2. The Gini coefficient is the ratio of the shaded area in figure 3.2 to the total area of the triangle AQZ. When multiplied by one hundred (as reported in table 3.2 and subsequent tables), the Gini coefficient thus represents the percentage of total income that would have to be redistributed in order to achieve perfect income equality.[4]

For the majority of countries included in the LIS database, we only have data for the 1980s and 1990s. To simplify matters and to maximize comparability across countries, table 3.2 presents the earliest post-1978 observations and the most recent observations of Gini coefficients available on the LIS website. Table 3.2 also records the lowest observation over the time period covered when this observation refers to any year other than the first or last year. When there is no figure recorded in the "lowest" column, this means that the earliest or the most recent observation is the lowest observation for that country. As indicated by table 3.2, the earliest and most recent observations refer to different years for different countries. To make it possible to compare the extent of change across countries, in the last two columns of table 3.2 I report the changes in Gini coefficients from the earliest observation and from the lowest observation as an annual average.

Table 3.2 shows that rising inequality of disposable household income is a rather pervasive trend across the OECD countries in the 1980s and 1990s. In ten of the sixteen countries included in table 3.2, the earliest available observation of Gini coefficients is also the lowest observation, meaning that inequality rose over the entire time period covered. In three other countries—Canada, France, and Italy—we observe an increase in equality in the 1980s, followed by a decrease in the 1990s. In the Canadian and Italian cases, the decline of equality in the 1990s was greater than the rise of equality in the 1980s. In the French case, the most recent Gini coefficient is smaller than the earliest observation, but it is noteworthy that the most recent French observation refers to 1994 whereas the most recent Canadian and Italian observations refer to 2000. While table 3.2 provides no indication of rising income inequality for the Netherlands, Switzerland, and Ireland, the Swiss data do not go beyond 1992. The Netherlands and Ireland would appear to be the only countries that can be said to have bucked the general trend toward a more inegalitarian distribution of disposable household income.

Among the countries for which increases of inequality are recorded in table 3.2, the United States does not stand out as a particularly egregious case. Over the period since 1979, we observe significantly larger increases in Gini coefficients for the United Kingdom and Austria and roughly comparable increases for Sweden and Finland. Also, table 3.2 indicates that income inequality increased substantially more in Italy over the 1990s than it did in the United States over the 1980s and 1990s taken together. In all of these countries, the growth of household income inequality since the lowest observation would be greater than in the United States if growth were expressed relative to initial levels or, in others, as percentage change. Absolute change strikes me as a more appropriate metric for comparison since it does not penalize more egalitarian countries.

From the varieties of capitalism perspective developed in chapter 2, the variation of inequality trajectories among Nordic and continental SMEs and also among LMEs constitutes an important feature of table 3.2. In each group, we find countries in which inequality has declined or held steady as well as countries in which inequality has grown significantly. Comparing group averages, the Nordic SMEs appear to have a more egalitarian distribution of disposable household income than the continental SMEs at the beginning as well as at the end of the time period covered by Table 3.2, but this difference is entirely attributable to Switzerland's exceptionally high level of inequality (by SME standards). Setting aside the Swiss case, there are no consistent differences between Nordic and continental SMEs with regard to the distribution of disposable household income in either the 1980s or the 1990s. However, the distinction between SMEs and LMEs clearly does correspond to an important divide among the OECD countries on this score. Again leaving Switzerland aside, the most egalitarian LME (the United Kingdom) was more inegalitarian than the least egalitarian SME (the Netherlands) in the early 1980s, and this was still true in the late 1990s (the most egalitarian LME now being Canada and the least egalitarian SME being Germany). Indeed, the gap between SMEs and LMEs increased in the course of the 1980s and 1990s. Inequality of disposable household income grew more consistently and, on average, more rapidly in LMEs than in SMEs.

The rise of disposable income inequality might be attributed to demographic changes, booming stock markets, cutbacks in welfare benefits provided by governments, and regressive tax reforms as well as inegalitarian labor market dynamics. Why do I think that labor market developments are particularly important? Let me begin to answer this question by introducing a new layer of cross-national evidence. For a more restricted set of countries, the LIS database allows us to calculate Gini coefficients for gross earnings of working-age households. Organized in the same manner as table 3.2, table 3.3 presents the results of these calculations. "Gross earnings" refer to pre-tax income from work and self-employment as well as "dependent" employment, and "working-age households" are here defined as households headed by someone aged between 25 and 59. Table 3.3 thus clears out the effects of taxes, transfer payments (public pensions in particular), and income from capital.[5]

Rising inequality emerges as a much more pronounced trend in the data on gross earnings for working-age households than in the data on disposable income for all households. In Norway and Australia, earnings inequality declined in the first half of the 1980s but increased sharply in the subsequent ten to fifteen years. In eight of the other nine countries, we observe quite large increases in Gini coefficients for gross earnings from the earliest to the most recent observation, ranging between an average annual increase of .12 in the Swiss case (for which we have no data beyond 1992) and an average annual increase of .62 in the British case. The Netherlands stands out as the only country in which earnings

Table 3.3 Distribution of gross earnings among working-age households, as measured by Gini coefficient, 1979–2000

	Earliest	Lowest	Most recent	Average annual change since earliest	Average annual change since lowest
Nordic SMEs	**29.7**		**34.9**		
Denmark (1987–97)	30.8		34.7	.39	
Finland (1987–00)	30.1		35.9	.45	
Norway (1979–00)	28.4	26.5 (1986)	31.8	.16	.38
Sweden (1981–00)	29.5		37.3	.41	
Continental SMEs	**32.8**		**35.0**		
Belgium (1997)			38.4		
Germany (1981–00)	28.5		34.6	.32	
Netherlands (1983–99)	38.3		34.1	−.26	
Switzerland (1982–92)	31.5		32.7	.12	
LMEs	**35.5**		**42.1**		
Australia (1981–94)	39.5	36.2 (1985)	39.7	.02	.39
Canada (1981–00)	33.5		39.6	.36	
United Kingdom (1979–99)	33.2		45.6	.62	
United States (1979–00)	35.6		43.4	.37	

Note. Working-age households are defined as households headed by someone between the ages of 25 and 59. As in table 3.2, the figures adjust for household size. Calculations by Lane Kenworthy from LIS database.

inequality declined during the 1980s and 1990s. In all of the other countries, Gini coefficients for gross earnings increased significantly more than Gini coefficients for disposable income. This is least true for the United States, where the Gini coefficient for earnings inequality increased by .37 per year while the Gini coefficient for disposable income increased by .32 per year from 1979–2000. At the other end of the spectrum, the Gini coefficient for gross earnings increased by .39 per year in Denmark from 1987 to 1997, but the Gini coefficient for disposable income only increased by .03 over the same period. As a group, the Nordic countries experienced at least as much growth of earnings inequality as the liberal market economies did in the 1980s and 1990s. (Relative to initial levels, the growth of earnings inequality in the Nordic countries was considerably greater.)

The discrepancy between changes in gross earnings inequality and disposable income inequality suggests that the Nordic welfare states, most particularly the Danish welfare state, have largely offset inegalitarian labor market trends or, in other words, compensated low-income households for their relative losses through more progressive income taxation or through redistributive transfer programs. With the notable exception of the Netherlands, all governments appear to have counteracted market forces to some degree. In the Dutch case, earnings inequality actually declined more than disposable income inequality, suggesting that the Dutch welfare state became less redistributive over this period. However, we must tread cautiously in drawing such inferences, keeping in mind that the figures for disposable income inequality include all households, while the figures for earnings inequality include only working-age households. I shall return to the question of the redistributive effects of taxation and social spending in chapters 7 and 8. For the time being, it suffices to note again that the U.S. data presented earlier in this section refer to gross family income. Following a detailed analysis of the effects of tax policy changes in the United States, Mishel, Bernstein, and Boushey conclude that "slower income growth and widening income inequality are primarily before-tax phenomena."[6]

As illustrated by figure 3.3, increases in gross earnings inequality correlate very closely with increases in disposable income inequality on a cross-national basis. This finding lends a great deal of plausibility to the claim that growing inequality of income from employment represents the primary reason why the distribution of disposable household income became more unequal in these countries between 1980 and 2000. Why, then, has earnings inequality grown in recent years? And why has earnings inequality grown more in some countries than in others? As noted at the outset, my answer to these questions has to do not only with (increasing) wage disparities among workers but also with changes in the distribution of employment across households.

Before moving on to my analysis of labor market dynamics, let me emphasize that I do not wish to deny the significance of wealth and financial market dynamics as a source of growing income inequality in the United States and elsewhere. For the United States, Mishel, Bernstein, and Boushey report that the share of total market-based personal income (defined as total income minus government transfers) accounted for by rent, interest, and dividends increased from 14.5 percent in 1973 to 20.0 percent in 2000, while the share accounted for by realized capital gains increased from 3.5 percent to 6.7 percent over the same period.[7] There is considerable evidence that the concentration of wealth also increased during the 1980s and 1990s. Even if this had not been the case, the increase in the share of capital income relative to the share of labor income would have entailed some increase in income inequality for the simple reason that income from financial assets is more unevenly distributed than income from employment.[8] As income from employment still accounts for more than two-thirds of total market-based personal income, however, it seems far-fetched to attribute the growth of income inequality primarily to changes in returns to capital and changes in the concen-

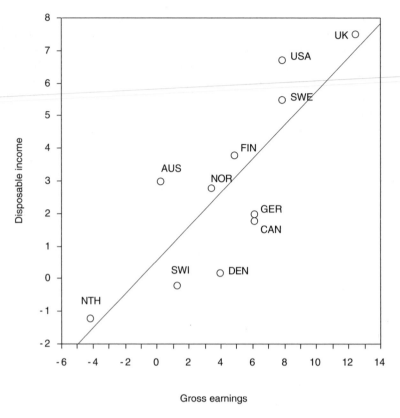

Correlation: .818
Note: Time periods vary by country, see tables 3.2 and 3.3.

Figure 3.3 Change in Gini coefficients for disposable income (all households) vs. change in Gini coefficients for gross earnings (working-age households), circa 1980–2000

tration of wealth. In addition, the shift from labor income to capital income and the stock market boom of the 1990s represent trends that can be observed across all the OECD countries. At least on the face of things, labor market dynamics constitute a more promising point of departure for an account of the growth of income inequality that sheds light on the considerable cross-national variation that we observe in the LIS data.

The demographic sources of growing income inequality should also be noted before we proceed. In the literature focusing on the U.S. experience, two developments pertaining to the changing composition of households have commonly been invoked to explain the growth of household income inequality. First, it is commonplace to attribute slow income growth at the lower end of the income distribution to an increase in the share of families with a single adult or, more specifically, single-mother families. Secondly, some scholars have suggested that a great deal of the growth of income inequality can be explained in terms of marital "homogamy" or, more prosaically, the correlation of spousal incomes. At least since the early 1970s, it has become increasingly the case that men with high incomes tend to be married to women with high incomes while men with low incomes tend to be married to women with low incomes.[9] Mishel, Bernstein, and Boushey argue convincingly that the first line of argument falters on timing: the negative effects of changes in household type were most pronounced in the 1970s, yet income growth across quintiles was more evenly distributed during this decade than during the subsequent two decades.[10] Again, however, it is first and foremost the comparative perspective adopted in this book that leads me to focus on labor market dynamics rather than demographics. The growth of single-parent families and marital homogamy are common trends across the OECD countries. These developments may well be invoked to explain why income inequality has grown in most OECD countries, but they do not seem to speak directly to the question of why income inequality has grown more in some countries than in others.

WAGE INEQUALITY

The OECD has compiled a reasonably comprehensive dataset on the distribution of wages in most member states. This dataset refers to individuals rather than households or families. "Wages" are defined in much the same way that LIS defines "gross earnings" (income from employment before taxes), but the OECD dataset is restricted to individuals in dependent employment. In other words, the dataset excludes the self-employed. For all countries except Norway, the OECD dataset is further restricted to full-time employees. The exclusion of part-time employees represents an important limitation that must be kept in mind as we look at the OECD data on relative wages.

The OECD dataset consists of measures of the gross earnings from employment for individuals at the different points in the earnings distribution. This does not allow us to calculate Gini coefficients. Instead, I will here use the 90-10 ratio as a summary measure of wage inequality. The 90-10 ratio is simply the ratio of the earnings of someone in the 90th percentile of the earnings distribution (the bottom of the top 10 percent of wage-earners) to the earnings of someone in the 10th percentile (the top of the bottom 10 percent of wage-earners). The 90-10 ratio thus measures the distance between two points at opposite ends of the earnings

43

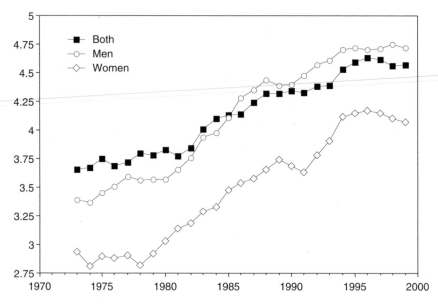

Source: OECD Directorate for Education, Employment, Labour and Social Affairs.

Figure 3.4 90–10 ratios for men and women in the United States, 1973–99

distribution while disregarding the tails of the distribution—in particular CEOs, investment bankers, specialist surgeons, and others who command extremely high salaries.

Using the OECD data, figure 3.4 tracks the evolution of 90-10 wage ratios for men and women separately and for both men and women combined in the United States from 1973 to 1998. In 1973, an American worker in the 90th percentile of the both-gender distribution earned 3.65 times as much as a worker in the 10th percentile. The both-gender 90-10 ratio rose quite steadily over the following two decades, reaching an all-time peak of 4.63 in 1996 and then fell slightly in 1997 and 1998. Measured in this fashion, overall wage inequality among full-time employees increased by just about 25 percent from 1973 to 1998. Treating men and women separately, we observe an even more dramatic increase of wage inequality from 1973 to 1998: 39.7 percent for men and 39.5 percent for women. As these figures indicate, the growth of within-gender inequality was partly offset by a pronounced narrowing of between-gender wage differentials from the mid-1970s onwards. According to Mishel, Bernstein, and Boushey, the median wage for women was 63.1 percent of the median wage for men in 1973. By 2001, this figure had increased to 78.1 percent.[11]

Table 3.4 90–10 wage ratios for full-time employees, 1980–2000

	Earliest	Lowest	Most recent	Average annual change since earliest	Average annual change since lowest
Nordic SMEs	**2.18**		**2.23**		
Denmark (1980–90)	2.13		2.16	.003	
Finland (1980–00)	2.47	2.29 (1996)	2.41*	−.003	.024
Norway (1980–00)	2.07		2.03*	−.002	
Sweden (1980–98)	2.03	1.95 (1983)	2.30*	.014	.021
Continental SMEs	**2.66**		**2.64**		
Belgium (1986–94)	2.40		2.24	−.022	
Germany (1984–95)	3.00	2.69 (1988)	2.86	−.013	.024
Netherlands (1980–97)	2.54	2.40 (1983)	2.83	.017	.031
Switzerland (1991–97)	2.71		2.62	−.013	
LMEs	**3.31**		**3.77**		
Australia (1980–00)	2.83	2.72 (1985)	3.07*	.010	.023
Canada (1981–94)	4.02		4.18	.012	
Ireland (1997)			3.93		
New Zealand (1984–97)	2.89	2.87 (1986)	3.41	.040	.049
United Kingdom (1980–00)	2.98		3.40	.021	
United States (1980–00)	3.83		4.64*	.039	
Italy (1986–96)	2.22		2.39	.017	
Japan (1980–98)	3.00		2.98	−.001	

Sources: Electronic data provided by the OECD Directorate for Education, Employment, Labour, and Social Affairs, supplemented by observations for 2000 (marked by an asterisk) reported in OECD, *Employment Outlook* (2004), 141.

For a small number of countries, the OECD dataset includes data for the 1970s, but most countries do not enter the dataset until the 1980s. The available data indicate that both-gender wage inequality began to increase in Australia and Canada, as well as the United States, in the second half of the 1970s, but in other countries (Finland, Sweden, the Netherlands, the United Kingdom, and Japan) wage inequality declined through the 1970s.[12] For the entire set of countries for which the OECD dataset provides comparable figures, table 3.4 summarizes the evolution of both-gender wage inequality from 1980 onwards. This table is organized in the same manner as tables 3.2 and 3.3: for each country, I report the earliest observation of 90-10 ratios available for the period 1980–2000 and also the most recent observation available. If there are observations for intervening years that are lower than both the earliest and the most recent observations, I also report the lowest observation in the time series for each country. As table 3.4 indicates, the time periods covered by the OECD dataset vary considerably from country to country. In particular, it should be noted that the Danish time series does not extend into the

1990s while the Swiss time series only begins in 1991. To make it possible to compare trends in wage inequality across country-specific time periods, I again report the average annual change from the earliest to the most recent observation and also the average annual change from the lowest to the most recent observation. The figures on average annual change in table 3.4 are much smaller than the corresponding figures in tables 3.2 and 3.3, but this is simply a result of 90-10 ratios being smaller numbers than Gini coefficients. Though I prefer to compare absolute changes rather than percentage changes, it is useful to keep in mind that the U.S. figure for average annual change (.041) represents a 21 percent increase of wage inequality over twenty years.

My primary interest is to compare trends in wage inequality, but a few preliminary observations about cross-national variation in levels of wage inequality are in order. Based on most recent available observations for each country, table 3.4 shows that the United States has by far the most inegalitarian wage structure of any of the OECD countries.[13] Norway occupies the opposite end of the cross-national spectrum. In 2000, an American in the 90th percentile of the earnings distribution earned nearly five times as much as someone in the 10th percentile, while the equivalent Norwegian earned only twice as much as someone in the 10th percentile.

My threefold typology of political economies turns out to be a very useful way to organize the data on relative wages. With respect to the most recent as well as the earliest observations, the Nordic SMEs, the continental SMEs and the LMEs represent three quite distinct bands on the cross-national spectrum measuring levels of wage inequality. The only exception to this pattern is Belgium, which falls within the Nordic range in the mid-1980s and mid-1990s alike. Setting the Belgian case aside, the distribution of wages in all Nordic SMEs has been consistently more egalitarian than the distribution of wages in all continental SMEs, and the distribution of wages in all continental SMEs has been consistently more egalitarian than the distribution of wages in all LMEs. (While Italy occupies an intermediate position between the Nordic and the continental SMEs, Japan occupies an intermediate position between the continental SMEs and the LMEs.) The absence of any convergence in levels of wage inequality among the three groups is another noteworthy feature of table 3.4.

For five out of fifteen countries (Denmark, Canada, the United Kingdom, the United States, and Italy), the earliest 90-10 ratio observation is also the lowest observation. In the Danish case, we observe only a very small increase of wage inequality from the earliest to the most recent observation, but, again, the Danish time series does not extend into the 1990s. In the other four countries that fall into this category, the increase of 90-10 ratios from the earliest to the most recent observation ranges

Table 3.5 Percentage change of 90–10 ratios for full-time employees, ca. 1983–98

	Men and women	Men only	Women only
SMEs			
Finland (1983–98)	–3.2	1.2	–1.9
Germany (1984–95)	–4.7	2.3	–15.4
Netherlands (1985–97)	13.2	19.8	4.9
Sweden (1983–98)	13.8	16.3	9.4
LMEs			
Australia (1983–99)	3.4	16.0	–2.5
Canada (1981–94)	3.9	8.4	7.2
New Zealand (1984–97)	18.0	30.5	16.0
United Kingdom (1983–99)	10.9	21.1	19.2
United States (1983–99)	13.7	19.8	23.7
Italy (1986–96)	7.7	16.7	–5.7
Japan	–4.5	1.5	1.4

Source: See table 3.4.

between .012 for Canada and .041 for the United States. For another four countries (Norway, Belgium, Switzerland, and Japan), the most recent observation is the lowest observation. For Belgium and Switzerland, the data show substantial declines of wage inequality, but these data cover relatively short time periods. As for Japan and Norway, the level of wage inequality was essentially unchanged from the 1980s to 1990s. For the remaining six countries (Finland, Sweden, Germany, the Netherlands, Australia, and New Zealand), we observe a decline of wage inequality through the first half of the 1980s (in the case of Finland, the first half of the 1990s) followed by substantial growth of wage inequality. In four of these cases (Sweden, the Netherlands, Australia, and New Zealand), the growth of wage inequality in the later period swamped the decline in the earlier period, but in two cases (Finland and Germany) the distribution of wages at the end period was still more egalitarian than the distribution of wages at the beginning. I hasten to point out that the OECD data for Germany do not include workers in the erstwhile East German states. For Germany as a whole, there can be little doubt that wage inequality increased significantly in the 1990s. The extremely sharp increase of wage inequality in Finland in the second half of the 1990s is also noteworthy. At most, table 3.4 allows us only to identify four countries that can be said to have bucked the tendency for wage inequality to rise over the last two decades: Norway, Belgium, Switzerland, and Japan.

The growth of wage inequality emerges as an even more pervasive and pronounced trend when we look at the distribution among male workers only. For a subset of the countries included in table 3.4, table 3.5 reports percentage increases for both-gender as well as separate male and female

90-10 ratios over roughly comparable periods of time. From the mid-1980s to the late 1990s, wage differentials among men increased in every country included in this table, and the growth of male wage inequality was always stronger than the growth of both-gender wage inequality—in some instances, much stronger. As in the United States, the gender gap in pay narrowed in virtually all OECD countries from the late 1970s through the mid-1990s. The only exception to this generalization is Sweden, where already in the late 1970s the earnings of full-time female workers averaged 84 percent of the earnings of male workers.[14] As table 3.5 indicates, wage inequality among women increased in the majority of countries, but this is not true for Finland, Germany, Australia, and Japan. In no country other than the United States did female wage inequality increase more than male wage inequality.

In sum, tables 3.4 and 3.5 show that the distribution of wages has become more inegalitarian in most OECD countries over the last two or three decades but also that the extent of this development and its timing varies a great deal across countries. Surely, the growth in wage inequality has been an important factor in the growth of household inequality, measured either in terms of gross earnings or disposable income. Yet the data presented above call into question the idea that wage inequality trends holds the key to cross-national differences in the growth of household inequality. Most obviously, the data for the Nordic countries pose a major puzzle from this point of view. By comparative standards, the growth of wage inequality appears to have been quite modest in the Nordic SMEs, yet these countries experienced a most dramatic increase in gross earnings inequality among working-age households from the mid-1980s through the 1990s. The flip side of the Nordic puzzle is the Dutch puzzle. While the Netherlands stands out in tables 3.4 and 3.5 as the SME in which wage inequality increased the most in the 1980s and 1990s, it stands out in table 3.3 as the only OECD country in which gross earnings inequality among working-age households actually declined over these two decades. Clearly, there is something missing from this picture. That the Netherlands achieved exceptionally rapid employment growth in the 1980s and 1990s while the Nordic SMEs experienced serious employment crises in the early 1990s suggests that employment is the key to resolving the puzzles that emerge when we try to match trends in wage inequality and trends in household earnings inequality.

ACCESS TO EMPLOYMENT AS A SOURCE OF INEQUALITY

As noted at the outset, the OECD data on relative wages reviewed in the preceding section are restricted to full-time employees. On average, part-time workers account for nearly one fifth (19.3 percent) of the employed labor force in the eighteen countries discussed in this book. The employed labor force in turn accounts for slightly more than two thirds (69.2 percent) of the working-age population, defined as people aged 15 to 64. Thus the OECD data on relative wages pertain to the distribution of earnings among people who constitute roughly 55 percent of the working-age population. In view of this, it is not so surprising that trends in the OECD data on relative wages fail to match trends in income inequality among working-age households.

To get a more complete understanding of trends in income inequality among working-age households, we must attend to the distributive impact of unemployment (or non-employment) as well as the distributive impact of part-time employment. Let us begin with part-time employment. As shown in table 3.6, there is a lot of variation in the incidence of part-time employment among the OECD countries, and this variation cuts across the distinction between liberal and social market economies. At one end of the spectrum, part-time employees currently constitute slightly more than one tenth of the employed labor force in Finland; at the other end of the spectrum, they represent more than one third of the employed labor force in the Netherlands. Table 3.6 also shows that women are heavily overrepresented among those employed part-time in all these countries and especially in the continental SMEs. Finally, table 3.6 shows that the incidence of part-time employment increased in most OECD countries from 1983 to 2003, often very dramatically, but four countries bucked this trend: Denmark, Norway, Sweden, and the United States.

Followed by Ireland and Australia, the Netherlands stands out as the country in which the growth of part-time employment relative to full-time employment over the last two decades has been the most pronounced. As we shall explore further in subsequent chapters, the employment growth for which the Netherlands became famous in the 1990s occurred almost entirely through the growth of part-time employment, and this feature is the principal source of divergent assessments of the Dutch "jobs miracle." Does the growth of part-time employment represent a solidaristic sharing of scarce employment opportunities, if not a progressive employer response to changes in the demand for employment associated with women's labor force participation, family needs, and affluence? Or does it represent the growth of precarious and poorly paid employment and a widening of the gulf between "insiders" and "outsiders" in the labor market?

For now, I am only concerned with the distributive impact of part-time employment. In all the OECD countries, part-time workers typically earn less, on an hourly basis, than full-time workers do. For a subset of coun-

49

Table 3.6 Incidence and composition of part-time employment, 1983–2003

	Part-time labor as % of total employment			Women's share in part-time employment,
	1983	2003	Change	2003
Nordic SMEs	**17.8**	**15.6**	**−2.2**	**68.4**
Denmark	19.2	15.8	−3.4	64.2
Finland	8.4	11.3	2.9	63.5
Norway	28.1*	21.0	−6.9	75.2
Sweden	15.5*	14.1	−1.4	70.8
Continental SMEs	**12.3**	**21.1**	**8.8**	**82.0**
Austria	8.4	13.6	5.2	87.3
Belgium	9.7	17.7	8.0	81.0
Germany	12.6	19.6	7.0	83.3
Netherlands	18.5	34.5	16.0	76.0
Switzerland		25.1		82.2
LMEs	**15.1**	**20.6**	**5.5**	**71.3**
Australia	17.5	27.9	10.4	67.2
Canada	16.8	18.8	2.0	68.9
Ireland	7.1	18.1	11.0	72.1
New Zealand	15.3	22.3	7.0	73.3
United Kingdom	18.4	23.3	4.9	77.3
United States	15.4	13.2	−2.2	68.8
France	8.9	12.9	4.0	80.0
Italy	7.8	12.0	4.2	74.7
Japan	17.5	26.0	8.5	66.7

Sources: OECD, *Employment Outlook* (1997), 177–78 and *Employment Outlook* (2004), 224.
Note: Part-time employment usually defined as working fewer than 30 hours per week in the main job. Marked by an asterisk, the Norwegian and Swedish figures for 1983 are based on a earlier data series, which tracks the main OECD series closely for 1990–96.

tries, table 3.7 shows the size of the hourly wage premium enjoyed by full-time workers in 1995. As figure 3.5 illustrates, cross-national variation in pay differentials between part-time and full-time workers broadly corresponds to cross-national variation in levels of inequality among full-time workers: on average, part-time workers tend to do better relative to full-time workers in countries with more compressed wages among full-time workers. This suggests that the incidence of part-time employment does not fundamentally alter comparative assessments of levels of wage inequality: that is to say, if our measure of wage inequality included part-time workers, all countries would be more inegalitarian, but the country rankings would remain more or less the same.

The incidence of part-time employment becomes a more relevant consideration when we compare countries in terms of change over time. Unfortunately, we do not have any cross-national data on changes in pay differentials between part-time and full-time workers over the 1980s and

Table 3.7 Median hourly earnings of part-time workers as percentage of median hourly earnings of full-time workers, 1995

Nordic SMEs	**81.3%**
Denmark	74.2
Finland	82.6
Sweden	87.2
Continental SMEs	**78.0**
Belgium	78.4
Germany	82.5
Netherlands	73.2
LMEs	**64.4**
Australia	89.4
Canada	55.9
United Kingdom	58.0
United States	54.3
France	73.0
Italy	87.4

Source: OECD, *Employment Outlook* (1999), 24.

1990s. Supposing that these differentials remained more or less unchanged, however, shifts in the incidence of part-time employment would have had important implications for overall wage inequality. For example, consider the following two-country comparison. In 1995, the hourly wage premium enjoyed by full-time workers was roughly the same in Sweden and Australia. From 1983 to 1999, both-gender wage inequality among full-time employees, measured by 90-10 ratios, increased by 13.8 percent in Sweden and by 3.4 percent in Australia. Over the same period of time, however, the incidence of part-time employment increased from 17.5 percent to 26.0 percent in Australia while it declined from 15.5 percent to 14.0 percent in Sweden. Relative to the average for all countries, the growth of Swedish wage inequality would probably be lower and the growth of Australian wage inequality higher if our measure of wage inequality included the wages of part-time workers.

This said, it is immediately apparent that shifts in the distribution of employment between part-time and full-time alone do not explain the Nordic and Dutch puzzles noted earlier. Based on changes in the incidence of part-time employment, we might have expected gross earnings inequality among working-age households to have grown less than wage inequality among full-time employees in the Nordic SMEs and more than wage inequality among full-time employees in the Netherlands. Clearly, the available data do not bear out these expectations. From the point of view of resolving the Nordic and Dutch puzzles, the distributive consequences of unemployment and employment growth would appear to be

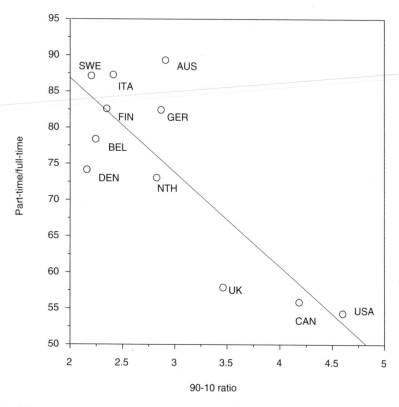

Correlation: −.824
Sources: Tables 3.4 and 3.7.
Note: Most recent observations of 90-10 ratios for countries with time series ending prior to 1995.

Figure 3.5 Median hourly earnings of part-time workers as percentage of median hourly earnings of full-time workers vs. 90-10 ratios for full-time workers, 1995

the crucial issue. With respect to unemployment, there is a great deal of evidence, from the United States and other countries, indicating that during economic downturns employers tend to hang on to skilled, well-paid employees while shedding unskilled, low-wage employees. The reasons for this behavior are not particularly mysterious: whereas unskilled workers are easily replaceable, reconstituting their skilled work-force as business activity picks up represents a potentially costly endeavor that employers wish to avoid. Persistently high levels of unemployment are likely to affect the relative bargaining power of unskilled and low-skill workers adversely, but in the short run rising unemployment tends to reduce wage inequality, as more low-wage workers than high-wage workers

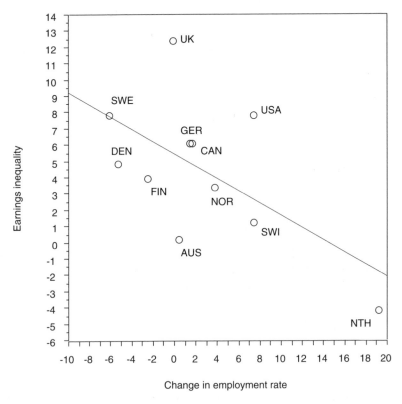

Correlation: .820
Note: See table 3.3 for (country-specific) time periods covered. Employment rates from OECD, *Employment Outlook* (various years).

Figure 3.6 Change in earning inequality among working-age households (Gini coefficients) vs. change in employment rate, 1980s and 1990s

drop out of the employed labor force. Needless to say, this does not mean that unemployment promotes equality. Even under the very generous unemployment insurance provisions of the Nordic countries, loss of employment invariably entails a loss of income, which is picked up in the data on household earnings but not in the data on the distribution of wages among employed workers.

Figure 3.6 plots changes in Gini coefficients for gross earnings among working-age households against changes in the rate of employment—the employed as a percentage of the population between ages 15 and 64. Over the time periods for which we have data on household earnings, these variables are rather closely associated with each other.[15] Generally speaking, inequality of household earnings grew less rapidly in countries that experienced more rapid increases in the percentage of the working-age population with jobs. In particular, figure 3.6 points to the expansion of employment as the key to the decline of household earnings inequality in the Netherlands. While the Dutch employment rate increased from 52.1 percent to 71.3 percent over the period covered by this analysis, Sweden, Denmark, and Finland all saw their employment rates decline.

Figure 3.6 suggests that employment contractions disproportionately hurt the employment opportunities and hence the income of low-income households while, conversely, employment growth disproportionately benefits low-income households. Low-income households in the Netherlands and, to a lesser extent, in the United States and some of the other liberal market economies appear to have compensated themselves for falling relative wages by increasing their employment, in terms the number of working household members and perhaps also the number of hours worked by employed household members. Low-income households appear to have been less able—or perhaps less willing—to engage in this type of compensatory behavior in those countries for which we observe no increase in wage inequality but a significant increase in household inequality (Finland, Denmark, Germany, Norway, and Switzerland) or, as in the Swedish case, a much larger increase in household inequality than in wage inequality. The information contained in the LIS database is too fragmentary to allow for a more systematic analysis of changes in employment across the income distribution, but it is noteworthy that the share of households in the bottom earnings quartile with no employed person decreased by 23 percentage points in the Netherlands from 1983 to 1999. For American married-couple families with children, Mishel, Bernstein, and Boushey show that the average number of hours worked per year by families in the bottom quintile increased by 15.8 percent from 1979 to 2000, while the average number of hours worked by families in the top quintile declined slightly (–.6 percent) over the same period.[16]

The existing literature suggests two possible reasons why the mechanism of "compensatory employment" might operate in some countries and not others. On the demand side, a combination of wage compression through centralized wage bargaining and high payroll taxes may have weakened relative demand for low-wage workers in the more egalitarian social market economies of northern Europe. On the supply side, continued real wage growth for low-wage workers and the public provision of relatively generous income support for unemployed workers may have reduced the need for low-income households in these countries to engage in compensatory employment. We shall return to these issues in subsequent chapters.

The cross-national association between the employment rate and household earnings inequality is reasonably close—but far from perfect. The main outliers in figure 3.6 are the United Kingdom, the United States, and Australia. In the United Kingdom and the United States, household earnings inequality has increased more than we would predict based on changes in the rate of employment, whereas as the opposite is the case for Australia. It is surely no accident that, among the eleven countries included in figure 3.6, the United Kingdom and the United States are the two countries in which wage inequality among full-time employees rose the most dramatically in the 1980s and 1990s. On the other hand, the growth of wage inequality in Australia was relatively moderate by comparative standards. These observations suggest that trends in wage inequality among full-time employees might indeed cast significant light on trends in earnings inequality among working-age households once we control for changes in employment rates. The fact that the time periods for which we have data on wage inequality do not match the time periods for which we have data on household earnings renders this exercise problematic, but table 3.8 reports the results of regressing changes in Gini coefficients for household earnings on observed changes in both-gender 90-10 ratios since 1980 as well as changes in employment rates over country-specific time periods that match the time periods for which we have observations on Gini coefficients. The coefficients for change in wage inequality and change in employment rates both clear the 90 percent confidence criterion for statistical significance. Though the coefficient for change in employment rates is considerably larger than the coefficient for change in wage inequality, the latter is also quite large—and certainly is substantively significant. We must not put too much stock in the results of a regression analysis based on only eleven observations and poorly matched data. Nonetheless, table 3.8 does suggest that trends in wage inequality and employment together shed quite a lot of light on the question of why income inequality among working-age households has grown more in some countries than in others.[17]

EXPLAINING TRENDS IN WAGE INEQUALITY

Two questions emerge from the preceding discussion. First, what accounts for cross-national variation in employment performance, most notably changes in employment rates? And second, what accounts for cross-national variation in the growth of wage differentials among employed workers? The first question will remain a central preoccupation throughout this book, and I will begin to tackle it in the next chapter. For now, let us briefly dwell on the second question. A rigorous comparative

Table 3.8 Determinants of change in earnings inequality among working-age households (Gini coefficients), OLS regression results

Constant	4.501
	(.0050)
Change in employment rate	−.732
	(.0145)
Change in 90–10 wage ratios	.450
	(.0922)
N	11
Adjusted R^2	.48

Note: Standardized (beta) coefficients with p-values (two-tailed tests) are in parentheses. The eleven countries included in this regression are the countries for which we have LIS observations of change in gross earning inequality over time (see table 3.3).

analysis of the determinants of wage inequality lies beyond the scope of this chapter. More modestly, I propose to review the factors that have been invoked to explain the growth of wage inequality in the United States and to explore the extent to which these factors also shed light on cross-national variation in the tendency for wage inequality to grow.[18]

Analyzing wage dispersion across industries since the 1920s, James Galbraith concludes that the movement of the rate of unemployment constitutes "the single most important statistical determinant of changing inequality in the modern American manufacturing wage structure."[19] This finding confirms that workers at the bottom of the wage hierarchy are more exposed to competition from the unemployed than are workers further up the wage hierarchy. In Galbraith's terms, more highly paid workers typically enjoy some degree of "monopoly power." As noted earlier, however, there is another side to the relationship between unemployment and wage inequality, one that runs counter to the straightforward association we would expect based the notion that unemployment disproportionately weakens the bargaining power of unskilled workers. To the extent that employers hang on to skilled, well-paid employees while shedding unskilled, low-wage employees during an economic downturn, increased unemployment will, in the short run, compress the earnings distribution among employed workers.

Galbraith's argument provides a compelling explanation for the improvement in the relative position of low-wage American workers that occurred in the late 1990s. Yet looking across the OECD countries, there is no consistent relationship whatsoever between wage inequality trends, measured as change in both-gender 90-10 ratios, and average rates of unemployment over the 1980–95 period. Nor do we find any consistent relationship between wage inequality and changes in the rate of unemployment from the early 1980s to the mid-1990s. The countervailing effects of unemployment for wage inequality seem to cancel each other out. More importantly for our present purposes, these effects are surely contingent on labor market institutions and government policies that vary across countries. It seems reasonable to hypothesize that the inegalitarian effect, operating through competition for low-wage jobs, is muted in countries that provide generous income support to the unemployed for long periods. On the other hand, the tendency for unemployment to be concentrated among low-skill workers is likely to be particularly strong in countries where worker skills represent a fixed investment by companies.

Labor economists typically explain the growth of U.S. wage inequality in terms of a mismatch between relative demand and supply of skilled labor. The standard argument along these lines posits that relative demand for well-educated workers has increased as a result of technological change—specifically, the "computerization" of many workplaces—and that the expansion of higher education has failed to keep up with this development. Some labor economists argue further that the relative supply of unskilled workers has increased as a result of immigration and, less obviously, as a result of the entry of more women into employment. While the education gap between men and women was never terribly large in the United States and effectively closed in the 1980s, increased female labor force participation still entailed an increase in the relative supply of workers with limited work experience. In a similar vein, increased trade with low-wage countries might be construed as a shift in the effective supply of unskilled labor relative to skilled labor. By the logic of supply and demand, increasing imports of less skill-intensive goods from low-wage countries puts downward pressure on the relative wages of unskilled workers.[20]

As noted by Mishel, Bernstein, and Boushey, it is exceedingly difficult to measure the extent and character of technological change; many demand-driven accounts of the American experience simply assume that, as Mishel, Bernstein, and Boushey put it, "whatever portion of wage inequality is unexplained by measurable factors can be considered to be the consequence of technological change."[21] The problems associated with comparing technological change across countries are, of course, even more daunting. In the absence of detailed evidence to the contrary, we have no reason to suspect that the countries that have experienced the most rapid growth of wage inequality since 1980 (the United States, New Zealand, the United Kingdom, the Netherlands, Sweden, and Italy) have all been at the forefront of technological change. As Richard Freeman and Lawrence Katz observe with regard to the 1980s, "all

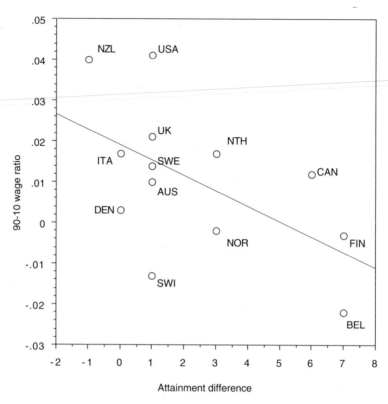

Correlation: −.564 (−.678 without Switzerland)
Sources: Table 3.4 and OECD, *Education at a Glance* (2004), 73–76.

Figure 3.7 Average annual change in both-gender wage ratio since 1980 vs. the difference between tertiary education attainment of 25–35 and 25–64 populations in 1995

advanced industrial countries experienced large, steady shifts in the industrial and occupational distribution of employment towards sectors and jobs that used a greater proportion of more educated workers."[22]

Freeman and Katz argue that the cross-national differences with respect to the supply of highly educated workers provide a better explanation of wage inequality trends. They point out that the expansion of higher education decelerated sharply in the United States from the late 1970s onwards, while Canada, France, Germany, and the Netherlands maintained their 1970s rate of growth into the 1980s. As figure 3.7 illustrates, this line of argument appears to be more generally relevant. The variable on the horizontal axis of this scatterplot is the difference between the percentage of 25- to 34-year-olds with some university education ("tertiary education," in the language of the OECD) and the percentage of 25- to

64-year-olds with some university education in 1995. This represents a proxy for growth of higher education over the preceding ten to fifteen years and turns out to be a reasonably good predictor of wage inequality trends, measured by average annual change in both-gender 90-10 wage ratios. It should be noted that figure 3.7 would be considerably more supportive of the proposition that the expansion of higher education has counteracted inegalitarian trends if the Swiss case were excluded, as it arguably should be, given that our data on Swiss wage inequality pertain to the 1991–97 period.[23]

Turning to the other supply-side variables posited by economists, there is no clear association, cross-nationally, between wage inequality trends and either increases in female labor force participation or increases in trade with low-wage countries from 1980 to 1995. To the extent that these variables constitute sources of rising wage inequality, their effects would seem to be sector-specific and perhaps contingent on institutional arrangements that vary across countries. The cross-national evidence regarding the inegalitarian effects of immigration is more ambiguous. Averaging annual net migration rates over the 1980–95 period, we observe much larger inflows of foreigners to Germany, Switzerland, and Canada than to any other OECD countries. Yet wage inequality declined in (West) Germany from 1984 to 1995, declined in Switzerland from 1991 to 1997, and increased only modestly in Canada from 1981 to 1994. Leaving these three countries out of the picture, however, we do find some support for the proposition that immigration has contributed to rising wage inequality by increasing the supply of unskilled labor, as illustrated by figure 3.8.

Yet another strand of research on the rise of wage inequality in the United States emphasizes the role of political and institutional developments, specifically the decline of unions and the failure of the federal government to maintain the real value of the minimum wage. From a comparative perspective, the argument about the minimum wage is of limited explanatory significance, for the simple reason that many countries do not have a statutory minimum wage. This holds for the majority of the social market economies. As noted in the introductory chapter, the social market economies are characterized not only by high rates of unionization but also by highly institutionalized forms of collective bargaining. As wage agreements negotiated by unions and employers associations typically apply to all workers in a given sector, irrespective of whether or not they are union members, collective bargaining rather than government legislation effectively determines the floor of the wage hierarchy. For the subset of countries with statutory minimum wages, the OECD reports that their real value declined by 21.5 percent in the Netherlands, 19.0 percent in the United States, and 4.4 percent in

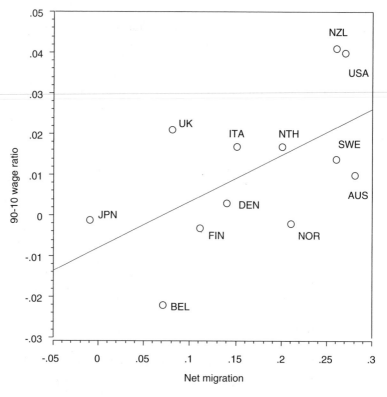

Correlation: .590
Sources: Table 3.4 and Firtz Scharpf and Vivien Schmidt, eds., *Welfare and Work in the Open Economy* (Oxford: Oxford University Press, 2000), vol. 1, 352.

Figure 3.8 Average annual change in both-gender wage ratio since 1980 vs. average annual net migration, 1980–95

Canada from 1980 to 1997. Over the same period, the real value of the minimum wage increased by 40.7 percent in Japan, 16.4 percent in France, 8.1 percent in New Zealand, and 5.0 percent in Belgium.[24] With the notable exception of New Zealand, where wage inequality increased despite the rise in the minimum wage, this pattern broadly corresponds to the wage inequality trends described earlier.

Unions approximate the logic of democratic decision-making (one person, one vote) more closely than markets do, and a majority of union members should favor redistributive wage demands (higher wage increases for workers with lower wages) whenever the mean wage exceeds the median wage. By this reasoning, unionized firms (or sectors) can be expected to have a more compressed wage distribution than their non-

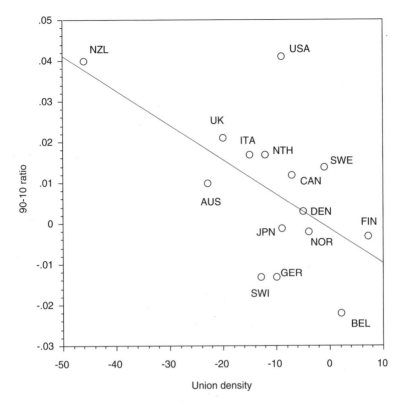

Correlation: −.592 (−.708 without the United States)
Sources: Tables 3.4 and 5.2.

Figure 3.9 Average annual change in both-gender wage ratio since 1980 vs. change in union density, 1980–2000

union counterparts. In addition, unionization will be associated with wage compression to the extent that unions primarily organize workers toward the bottom of the wage distribution and are able to deliver a wage premium to their members. Recent econometric studies indicate that de-unionization accounts for roughly one-fifth of the rise of wage inequality in the United States from the mid-1970s to the late 1980s.[25] As figure 3.9 illustrates, changes in union density from 1980 to 2000 turn out to be a rather good predictor of wage inequality trends across the OECD countries. The United States is the most significant outlier, with wage inequality rising more rapidly than the cross-national association between changes in union density and wage inequality would lead us to expect. The American case might be explained by the fact that union density was from the outset much lower in the United States than any of the

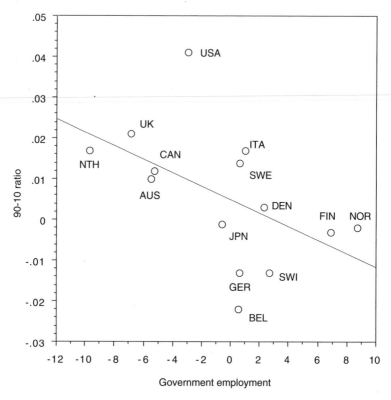

Correlation: −.515 (−.552 without the United States)
Sources: Tables 3.4 and 8.3.

Figure 3.10 Average annual change in both-gender wage ratio since 1980 vs. change in the government's share of total employment, 1980–95

other countries included in figure 3.9. Arguably, unions are so weak in the United States that the effects of any further weakening are quite limited.

Finally, figure 3.10 suggests that wage inequality trends are also correlated with changes in the size of the public sector (government employment as a percentage of total employment) from 1980 to 1995, though this association is clearly not as strong as that between rising wage inequality and de-unionization. In the United States and elsewhere, government employers played a leading role in eliminating gender-based wage differentials in the 1960s and 1970s. More generally, government employers seem to have been more receptive to egalitarian wage demands in this period, being sheltered from competition in product markets and accountable to elected officials. As I discuss further in subsequent chapters, welfare states not only failed to offset inegalitarian labor market trends in the 1980s and 1990s; to some degree, public sector retrenchment and restructuring also seem to have contributed to inegalitarian labor market trends. (The United States again represents something of an outlier in figure 3.10, which might be explained by the public sector's share of total employment being comparatively small to begin with.)

Since public sector workers are better organized than private sector workers in all the OECD, changes in unionization and the size of the public sector are obviously related to each other, but the small number of cases in this analysis makes it impossible to estimate their independent effects on wage inequality. Suffice it to note here that multiple regression models based on pooling time series observations across countries show that both variables have had significant effects.[26] Along with trends in higher education enrollments, these would appear to be the most important factors explaining cross-national variation in the rise of wage inequality. Less consistently, immigration and minimum wage legislation also appear to have played some role in generating different inequality trajectories.

WAGE COMPRESSION AS INDUSTRIAL POLICY

Across the OECD countries, unions have been a force pushing for the compression of wage differentials or, more recently, resisting the dispersion of wage differentials. In many cases, this has simply been a result of union leaders seeking to gain (or maintain) the support of workers toward the bottom of the wage distribution. However, labor movements in the Nordic countries and, to a lesser degree, other European labor movements embraced the idea of "solidaristic wage policy" as part of a long-term, political-economic strategy in the 1960s and 1970s. Sweden's powerful confederation of blue-collar unions, Landsorganisationen (LO), assumed a leading role in this respect. The origins, modalities, and consequences of solidaristic wage bargaining in Sweden has been the subject of many studies and need not detain us here, but the motivations behind the egalitarianism of the so-called "Rehn-Meidner model" are relevant to our present concerns.

As economists working for LO in the 1950s, Gösta Rehn and Rudolf Meidner asserted that a solidaristic approach to wage bargaining would not only be good for low-wage workers but for the Swedish economy as well. Wage compression, Rehn and Meidner argued, would boost productivity growth by squeezing corporate profits selectively. On the one hand, a concerted union effort to provide low-wage workers with higher increases than market forces dictated would squeeze the profits of less efficient firms (sectors) and force them either to rationalize production or to go out of business. On the other hand, the wage restraint by well-paid workers implied by the principle of wage solidarity would promote the expansion of more efficient firms (sectors). The net effect of this differentiated pressure on firms would be to raise average productivity in the economy and thereby make it possible for average wages to rise without threatening macro-economic stability. Critically important, the Rehn-Meidner strategy required the government to develop active labor market measures—relocation subsidies as well as retraining programs—designed to ease the transition of workers from less efficient to more efficient firms and sectors and also to curtail wage drift caused by bottlenecks in the supply of labor.[27]

The insight at the core of this strategic vision is the idea that low wages represent a subsidy to inefficient capital. At the same time, Rehn and Meidner recognized that wage differentials were necessary as an incentive for workers to acquire skills and to take on more responsibility in the production process. The goal of union wage policy should be to eliminate differentials based on corporate profitability while maintaining differentials based on skill and performance. In other words, the goal of union wage policy should be "equal pay for equal work" as distinct from "equal pay for everyone."

In practice, it proved difficult for Swedish unions to maintain the distinction between "good" and "bad" wage differentials, and most observers agree that solidaristic wage policy became too egalitarian in the course of the 1960s and 1970s, producing a generalized profits squeeze and, ultimately, an employer campaign to decentralize wage bargaining.[28] Still, the insights of the Rehn-Meidner model remain relevant and extend beyond the Swedish case. In particular, the idea that low wages represent a subsidy to inefficient capital casts a critical light on the expansion of low-paying service jobs in the 1980s and 1990s. We ought not conflate efficiency and employment, nor should we conflate the productivity of workers and the productivity of firms. Only some of the dramatic growth of wage inequality that has occurred in the United States and some other countries could possibly be justified in terms of productive efficiency.

SUMMARY

Wage differentials among male workers have grown in all OECD countries for which we have time series covering most of the 1980s and 1990s, but there is a great deal of cross-national variation in the extent to which male wage inequality has grown. Also, wage inequality among female workers declined over these two decades in some countries. Even where we do observe inegalitarian trends for women as well as men, as in the United Kingdom and the United States, these trends have been partly offset by the narrowing of between-gender differentials. The cross-national diversity in the data on relative wages among full-time employees is more impressive than the common tendency for wage inequality to rise.

The expansion of part-time employment relative to full-time employment in most countries since the early 1980s represents a source of inequality that is not captured by the OECD data on relative wages (although it does show up in the LIS data on gross earnings by household). Given that women constitute the vast majority of part-time employees, the issue of part-time employment also bears on between-gender differentials and wage differentials among women. In countries where the incidence of part-time employment has grown significantly, there has been more wage differentiation among women than the data on the wages of full-time employees would have us believe. As a group, women have perhaps not fared as well relative to men as these data suggest.

Political and institutional factors are critically important for understanding why wage inequality has grown more in some countries than in others. Labor economists engaged in comparative analysis recognize this point, but in their account labor market institutions typically play the role of constraining market forces that generate wage differentiation. For example, Francine Blau and Larry Kahn remark that slower growth of wage inequality indicates that in other countries wage-setting institutions have played an important role in "moderating the negative effect of recent trends in technological change and international trade on low-skilled workers."[29] In the preceding discussion, by contrast, institutional change—specifically, union decline and public sector retrenchment—itself emerges as a source of inegalitarian labor market trends. The rise of income inequality has been "market-driven" in the sense that gross earnings inequality has increased more than disposable income inequality: in general, taxes and government transfers have counteracted the effects of rising of gross earnings inequality. However, we ought not conflate "politics" with "redistribution." My comparative analysis of wage inequality trends suggests that there is an important political dimension to the processes whereby gross earnings are distributed.

Changes in the distribution of wages have contributed to rising earnings inequality among working-age households, but changes in the distribution of employment appear to constitute an even more important consideration. For many countries, it would appear that wages and employment have both become more unevenly distributed, but some of the data presented above suggest that differentiation of wages and differentiation of employment opportunities might be conceived as alter-

native paths to higher levels of earnings inequality. The preceding discussion should motivate us to pursue the question of whether or not wage
inequality and employment growth are somehow at odds with each other.
Did rising wage inequality make it possible for low-income Dutch households to increase their employment and hence their earnings in the 1980s
and 1990s? Conversely, did continued wage compression reduce the
employment opportunities of low-income households in the Nordic countries in the 1990s?

CHAPTER 4

Employment Performance

This chapter compares countries in terms of three dimensions (or indicators) of employment performance: unemployment, employment levels, and employment growth. For working-age adults and their dependents, unemployment is the principal source of economic insecurity in capitalist societies. Invariably associated with some income loss, unemployment generates inequality to the extent that poorly paid workers are more likely to lose their jobs than better-paid workers during economic downturns. More indirectly, unemployment also promotes inequality by weakening the relative bargaining position of unskilled workers and perhaps by weakening the ability of unions to mobilize their members behind solidaristic wage demands. At the same time, mass unemployment is a source of fiscal pressures on the welfare state: as unemployment rises, the number of taxpayers declines and the number of welfare claimants increases.

As noted in the introductory chapter, comparing rates of unemployment in recent years undercuts strong claims about the superiority of liberal market economies relative to social market economies. By comparative standards, unemployment in Finland, Belgium, and Germany was quite high in 2000–03. On the other hand, the four OECD countries with the lowest rates of unemployment in this period—the Netherlands, Switzerland, Norway, and Austria—were also SMEs, and the unemployment rates of Denmark and Sweden compare favorably with those of most liberal market economies. On average, unemployment rates in SMEs and LMEs were virtually identical in this period. There are at least two counts on which proponents of the liberal market model might reasonably object to this comparison. First, proponents of the liberal market model might object that the figures presented in the introductory chapter fail to convey that *trends* in unemployment rates have been more favorable in LMEs since the early 1990s. Second, they might argue that rates of *long-term* unemployment constitute a more appropriate metric for assessing the relative merits of the liberal and social market models. In what follows, I present data pertaining to both these issues and also address the question of how unemployment affects different categories of workers.

We can distinguish two different conceptions of full employment as a public policy goal. In the first conception, "full employment" simply means the absence of unemployment. Recognizing that many people who do not actively seek employment would in fact do so under certain circumstances, the second, more ambitious conception implies an abundance of good jobs that pull people into the labor force. From this perspective, firmly embraced by social democrats in Scandinavia during the 1960s and 1970s, the employment rate (the number of employed people as a percentage of the working-age population) constitutes a better measure of success than the unemployment rate (the number of unemployed people as a percentage of the labor force).

Many European countries, especially continental SMEs, used disability pensions and early retirement schemes to prevent employment losses from translating into high unemployment in the 1970s and the 1980s (see chapter 7). However necessary or beneficial such policies may have been from a social point of view, reducing unemployment through labor force exit can hardly be considered a step toward "full employment." As this example illustrates, moreover, the employment rate is most relevant to the fiscal politics of public welfare provision, for nonworking adults outside the labor force may be just as dependent on public support as the unemployed.

By definition, the employment rate is a function of three variables: (a) the size of the working-age population; (b) the number of people who are in the labor force or, in other words, want jobs; and (c) the number of jobs available. Political-economic institutions and government policies affect all three of these variables, but the question of how institutions and policies affect the rate of job creation is of particular interest in this context. As we saw in the introductory chapter, since 1990 the number of people in employment has generally grown more rapidly in liberal market economies than in social market economies. The following discussion provides further data on patterns of employment growth and takes a first stab at the question of a trade-off between employment growth and wage inequality by asking whether these variables correlate on a cross-national basis. Finally, I propose to look a little closer at the case of the Netherlands, which stands out as the social market economy with the strongest record of employment creation over the last two decades.

UNEMPLOYMENT

It is a commonplace that the international recession of 1974–75 marked the end of full employment in the OECD world. From 1960 to 1973, the U.S. rate of unemployment averaged 4.8 percent. By comparative standards, this was a very high figure at the time. Comparable rates of unemployment were found in Ireland (5.2 percent), Canada (5.0 percent), and Italy (4.5 percent), but in none of the other countries covered in this book did the average rate of unemployment over the period 1960–73 exceed 2.2 percent. For Ireland and Italy, high rates of unemployment might be attributed to economic backwardness. For Canada and the United States, high rates of labor mobility, with many workers quitting their jobs to better themselves, surely played some role, but high rates of unemployment in these countries also reflected the absence of the kind of political commitment to full employment that existed in Western Europe at this time.

Unemployment rates shot up sharply in the mid-1970s in all OECD countries except for Japan, Switzerland, Austria, Norway, and Sweden. As table 4.1 documents, these five countries successfully resisted mass unemployment through the 1980s. In the other thirteen countries, unemployment remained much higher in the 1980s than it had been in the 1960s—in some cases, such as Belgium, the Netherlands, and France, four or even five times as high as it had been in the 1960s. In the United States, Denmark, Finland, and Sweden, the rate of unemployment declined in the course of the 1980s, but in the other countries the rate of unemployment either increased or remained essentially unchanged over the decade. While the international recession of the early 1990s again boosted the ranks of the unemployed in most countries, the increase of unemployment during this recession was generally less dramatic than it had been during the recessions of 1974–75 and 1980–81. However, the employment situation of the Nordic SMEs, most especially Finland and Sweden, deteriorated very sharply in the first half of the 1990s. With much of Finnish industry specializing in trade with the Soviet Union, the Finnish economy entered a deep adjustment crisis at this time, pushing the unemployment rate above that of France and Italy. Meanwhile, Sweden moved from having had the lowest unemployment rate after Switzerland in the second half of the 1980s to being an average European country in the mid-1990s. While Denmark and Norway recovered

Table 4.1 Unemployment rates, 1980–2003

	1980–84	1985–89	1990–94	1995–99	2000–03
Nordic SMEs	**5.6%**	**4.1%**	**7.8%**	**8.0%**	**5.8%**
Denmark	9.6	6.6	8.7	5.9	4.8
Finland	5.1	4.6	10.9	12.9	9.3
Norway	2.6	3.0	5.7	4.1	3.9
Sweden	2.8	2.1	5.8	9.1	5.3
Continental SMEs	**6.1**	**6.5**	**5.4**	**6.4**	**5.2**
Austria	3.1	3.4	3.6	5.0	4.0
Belgium	11.0	11.0	7.9	9.2	7.3
Germany	5.9	7.5	6.0	8.9	8.4
Netherlands	9.9	9.7	6.3	5.4	3.0
Switzerland	0.5	0.7	3.2	3.7	3.2
LMEs	**8.4**	**9.2**	**9.9**	**7.6**	**5.6**
Australia	7.5	7.5	9.6	8.0	6.4
Canada	11.3	10.1	10.3	9.0	7.3
Ireland	11.6	16.9	14.7	9.7	4.3
New Zealand	4.1	4.9	9.2	6.6	5.3
United Kingdom	9.5	9.6	9.2	7.3	5.1
United States	8.2	6.1	6.6	5.0	5.1
France	8.0	10.1	10.6	12.0	9.0
Italy	8.6	11.3	9.6	12.1	9.4
Japan	2.4	2.6	2.4	3.9	5.1

Sources: OECD, Historical Statistics (1996), and OECD, *Employment Outlook* (2004), 293.

Note: Except for Austria 1990–94, post-1990 figures are based on a standardized definition of unemployment; figures for 1980s are based on national definitions. German figures prior to 1993 refer to West Germany.

relatively quickly from their employment crises in the early 1990s, Finland and Sweden saw their unemployment rates continue to rise through the mid-1990s. Among the other countries that had previously maintained more or less full employment, Switzerland also experienced a significant increase in unemployment in the early 1990s while Austria and Japan did so in the second half of the 1990s.

The average rate of unemployment increased from the first to the second half of the 1990s in Belgium, Germany, France, and Italy as well as Finland, Sweden, Switzerland, Austria, and Japan. By contrast, the average rate of unemployment declined in all the liberal market economies from the first half to the second half of the 1990s. Except for Japan, every single country included in table 4.1 recorded some decrease in the rate of unemployment in 2000–03, yet mass unemployment persists in Italy, Finland, France, Germany, Belgium, and Canada.

As noted in the introductory chapter, Germany's high rate of unemployment since the early 1990s has featured prominently in editorials in the business press claiming that social protection causes slow growth and high unemployment. By contrast, I am struck by the fact that the collapse of communism and the unification of Germany did not translate into an even sharper rise in German unemployment, especially in light of the Finnish experience. When the former East Germany was included in the OECD statistics for Germany in 1993, the standardized German unemployment rate increased from 6.4 percent to 7.7 percent.[1] The modesty of this increase partly reflects the fact that East Germany was much smaller than West Germany (in the OECD's statistics, the total German labor force increased from 30.9 million in 1992 to 38.7 million in 1993), but the German government also took extraordinary measures to counteract the employment consequences of the dismantling of the East German economy. With virtually no viable businesses in the East at the beginning of the 1990s, it is hardly surprising that mass unemployment has been especially persistent in Germany.

This said, I hasten to acknowledge that the data presented in table 4.1 indeed indicate that the liberal market economies have been more successful than other OECD countries in combating unemployment over the last fifteen years. From 1990–94 to 1995–99 and again from 1995–99 to 2000–03, the average rate of unemployment fell in every one of the liberal market economies except for a very small increase from 1995–99 to 2000–03 in the United States. This observation holds for only three out of nine social market economies (Denmark, Norway, and the Netherlands).

The discussion so far treats unemployment as an undesirable condition that has the same meaning or implications for all unemployed workers. Needless to say, perhaps, in the real world this is not the case. Most obviously, we need to distinguish between transitory and more durable forms of unemployment. This distinction matters not only for the welfare of individuals and households but also for economic performance, for politics, and for the social fabric of communities. Long-term unemployment represents a particularly invidious form of unemployment on several counts. To begin with, it erodes employability: as people stay unemployed for extended periods of time, they lose some of their skills, including social skills, and perhaps also some of their motivation to work. Long-term unemployment thus reduces the productive potential of the economy at the same time that it renders individuals dependent on government support. In addition, long-term unemployment tends to be associated with nonvoting and other manifestations of political disaffection in virtually all countries.

The first two columns of table 4.2 show the percentage of unemployed people who had been unemployed for more than six months and more than twelve months in 2003. Multiplying aggregate unemployment rates by these percentages expressed as fractions yields rates of long-term

Table 4.2 Long-term unemployment, 2003

	Long-term unemployment as % of total unemployment		Long-term unemployment (>6 months) as % of labor force
	>6 months	>12 months	
Nordic SMEs	**34.6**	**17.2**	**2.8**
Denmark	40.9	19.9	2.2
Finland	41.4	24.7	3.8
Norway	20.6	6.4	0.9
Sweden	35.4	17.8	2.1
Continental SMEs	**54.4**	**35.4**	**3.4**
Austria	41.0	24.5	1.9
Belgium	64.7	46.3	5.0
Germany	68.5	50.0	6.4
Netherlands	49.2	29.2	1.8
Switzerland	48.8	27.0	2.0
LMEs	**33.6**	**19.4**	**1.7**
Australia	39.7	22.5	1.9
Canada	18.6	10.1	1.4
Ireland	56.6	35.4	2.5
New Zealand	27.4	13.3	1.3
United Kingdom	37.3	23.0	1.8
United States	22.0	11.8	1.3
France	53.4	33.8	5.0
Italy	74.1	58.2	6.4
Japan	50.9	33.5	2.7

Source: OECD, *Employment Outlook* (2004), 315.

unemployment, that is to say, the long-term unemployed as a percentage of the total labor force. The last column of table 4.2 reports the results of this exercise for 2003, with long-term unemployment defined as unemployment spells exceeding six months.

With 22 percent of the unemployed having been unemployed for more than six months, the U.S. long-term unemployment rate in 2003 was 1.3 percent. Only one other OECD country, Norway, performs better than the United States on this count, while New Zealand and Canada perform about the same as the United States. All other OECD countries have significantly higher rates of long-term unemployment. Belgium, Germany, France, and Italy—to a lesser extent Finland—again stand out as the OECD countries with the worst unemployment performance by this measure. In Canada, the long-term unemployed constitute a smaller percentage of all unemployed workers than in any other country included in table 4.2, and taking the duration of unemployment into account dramatically transforms our comparative assessment of Canada's labor market performance. With respect to aggregate unemployment rates,

Canada ranks near the top of the top of the OECD league (tied for fifth place among the countries included in table 4.1), but with respect to long-term unemployment Canada ranks near the bottom (fourth place from the bottom in table 4.2).

Table 4.2 suggests that long unemployment spells represent a particular problem for the economies of continental Europe—the continental SMEs along with the southern European member states of the European Union. Among the continental SMEs, the proportion of the unemployed who have been unemployed for more than six months ranges from 41.0 percent in Austria to 68.5 percent in Germany. The contrast with the LMEs is particularly striking if we disregard the Irish case, which is distinguished by a very high incidence of long-term unemployment as well as a fairly low aggregate rate of unemployment (and thus represents a mirror image of the Canadian case). Among the remaining LMEs, the proportion of the unemployed who have been unemployed for more than six months ranges from 18.6 percent in Canada to 39.7 percent in Australia. The group averages suggest that the problem of long unemployment spells is no greater in the Nordic SMEs than in the LMEs, but these averages are misleading because of the exceptionally low incidence of long-term unemployment in Norway as well as the exceptionally high incidence in Ireland. It seems more judicious to say that the Nordic SMEs fall between the LMEs and the continental measures on this measure of employment performance.

With the Netherlands and the United States as their concrete examples, Jelle Visser and Anton Hemerijck elaborate on the contrast between LMEs and continental SMEs as follows:

> Like most EU countries, the Netherlands has a severe problem of long-term unemployment. Unlike the U.S., the biggest risk is not to become unemployed when holding a job, but to stay unemployed once a job is lost. In 1992, when the unemployment rate (6.7 percent) was marginally lower than in the U.S. (7.3 percent), this reflected quite different realities. In the U.S., on a monthly basis, about two percent of all workers lost their job, in the Netherlands less than half a percent. In the U.S. forty percent of the unemployed found a new job within a month, against five to six percent in the Netherlands.[2]

Another way to put this point is to say that unemployment tends to be more concentrated in SMEs than LMEs. In the former group of countries, a relatively small percentage of the labor force accounts for a very large percentage of unemployment. This observation resonates with a rather common argument among critics of the social market model, namely that this model entails a sharp divide between insiders and out-

Table 4.3 Unemployment rates of different categories of workers as ratio of the national unemployment rate, 2003

	Women	Aged 15–24	Less than high school education (aged 25–64)
Nordic SMEs	**1.0**	**2.3**	**1.1**
Denmark	1.0	1.8	1.1
Finland	1.0	2.4	1.4
Norway	0.9	2.6	0.8
Sweden	0.9	2.5	1.0
Continental SMEs	**1.0**	**1.8**	**1.1**
Austria	1.0	1.7	1.6
Belgium	1.0	2.3	1.3
Germany	1.0	1.1	1.6
Netherlands	1.0	1.7	1.0
Switzerland	1.1	2.1	1.1
LMEs	**1.0**	**2.0**	**1.4**
Australia	1.0	1.9	1.2
Canada	0.9	1.8	1.4
Ireland	0.9	1.7	1.3
New Zealand	1.1	2.2	1.2
United Kingdom	0.8	2.4	1.7
United States	1.0	2.1	1.7
France	1.1	2.2	1.3
Italy	1.4	3.1	1.0
Japan	1.0	1.9	1.2

Source: OECD, *Employment Outlook* (2004), 294–309.

siders in the labor market, with "insiders" defined as workers with secure, well-paid jobs protected by government legislation as well as by strong unions.[3]

Challenging the notion that the social market economies of northern and central Europe represent an egalitarian alternative to the American model, the insider-outsider theme will come up again later in this chapter and in subsequent chapters. For now, let us probe this issue just a bit further by asking whether the more concentrated nature of unemployment in many social market economies implies that unemployment is more unevenly distributed across categories of workers. Table 4.3 presents data that show how women, youth, and unskilled workers fare with respect to unemployment in different OECD countries. "Youth" is here defined as individuals between the ages of 15 and 24 while "unskilled workers" are defined as individuals between the ages of 25 and 64 without a high school degree. Taken directly from official OECD statistics, these categories can be treated as rough proxies for outsider status in the labor market. (Unfortunately, there are no readily accessible comparative data on unemployment rates for immigrants or ethnic/racial minorities.) Construed as a critique of the social market model, the insider-outsider perspective leads us to expect that unemployment rates among women, youth, and unskilled workers should be higher in SMEs than LMEs if we control for aggregate rates of unemployment. In table 4.3, the unemployment rates of women, youth, and unskilled workers are expressed as ratios of the national unemployment rate in 2003. A number greater than one means that the unemployment rate for the group in question is higher than the unemployment rate for the labor force as a whole (2.0 means that it is twice as high).[4]

The evidence presented in table 4.3 can be summarized as follows. To begin with, rates of unemployment among women are very similar to national rates of unemployment in virtually all of these countries. The major exception to this generalization is Italy, where the female rate of unemployment is considerably higher than the national rate of unemployment. While women are somewhat more likely to be unemployed than men in Switzerland, New Zealand, and France, they are less likely to be unemployed in Norway, Ireland, the United Kingdom, and the United States. Overall, neither LMEs nor SMEs display any pronounced gender bias with respect to unemployment. Second, table 4.3 shows that youth unemployment rates exceed national unemployment rates in all OECD countries, often by a very large margin. In ten out of eighteen countries, the rate of youth unemployment is more than twice as high as the national unemployment rate. Youth unemployment appears to be a particularly pronounced problem in Finland, Norway, and Sweden, along with Italy, but this is not true for other social market economies. Largely because of the very low rate of youth unemployment in Germany, the continental SMEs actually perform better than both the LMEs and the Nordic SMEs by this measure. Finally, high school dropouts are more likely to be unemployed than more educated workers in all but four countries: Norway, Sweden, the Netherlands, and Italy. The evidence in table 4.3 does not support the proposition that unskilled workers fare worse in SMEs than in LMEs. Relative to national unemployment rates, unemployment among unskilled workers is actually higher, on average, in LMEs, something that is particularly true of the United Kingdom and the United States.

Low relative rates of youth unemployment in Denmark and the continental SMEs (except Belgium) reflect the strength of vocational training in these countries, which translates into higher school retention rates among less academically gifted youth. Poorly trained persons probably account for a larger proportion of labor force aged 15 to 24 in the United States than they do in Germany. Controlling for skill levels and other employability attributes, we might well find that German youth face obstacles to employment at least as great as American youth do, but it is not obvious to me why we should control for skills when assessing how youth fare in different institutional settings. To the extent that Germany and other SMEs use training to improve the employment prospects of young people, this should be counted in their favor rather than discounted.

Table 4.3 provides precious little evidence to support the contention that social market institutions discriminate against "outsiders" to a greater extent than liberal market institutions. Still, long-term unemployment clearly represents a serious problem for the social market economies of northern and central Europe. Arguably, the high incidence of long-term employment constitutes an important reason why high levels of unemployment have proved so stubbornly persistent in continental Europe, particularly Belgium, Germany, France, and Italy. The long-term employed are not likely to search very hard for jobs. Along these lines, Francine Blau and Lawrence Kahn speculate that "when unemployment becomes long term, it takes higher and higher levels of overall unemployment to establish the downward real-wage pressure needed to induce firms to hire more labor."[5]

From a comparative perspective, the reduction of the overall unemployment rate that the United States achieved in the course of the 1980s and 1990s is indeed impressive, as is the very low rate of long-term unemployment in the United States. As Bruce Western and Katherine Beckett show, however, taking into account rates of incarceration casts the American experience in a less favorable light. For thirteen European countries, the average male rate of unemployment in 1995 increases from 8.3 percent to 8.5 percent if we count prisoners as part of the unemployed population. In the United States, by contrast, this adjustment raises the 1995 male rate of unemployment from 5.6 percent to 7.5 percent. Most importantly, Western and Beckett's analysis indicates that the expansion of the U.S. prison population accounts for a large part of the decline of male unemployment in the United States relative to Europe from 1983 to 1995.[6] Needless to say, perhaps, the costs of the American prison system are considerably greater than what European welfare states spend on income maintenance for the long-term unemployed.

EMPLOYMENT RATES

Table 4.4 reports on employment rates in 1983 and 2003. The employment rate is the percentage of the working-age population in employment, with "working-age population" defined as the population between the ages of 15 and 64. For each country, table 4.4 provides employment rates for men and women separately as well as total (both-gender) employ-

Table 4.4 Employment rates by gender, 1983 and 2003

	Men and women		Men		Women	
	1983	2003	1983	2003	1983	2003
Nordic SMEs	**75.6%**	**73.2%**	**82.2%**	**75.8%**	**70.0%**	**70.5%**
Denmark	71.8	75.1	78.4	79.7	65.2	70.5
Finland	73.2	67.4	77.4	69.0	69.0	65.7
Norway	77.3	75.9	88.2	78.8	70.1	72.9
Sweden	80.2	74.3	84.7	75.6	75.5	72.8
Continental SMEs	**57.7**	**68.7**	**73.9**	**75.8**	**41.6**	**61.5**
Austria	62.9	68.2	79.4	75.3	47.1	61.2
Belgium	53.5	59.3	70.4	67.1	36.6	51.4
Germany	62.2	64.6	76.6	70.4	47.8	58.7
Netherlands	52.0	73.6	69.1	81.2	34.7	65.8
Switzerland		77.8		84.9		70.6
LMEs	**62.9**	**70.5**	**77.4**	**77.2**	**48.4**	**63.9**
Australia	62.1	69.3	77.3	76.4	46.7	62.2
Canada	64.8	72.1	75.5	76.5	54.2	67.7
Ireland	54.0	65.0	73.9	74.5	33.6	55.4
New Zealand	61.6	72.5	80.3	79.3	42.8	65.8
United Kingdom	67.0	72.9	78.7	79.3	55.3	66.4
United States	68.0	71.2	78.9	76.9	57.7	65.7
France	62.0	61.9	74.4	67.7	49.7	56.0
Italy	55.0	56.2	76.6	69.7	34.4	42.7
Japan	71.0	68.4	86.6	79.8	55.7	56.8

Sources: OECD, *Employment Outlook* (1997), 164–65, and *Employment Outlook* (2004), 295–96.

ment rates. In contrast to unemployment rates, the employment rates of men and women remain significantly different in most OECD countries.

In the data for 1983, the Nordic SMEs clearly stand out as a group, with much higher overall rates of employment than any other OECD countries but Japan and possibly Switzerland (for which we lack 1983 data). With a both-gender employment rate of 80.2 percent, Sweden represents the upper end of the entire OECD range, while Denmark represents the lower end of the Nordic range at 71.8 percent. Along with Ireland, France, and Italy, the continental SMEs constitute a distinct band of low-employment countries, ranging from 52.0 percent for the Netherlands to 62.9 percent for Austria. The average for the LMEs is dragged down by Ireland's exceptionally low employment rate. Leaving the Irish case aside, the LMEs range between 61.6 percent for New Zealand and 68.0 percent for the United States.

The employment rate among men was higher in the Nordic countries than in most other OECD countries in 1983, but table 4.4 makes it very clear that high employment rates among women constitutes the most distinctive feature of the Nordic countries. For men only, the range of variation in employment rates among the OECD countries in 1983 is much less pronounced than the range for women, and the threefold grouping of countries that I have proposed does not capture the 1983 data as well. Norway leads the OECD league, followed by Japan, but male employment rates for Austria, New Zealand, the United Kingdom, and the United States are higher than those for Denmark and Finland.

The employment rate of women increased sharply in all the Nordic countries in the 1960s and 1970s. The contrast between the Nordic countries and continental Europe on this score is particularly stark. Public policy differences are central to this contrast, though such differences might of course be attributed in turn to more deep-seated cultural differences. In the Nordic countries, a broad consensus crystallized in the 1960s behind policies to promote or facilitate women's employment. Specifically, this consensus translated into the abandonment of household taxation in favor of individual taxation (reducing the disincentives that high marginal tax rates implied for two-income families), the introduction of generous parental leave insurance schemes, and the expansion of public child care provision. The expansion of public sector employment also promoted female employment in the Nordic countries in the 1970s and 1980s. Partly on account of the prominent role played by Christian Democratic parties, the commitment to such policies has been much weaker in the social market economies of continental Europe. In the absence of employment-promoting policies, the provision of generous family allowances may actually have encouraged women to stay home and take care of their children in the continental SMEs.[7]

In all of the liberal market economies, the employment rate of men remained essentially unchanged while the employment rate of women increased substantially from 1983 to 2003. As a result, overall employment rates also increased substantially in all the LMEs over these two decades. The increase was greatest in Ireland and New Zealand, the two LMEs that had the lowest employment rates in 1983, and smallest in the United States, the LME with the highest employment rate in 1983. Denmark registered a small increase in the employment rate of men, and the Netherlands stands out as the OECD country in which the employment rate of men increased the most from 1983 to 2003. In the other Nordic and continental SMEs, the employment rate of men declined over these two decades. This also holds for France, Italy, and Japan. The decline in male employment rates was particularly dramatic in Finland and Sweden, and these two countries also experienced declines in female employment rates. Since female rates fell less than male rates, however, gender differences in employment rates continued to decline in Finland and Sweden. In all other countries in which the male employment rate declined, this decline was at least partly offset by rising female employment rates. The extensive entry of women into employment in the continental SMEs during an era of mass unemployment is particularly noteworthy. Again, the Dutch case stands out, with the female employment rate nearly doubling from 1983 to 2003.

Declining rates of employment among men obviously reflect rising rates of unemployment, but they also reflect changes in the patterns of entry into and exit from the labor force. Young people postpone entry into the labor force by continuing their education, and they are especially likely to make this choice in the face of poor job prospects. At the same time, unemployed workers who are unable to find new employment commonly drop out of the labor force when their unemployment benefits expire. From a comparative perspective, falling male employment rates tend to be associated either with unusually high unemployment, exemplified by southern Europe for all of the 1980s and 1990s and by the Nordic SMEs in the first half of the 1990s, or with public schemes encouraging older unemployed workers to exit the labor force, exemplified by the continental SMEs for most of this period.

The Nordic SMEs recovered rather swiftly from the employment crisis of the early 1990s. High employment rates remain a characteristic of these economies, but their employment rates no longer stand out as clearly. The data in table 4.4 show a clear tendency for employment rates to converge across the OECD countries. Generally speaking, countries that started the 1980s with relatively low employment rates achieved larger increases in employment rates over the ensuing two decades than countries that started with relatively high employment rates. (For men and women combined, the correlation between employment rates in 1983 and changes in employment rates from 1983 to 2003 is $-.731$.) Related to this, table 4.4 also shows that gender differences in employment rates diminished in all the OECD countries from 1983 to 2003.

The observation that gender differences in employment rates have diminished requires some qualification. As we saw in chapter 3 (table 3.6), the incidence of part-time employment has increased significantly since the early 1980s in many countries, and part-time employment is heavily concentrated among women in all countries. Adjusting for the number of hours worked, the differences between the employment of men and women would be greater than they are in table 4.4. As figure 4.1 illustrates, changes in female employment rates correlate closely with changes in the incidence of part-time employment on a cross-national basis. To a large extent, the expansion of part-time employment can be seen as a response to the growing importance of women as a source of labor supply and the problems that women face in reconciling work with child care and other "domestic duties," especially in countries with limited public child care provisions.

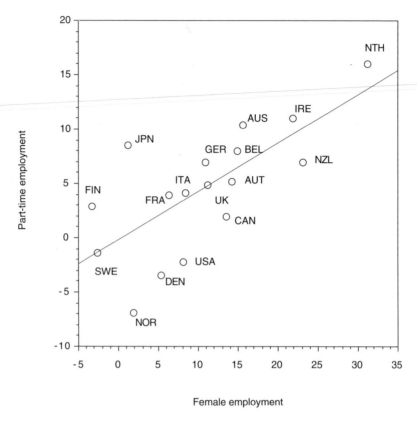

Correlation: .711
Sources: Tables 3.6 and 4.4.

Figure 4.1 Change in the incidence of part-time employment vs. change in the female employment rate, 1983–2003

The cross-national convergence of employment rates that has occurred since the early 1980s clearly involves a "ceiling effect." Given that the working-age population includes students and disabled people, that labor mobility inevitably involves some unemployment, and that some individuals prefer to assume household responsibilities to working, it is hard to imagine a society with an overall employment rate much higher than that which Sweden achieved in the early 1980s (80 percent). As the employment rate approaches this ceiling, further increases become more difficult to achieve. Yet this ceiling effect alone obviously does not explain why employment rates fell in the Nordic countries from 1983 to 2003, nor does it explain the considerable variation that exists among countries that started this period at similar levels of employment. For example, Australia,

Table 4.5 Average annual growth of civilian employment, 1980–2002

	Employed persons		Hours worked, 1990–2002
	1980–90	1990–2002	
Nordic SMEs	**0.7%**	**0.1%**	**−0.2%**
Denmark	0.7	0.2	0.2
Finland	0.8	−0.4	−0.8
Norway	0.6	1.1	0.5
Sweden	0.6	−0.5	−0.8
Continental SMEs	**1.3**	**0.8**	**0.3**
Austria	1.1	0.9	−0.1
Belgium	0.2	0.5	
Germany	0.8	−0.2	−0.8
Netherlands	2.3	2.0	1.4
Switzerland	1.9	0.7	0.5
LMEs	**1.4**	**1.7**	**1.4**
Australia	2.2	1.5	1.3
Canada	1.8	1.4	1.3
Ireland	0.1	3.5	2.3
New Zealand	1.6	2.0	2.0
United Kingdom	0.7	0.5	0.4
United States	1.8	1.2	1.1
France	0.3	0.8	0.2
Italy	0.4	0.2	−0.1
Japan	1.2	0.1	−0.9

Sources: OECD, *Labour Force Statistics* (2003), 20–21, 28–32, and OECD, *Employment Outlook* (2003), 322.

Note. German figures for 1980–90 refer to West Germany; German figures for 1990–2002 refer to unified Germany, 1991–2002.

Canada, and New Zealand achieved much greater increases in employment rates than Germany and France in the 1980s and 1990s even though all of these countries operated at employment rates in the 62–65 percent range in the early 1980s. Similarly, the Netherlands and Ireland outperformed Italy from comparable starting points (52–55 percent). Controlling for initial levels of employment, some economies have clearly been more able to generate new jobs than others.

EMPLOYMENT GROWTH

As noted in the introductory chapter, the claim that liberal market institutions produce better employment outcomes than social market institutions is most clearly supported by data on employment growth or, in other words, job creation. The first column of table 4.5 reports average annual growth rates of the total number of people in civilian employment over the 1980–90 and 1990–2002 periods. The data for the 1980s in table 4.5

present a mixed picture. During this decade, total employment grew very slowly, by less than one-half of 1 percent per year, in Belgium, Ireland, France, and Italy. On the other hand, total employment growth averaged more than 1.5 percent per year in the Netherlands, Switzerland, Australia, Canada, New Zealand, and the United States. The remaining countries, which include all the Nordic SMEs, fall in the range from 0.6 percent to 1.2 percent. The distinction between SMEs and LMEs emerges more clearly in the more recent figures. Over the period from 1990 to 2002, only two SMEs achieved employment growth rates above 1 percent, and the Dutch experience stands out as very exceptional. In Germany as well as in Finland and Sweden, the total number of people in employment actually declined over this period. By contrast, all LMEs except the United Kingdom maintained very healthy rates of employment growth in the 1990s and early 2000s, ranging from 1.2 percent for the United States to a spectacular 3.5 percent for Ireland.

To take into account the differential growth of part-time employment among OECD countries, the last column of table 4.5 presents my calculations of average annual growth of total employment measured in terms of hours worked (rather than individuals in employment) for the 1990–2002 period. Adjusting for hours worked does not significantly change employment growth rates in any of the LMEs except for Ireland.[8] The same is true for Denmark. For all other countries included in these tables, however, employment growth measured in hours was lower than employment growth measured in people. In particular, adjusting for hours worked makes the Dutch and Irish jobs miracles look considerably less impressive. It is also noteworthy that this adjustment puts the Austrian, German, Italian, and Japanese employment growth rates into negative territory.

Much of the existing literature implies that the poor employment performance of the social market economies derives from the manufacturing bias of these economies and their failure to generate new service jobs. One version of this argument holds that services are inherently more labor-intensive than manufacturing and that the room for productivity growth is more restricted in services. As a result, the expansion of the service sector—at least large parts of what is after all a very heterogeneous field of economic activities—depends critically on the ability of employers to hire unskilled workers at low wages. From this perspective, the wage floors and the compression of wage differentials produced by the collective bargaining arrangements characteristic of SMEs represent barriers to the growth of service employment.[9] In a similar vein, one might perhaps also argue that the employment protection measures characteristic of SMEs represent more of a barrier to the growth of employment in services than in industry.

Table 4.6 Average annual growth of employment in industry and services, 1980–2002

	Industry		Services	
	1980–90	1990–2002	1988–90	1990–2002
Nordic SMEs	**−0.6%**	**−1.2%**	**1.7%**	**0.9%**
Denmark	−0.3	−0.8	1.3	0.8
Finland	−0.6	−1.4	2.3	0.5
Norway	−1.2	0.0	1.7	1.7
Sweden	−0.4	−2.4	1.4	0.4
Continental SMEs	**−0.2**	**−1.1**	**2.4**	**1.8**
Austria	0.2	−0.9	2.2	2.2
Belgium	−1.8	−0.9	1.2	1.1
Germany	−0.4	−2.3	2.1	1.3
Netherlands	0.6	−0.1	3.1	2.9
Switzerland	0.2	−1.3	3.3	1.6
LMEs	**−0.4**	**0.5**	**2.4**	**2.4**
Australia	0.8	0.0	3.2	2.1
Canada	0.1	0.8	2.6	1.7
Ireland	−1.1	3.2	1.4	4.7
New Zealand	−1.6	1.3	3.2	2.4
United Kingdom	−0.8	−2.0	1.6	1.5
United States	0.3	−0.5	2.5	1.7
France	−1.6	−1.1	1.8	1.8
Italy	−1.2	0.1	2.5	0.7
Japan	0.8	−1.0	2.1	1.0

Source: OECD, *Labour Force Statistics* (2003), 28–32.
Note: German figures for 1980–90 refer to West Germany; German figures for 1990–2002 refer to unified Germany, 1991–2002.

Reporting on annual employment growth in services and industry separately for the 1980–90 and 1990–2002 periods, table 4.6 raises some doubts about these arguments. In the 1980s, the continental SMEs performed, on average, just as well as the LMEs as far as the growth of service employment is concerned; even the Nordic SMEs expanded service employment at rather healthy rates. Over the 1990–2002 period, the average growth rate of service employment in LMEs outpaced that of continental SMEs, but the difference in group averages appears to be entirely attributable to Ireland's exceptional growth rate. At least for the most recent period, the most important thing that distinguishes the continental SMEs from the LMEs seems to be the sizable employment losses the continental SMEs suffered in the manufacturing industry, which happened to only one of the LMEs, the United Kingdom. Table 4.6 also suggests that contractions of industrial employment were the key feature in the employment crises that the Nordic countries experienced in the first half of the 1990s. As figure 4.2 illustrates, there is a rather close positive correlation between employment growth in industry and services. It does

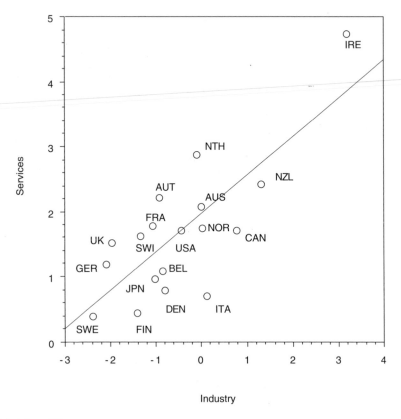

Correlation: .772
Source: Table 4.6.

Figure 4.2 Annual growth of employment in services vs. annual growth of employment in industry, 1990–2002

not appear to be the case that some countries are better at generating industrial jobs while others excel at generating service jobs. At this level of aggregation, countries with strong employment performance appear to be strong across all sectors while countries with weak employment performance appear to be weak across all sectors.

One might well object that the data in table 4.6 ignore the distinction between public and private services. Arguably, it is private sector service employment that represents the Achilles' heel of the social market economies. Government employers are less subject to competitive pressures and therefore more able to live with the constraints associated with social market arrangements. Unfortunately, the data series on government employment previously published in the OECD's *Historical Statistics*

Table 4.7 Average annual growth of employment in private and public services, 1980–97

	Public	Private
Nordic SMEs	**1.2%**	**1.0%**
Denmark	0.9	1.2
Finland	1.4	0.7
Norway*	2.8	1.0
Sweden	−0.5	1.0
Continental SMEs	**1.4**	**2.5**
Austria*	2.7	2.3
Belgium	0.2	1.4
Germany	0.0	2.7
Netherlands*	0.8	3.6
Switzerland*	3.3	2.3
LMEs	**0.1**	**2.5**
Australia*	0.2	4.1
Canada	1.4	2.2
Ireland	0.1	3.3
United Kingdom*	−2.4	2.7
United States	0.2	2.8
France	3.0	0.8
Italy	0.4	1.8
Japan	0.3	1.9

Sources: OECD, *Labour Force Statistics* (2003), 30–31, and OECD, *Historical Statistics* (2000).

Note: Figures for countries marked by an asterisk refer to 1980–95. German figures are for West Germany, 1980–90, and unified Germany, 1991–97.

has been discontinued. Based on the most recent data available, table 4.7 reports on annual employment growth rates for public and private services separately over the 1980s and the first half of the 1990s. Over this period, public sector employment increased in Canada, contracted sharply in the United Kingdom, and grew at anemic rates in the other LMEs. By contrast, significant public sector employment expansion occurred in six out of nine SMEs. When we look at employment growth in private services, however, the comparison does not turn decisively in favor of the LMEs. Furthermore, plotting employment growth rates in private services against employment growth rates in public services does not yield any consistent association between these two variables (see figure 4.3). Based on the evidence presented in table 4.7, it is not obvious that the expansion of employment in public services crowds out employment in private services.

As noted above, employment contracted sharply in the Nordic countries, particularly Finland and Sweden, in the early 1990s, but these countries have subsequently recovered from their employment crises. By

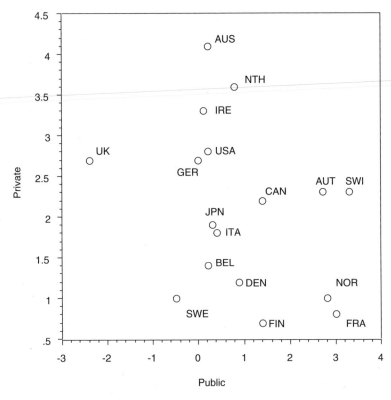

Source: Table 4.7.

Figure 4.3 Annual growth of employment in private services vs. annual growth of employment in public services, 1980–97

averaging employment growth rates over the 1990–2003 period, tables 4.5 and 4.6 fail to capture this turnaround, which is evident in earlier unemployment figures. Table 4.8 presents annual growth rates of total (civilian) employment for the 1995–2002 period. Comparing the figures in table 4.8 to those for 1990 through 2002 in table 4.5, almost all countries have generated more employment since 1995 than they did in the first half of the 1990s, but this improvement has been far more pronounced in the United Kingdom and the Nordic countries than in other countries. (Employment growth has apparently slowed down in Austria, New Zealand, and Japan.) On average, LMEs still outperform SMEs, but the continental SMEs no longer outperform the Nordic SMEs over this more recent time period.

As a group, the liberal market economies are characterized by higher-than-average employment growth rates, but not by lower-than-average

Table 4.8 Average annual growth of total employment, 1995–2002

Nordic SMEs	**1.2%**
Denmark	0.7
Finland	1.8
Norway	1.5
Sweden	0.9
Continental SMEs	**0.9**
Austria	0.3
Belgium	0.9
Germany	0.1
Netherlands	2.2
Switzerland	0.8
LMEs	**2.1**
Australia	1.8
Canada	2.0
Ireland	4.5
New Zealand	1.7
United Kingdom	1.3
United States	1.3
France	1.5
Italy	1.2
Japan	−0.3

Source: OECD, *Labour Force Statistics* (2003), 20–21.

unemployment rates, nor by higher-than-average employment rates. The explanation for this apparent disconnect has to do with working-age population growth. As table 4.9 shows, the rate of working-age population growth over the 1980–2002 period was much greater in all liberal market economies, with the notable exception of the United Kingdom, than in any of the other OECD countries. Leaving the United Kingdom aside, the United States is the liberal market economy in which the working-age population grew the slowest in the 1980s and 1990s, yet its growth rate of 1.1 percent per year was significantly higher than that for the fastest-growing countries outside the LME group—the Netherlands and Switzerland, at 0.7 percent per year.

In part, cross-national differences in working-age population growth reflect patterns of emigration and, above all, immigration (in the Irish case, the return of expatriates), but the correlation between working-age population growth and net migration is far from perfect.[10] Other demographic variables would also have to be considered to explain the data presented in table 4.9. For our present purposes, suffice it to note that a country with a rapidly growing working-age population must generate more new jobs to maintain a given employment rate than a country with a less rapidly growing working-age population. In a narrow sense, popu-

Table 4.9 Average annual growth of working-age population
(ages 15–64), 1980–2002

Nordic SMEs	**0.4%**
Denmark	0.3
Finland	0.3
Norway	0.6
Sweden	0.4
Continental SMEs	**0.5**
Austria	0.6
Belgium	0.2
Germany	0.3
Netherlands	0.7
Switzerland	0.7
LMEs	**1.1**
Australia	1.5
Canada	1.2
Ireland	1.3
New Zealand	1.2
United Kingdom	0.4
United States	1.1
France	0.5
Italy	0.2
Japan	0.4

Source: OECD, *Labour Force Statistics* (2003), 8–9.

lation growth might be said to constitute a liability for the liberal market economies relative to the social market economies, making it harder for them to raise the rate of employment (or reduce the rate of unemployment). From a broader perspective, however, population growth is surely a good thing, as it is associated with more rapid economic growth and mitigates the fiscal problems that increased life expectancy poses for the public provision of social welfare in the advanced capitalist countries.

IS THERE A TRADE-OFF BETWEEN EMPLOYMENT AND EQUALITY?

As noted earlier, it is a commonly held view, among both European and American economists, that the poor employment performance of Europe's social market economies stems from the lack of labor market flexibility. The proponents of this view argue that some combination of institutionalized collective bargaining, minimum wage legislation, and social welfare provisions—generous unemployment insurance in particular—has prevented the natural market response to rising unemployment: falling wages giving rise to increased demand for labor. Commonly, the argument focuses on the supply and demand for unskilled labor. The problem with the social market economies, we are told, is not simply or even primarily that average wages are too high for labor markets to clear: the real problem is that wages are too compressed. In the name of solidarity, unions have prioritized wage increases (or resisted wage cuts) for the lowest paid of their members and, in so doing, have priced unskilled labor out of the market.

It is not altogether clear why unions should engage in such apparently irrational behavior. One might perhaps argue that unions are more responsive to the interests of skilled rather than unskilled workers, but then the question becomes, why did they pursue wage compression in the first place? Setting this question aside, let us briefly consider whether the core empirical proposition of market liberals—that there exists a trade-off between good employment performance and egalitarianism—is borne out by cross-national evidence. Since the conventional argument hinges on the relative wages of less skilled workers, for this purpose the 50-10 ratio (the ratio of earnings at the median of the wage distribution to earnings in the 10th percentile) represents a more appropriate measure of wage inequality than the 90-10 ratio.[11]

To begin with, figure 4.4 plots 2001 employment rates for high school dropouts against the most recent observations of the wage spread in the bottom half of the wage distribution. It is immediately apparent that there is no simple linear relationship between these variables. It is certainly not the case that unskilled workers are generally less likely to be employed in more egalitarian countries. Sweden, Switzerland, and Japan (and, to a lesser extent, Denmark) are distinguished by high levels of employment among unskilled workers as well as low levels of inequality. And despite high levels of inequality, Canada, the United States, and Ireland do not exhibit particularly high levels of employment among unskilled workers. Similarly, plotting relative unemployment rates for unskilled workers (as measured in table 4.3) against 50-10 ratios does not yield anything like the picture that the trade-off thesis would lead us to expect. As noted earlier, unskilled workers do not appear to be particularly vulnerable to unemployment in countries where wages are compressed.

Plotting overall employment rates against observations of wage inequality in the 1990s also does not yield any support for the trade-off thesis. Again, the Nordic SMEs cut against the trade-off thesis, combining low levels of inequality with high levels of employment. On the other hand, figure 4.5 shows that there is a reasonably consistent and strong association between higher 50-10 wage ratios in the early 1990s and more rapid growth of total employment over the 1990–2002 period. This association also appears if we plot employment growth over the 1980–90 period against 50-10 wage ratios in the early 1980s. Curiously, however, levels of wage inequality do not correlate as strongly with growth of employment

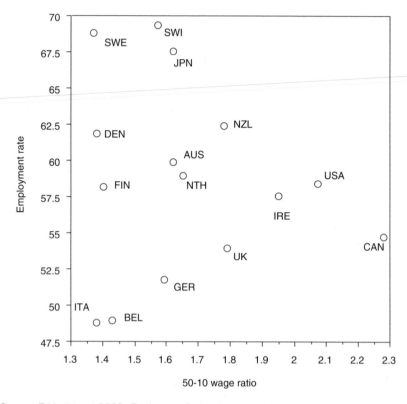

Sources: Table 3.4 and OECD, *Employment Outlook* (2004), 316–18.

Figure 4.4 Employment rate of workers with less than high school education in 2001 vs. most recent observation of 50-10 wage ratio

in the service sector for the 1990–2002 period or with growth of employment in private services for the 1980–97 period.[12] In general, more inegalitarian countries generated more new jobs than less inegalitarian countries over the last two decades of the twentieth century, but this association does not appear to be specifically due to the dynamics of job creation in private services. To gain a clearer understanding of the implications of wage inequality for employment growth, we would have to disaggregate "services" further and also disaggregate "industry."

To sum up, the evidence presented here suggests that wage inequality is indeed conducive to employment growth, but employment growth does not translate into relative employment gains for unskilled workers, at least not for unskilled male workers. By itself, allowing for increased wage differentiation is unlikely to eliminate the problem of long-term unemployment among unskilled workers. Also, I hasten to add that the association

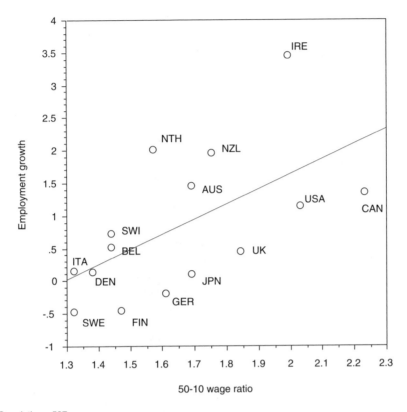

Correlation: .587
Sources: See tables 3.4 and 4.5.

Figure 4.5 Average annual growth of total employment 1990–2002 vs. 50–10 wage ratio, circa 1990

between wage inequality and employment growth established by figure 4.6 does not imply that egalitarian wages are the principal source of the SMEs' poor employment performance in the 1990s. As this study emphasizes, egalitarian wages are part of a bundle of characteristics that set SMEs apart from LMEs; as we shall see in subsequent chapters, other elements of the social market model are also associated with sluggish employment growth. The association between wage inequality and employment growth could indeed be entirely spurious, but multiple regression results reported by Lane Kenworthy suggest that this is not the case.[13] The more important point is that allowing wage inequality to rise is not the only way for the social market economies to address the problem of stimulating employment growth. Other institutional reforms may be equally or more effective and perhaps more desirable.

THE DUTCH "JOBS MIRACLE"

Among Europe's social market economies, the Netherlands stands out as the country with the best employment performance over the last two decades.[14] Averaging 9.9 percent in the 1980–84 period, the Dutch unemployment rate fell steadily over the next fifteen years, reaching 2.8 percent in 2000. With the total number of people in employment increasing by 61 percent from 1980 to 2002, the Dutch employment rate (employed people as percentage of population aged 15 to 64) rose from 52 percent in 1983 to 73.6 percent in 2003. The Dutch "jobs miracle" becomes slightly less impressive once one considers that 60 percent of the jobs created between 1987 and 1996 were part-time jobs. In relation to the total labor force, the number of people "usually working less than 30 hours per week" increased from 18.5 percent in 1983 to 34.5 percent in 2003, by far the largest increase of part-time employment in any of the OECD countries during this period (see table 3.6). Still, there is no gainsaying Dutch success in generating and sustaining employment growth.

For our purposes, the crucial question is whether the Netherlands has achieved employment growth by embracing the American model of deregulated labor markets or whether the Dutch experience should rather be viewed as a distinctive approach to employment growth, preserving core features of the social market model. On balance, the latter interpretation comes closer to the truth. The Dutch turnaround in the early 1980s coincided with the formation of a government committed to liberalization, cutting back the size of government and freeing market forces, and this view has informed the policies of subsequent governments as well. However, the Netherlands can hardly be characterized as a case of dismantling collective bargaining or social protections; rather, it is a case of more or less consensual policy adjustment within existing institutions. Indeed, the Dutch jobs miracle has involved a strengthening of social partnership and coordinated wage bargaining.

By all accounts, coordinated wage restraint has been the key to the Dutch jobs miracle. In the early 1980s, Dutch union leaders came to recognize that corporate profitability would have to be boosted in order to tackle the problem of mass unemployment. In a historic agreement with private employers signed in 1982, the unions agreed to restrain wage demands and to scrap automatic cost-of-living adjustments in return for the average work week being reduced from 40 to 38 hours. Over two years (1983–84), average real wages fell by 9 percent and labor's share of net enterprise income fell from 89 percent to 83.5 percent. While the employers staunchly resisted any further reduction of the work week, the unions continued to exercise wage restraint. From 1980 to 1994, the increase of average Dutch labor costs (57.5 percent) was nearly half as large as the increase of German labor costs (102.4 percent) and also considerably less than labor cost increases in the UK (63.1 percent) and the United States (68.3 percent).[15]

Government policy played an important role in sustaining this employment pact in the 1980s and 1990s. In the early 1990s, the government relieved some of the pressure on the unions by imposing a temporary wage freeze. More importantly, the statutory minimum wage has been cut several times, falling from 64.4 percent of the average wage in the 1980s to 51 percent in 1995. Also, public sector wages have effectively been "decoupled" from private sector wages, allowing the latter to grow more rapidly than the former. Finally, reforms of the Dutch welfare state (to be discussed further in chapters 7 and 8) have contributed to the jobs miracle in two different ways. On the one hand, more restrictive eligibility requirements for disability insurance and early retirement have boosted the supply of labor, dampening wage pressure in the economy. On the other hand, a significant reduction of government spending has made it possible to use tax cuts as a way to compensate workers for wage restraint.

The impact of wage restraint on household spending has also been cushioned by the entry of married women into employment. As commonly noted, the jobs miracle has involved a sharp shift from households with a single breadwinner to a "one-and-a-half jobs model." Arguably, employment based on wage restraint was made possible by the fact that the female employment rate was exceptionally low at the outset of this period. In this sense, the applicability of the Dutch model may be more limited than current debates in Europe suggest.

As we saw in the preceding chapter, the Netherlands has experienced a sharper increase of wage inequality than any of the other social market economies since the early 1980s. The 90-10 ratio for full-time employees increased by 17.5 percent, from 2.40 in 1983 to 2.82 in 1995 (see table 3.4). As most of this increase occurred in the mid-1990s, increased wage inequality appears to have been a consequence of employment growth rather a precondition for employment growth. Still, we cannot claim that coordinated wage restraint has enabled the Dutch to generate employment without the inegalitarian consequences observed in liberal market economies. To the extent that unions have been able to influence the pattern of employment growth, their influence has rather manifested itself in some reduction of work hours and, more importantly, better employment terms and more legal protection for part-time and temporary employees.

In addition to increased wage inequality, two other blemishes on the Dutch model must be noted. First, long-term unemployment remains a serious problem, particularly for unskilled workers. Secondly, it should perhaps not come as a big surprise that the Dutch low-wage strategy to boost employment, especially employment in private services, has translated into relatively sluggish productivity growth. From 1982 to 1995, GDP per hours worked grew at an annual rate of 2.6 percent, as compared to an average annual rate of 3.8 percent for the EU as a whole.[16] The Dutch model leaves a great deal to be desired, but it also shows that employment growth can be achieved and sustained under social market arrangements.

SUMMARY

A number of social market economies have consistently had lower rates of unemployment than the average for the liberal market economies. And even without far-reaching deregulation of labor markets, unemployment rates have fallen sharply in most social market economies over the last few years. The employment performance of the social market economies of northern Europe has been inferior to that of liberal market economies on two counts: the duration of unemployment and job creation. The former problem pertains primarily to the continental SMEs. Considered as a group and juxtaposed to the liberal market economies, the social market economies look worse with respect to job creation. Egalitarian wages appear to have inhibited employment growth in the social market economies, but it is by no means clear that this is the main obstacle to employment growth. As subsequent chapters will explore, other factors may represent more significant constraints on the ability of the social market economics to improve their employment performance.

Macro-Economic Management and Wage Bargaining

It is commonplace to attribute the persistence of high unemployment in Europe to economic policies and institutional conditions that have inhibited economic growth or, alternatively, promoted "jobless growth." From this viewpoint, Europe's poor employment performance is a long-term problem and essentially a micro-economic problem. As I discuss in other chapters, the conventional view certainly contains some elements of truth, but it is often couched too sweepingly and thus fails to address the crucial question of *which* policies and institutions need to change to achieve more satisfactory employment performance. In this chapter I argue that the macro-economic dimension of comparative employment performance is more important than the conventional view suggests.

For reasons articulated below, we ought to adjust for the balance of current accounts when we compare unemployment rates across countries. As we shall see, this adjustment lowers the unemployment rates of the social market economies while it increases the unemployment rates of the liberal market economies. Two questions arise: Why is the "minimum sustainable rate of unemployment" generally lower in social market economies than liberal market economies? And why have governments apparently pursued more restrictive macro-economic policies in the social market economies than the liberal market economies, failing to reduce unemployment to the extent that they could have done?

The bulk of this chapter addresses the first question. Drawing on an extensive literature, I argue that the institutional arrangements of social market economies facilitate the exercise of wage restraint. The more encompassing and more centralized nature of wage bargaining constitutes the key contrast between social and liberal market economies for the purposes of this argument. To appreciate fully the logic of wage restraint in social market economies, however, we must also take into account the interplay between wage bargaining and monetary policy. While de-unionization and decentralization of wage bargaining have occurred in some social market economies over the last two decades, these tendencies have been more pronounced in the liberal market economies. Coordinated wage bargaining remains a source of comparative institutional advantage for the social market economies. The empirical evidence indicates that more coordinated wage bargaining was associated with better macro-economic performance in the 1990s as well as the 1980s.

The deflationary bias exhibited by the social market economies in the 1990s should first and foremost be seen as a manifestation of the impact of German unification and the politics of European monetary cooperation rather than an inherent feature of social market arrangements. This in turn raises the question of the implications of the introduction of the Euro for coordinated wage bargaining and macro-economic management. I will briefly address this question toward the end of the chapter.

THE MACRO-ECONOMIC DIMENSION OF UNEMPLOYMENT

Like the pre-Keynesian economic orthodoxy of the 1920s, the currently dominant view among economists holds that macro-economic policies have little or no effect on the rate of unemployment. Rational expectations ensure that firms, unions, and other private actors anticipate and discount any government efforts to stimulate aggregate demand and that any new jobs created by the government will be matched by job losses in the private sector. In each country, there is a unique equilibrium rate of unemployment, and over the medium term, if not the short term, the actual rate of unemployment will coincide with the equilibrium rate. The equilibrium rate of unemployment varies across countries for reasons having to do with micro-economics or, in other words, institutional arrangements. If governments want to reduce the rate of unemployment, they must intervene at this level; that is, they must implement structural reforms that render labor markets more flexible and efficient, allowing for the downward adjustment of wages.[1]

Drawing on neo-Keynesian ideas, recent work by David Soskice challenges the neoclassical claim that macro-economic policy does not matter to unemployment.[2] Soskice argues that the neoclassical idea of a unique equilibrium rate of unemployment makes sense in a closed economy. In an open economy, however, firms must conform, more or less, to world prices—their pricing behavior cannot be understood simply as a markup on unit costs of production—and from this follows the existence of multiple unemployment equilibria. In Soskice's model of the open economy, aggregate demand determines the equilibrium rate of unemployment, but the external balance constrains the ability of the government to stimulate aggregate demand.

To provide a rough estimate of minimum sustainable rates of unemployment, Soskice subtracts the current account balance, expressed in percent of GDP, from the actual rate of unemployment.[3] The current account balance measures the balance of trade in goods and services, plus net rents, profits, dividends, and current transfer payments. A negative balance implies that a country imports more goods, services, and capital than it exports. Assuming that current account deficits are unsustainable over the long run and that short-term measures to close the current account deficit (for example, increasing interest rates) entail an increase of unemployment, the actual level of unemployment in countries with negative current account balances can be characterized as unsustainably low.

Using standardized unemployment rates, table 5.1 calculates minimum sustainable unemployment rates for the 1995–2000 period in the manner proposed by Soskice. While the actual unemployment rate was, on average, somewhat lower in social market economies than liberal market economies in this period, the liberal and social market economies diverged most sharply with respect to the current account balance. Except for Ireland, all the liberal market economies had negative current account balances in this period and the deficits were quite sizable in the cases of Australia, New Zealand, and the United States. By contrast, all but two social market economies, Austria and Germany, ran current account surpluses, as did also France, Italy, and Japan.

Subtracting current account balances from actual unemployment rates casts the performance of the liberal market economies in the second half of the 1990s in a very unfavorable light. By this way of reckoning, the minimum sustainable unemployment rate ranges between 7.4 percent (the United States) and 12.4 percent (Australia) under LME conditions, while it ranges between −6.4 percent (Switzerland) and 8.3 percent (Germany) under SME conditions. The average rate for the liberal market economies is nearly three times as high as that for the nine social market economies, 9.2 percent as compared to 3.4 percent.

The point of this exercise is not to generate exact measures of the natural rate of unemployment. The U.S. figure is higher than any current estimates, and Switzerland surely does not have a natural rate of unemployment of −6.4 percent. It is the country rankings in the third column of table 5.1, not the specific estimates of minimum sustainable unemployment, that matter. The main message of table 5.1 is that most social

Table 5.1 Minimum sustainable unemployment rates, 1995–2000

	A: Actual unemployment	B: Current account balance in percent of GDP	A minus B
Nordic SMEs	**7.6**	**3.7**	**3.9**
Denmark	5.8	0.8	5.0
Finland	12.3	5.5	6.8
Norway	4.0	5.3	−1.3
Sweden	8.3	3.0	5.3
Continental SMEs	**6.1**	**3.1**	**3.0**
Austria	4.1	−2.8	6.9
Belgium	9.1	4.3	4.8
Germany	8.9	−0.6	8.3
Netherlands	4.8	5.0	−0.2
Switzerland	3.5	9.8	−6.4
LMEs	**7.2**	**−2.0**	**9.2**
Australia	7.9	−4.5	12.4
Canada	8.5	−0.4	8.9
Ireland	8.5	1.6	6.9
New Zealand	6.6	−5.6	12.2
United Kingdom	7.0	−0.7	7.7
United States	4.8	−2.6	7.4
France	11.5	2.0	9.5
Italy	11.4	1.7	9.7
Japan	3.9	2.3	1.6

Sources: OECD, *Employment Outlook*, 2001, p. 209, and OECD, *Economic Outlook*, no. 69, 2001, p. 280.

market economies could have reduced unemployment by stimulating aggregate demand in the second half of the 1990s, while the liberal market economies could not have done so.

Why, then, does the minimum sustainable rate of unemployment tend to be lower in social market economies than liberal market economies? The argument to be developed below holds that the coordination of wage bargaining characteristic of the social market economies provides an effective mechanism to ensure that wage growth remains consistent with the requirements of non-inflationary growth and international competitiveness. Lacking such institutions, the liberal market economies must rely on unemployment to discipline labor.

Unions and Wage Restraint

For the discussion in this chapter, the key point of contrast between social and liberal market economies is that collective bargaining plays a much more important role in the process of wage formation in the former

Table 5.2 Wage bargaining institutions, 1980 and 2000

	Union density			Collective bargaining coverage		
	1980	2000	Change	1980	2000	Change
Nordic SMEs	**72%**	**71%**		**78%**	**83%**	
Denmark	79	74	−5	70	80	+10
Finland	69	76	+7	90	90	
Norway	58	54	−4	70	70	
Sweden	80	79	−1	80	90	+10
Continental SMEs	**42**	**32**		**77**	**75**	
Austria	57	37	−20	95	95	
Belgium	54	56	+2	90	90	
Germany	35	25	−10	80	68	−12
Netherlands	35	23	−12	70	80	+10
Switzerland	31	18	−13	50	40	−10
LMEs	**47**	**26**				
Australia	48	25	−23	80	80	
Canada	35	28	−7	37	32	−5
Ireland	57	38	−19			
New Zealand	69	23	−46	60	25	−35
United Kingdom	51	31	−20	70	30	−50
United States	22	13	−9	26	14	−12
France	18	10	−8	80	90	+10
Italy	50	35	−15	85	80	−5
Japan	31	22	−9	25	15	−10

Source: OECD, *Employment Outlook* (2004), 145.

Note: Depending on the country, union density refers either to employed union members or employed and unemployed union members as a percentage of the employed labor force. Retired persons who retain their union membership are generally not included.

set of countries than in the latter. This observation involves two analytically distinct considerations: the rate of unionization and the extent to which the wages of non-union workers are determined by collective bargaining between unions and employers. Looking at the data for 2000 in the first panel of table 5.2, we observe that the unionization rate of the least unionized SME (Switzerland) is five percentage points higher than the unionization rate of the least unionized LME (the United States) and, similarly, that the unionization rate of the most unionized SME (Sweden) is much higher than the unionization rate of the most unionized LME (Ireland). However, it is immediately apparent from table 5.2 that the weakness of American unions is unique and that high unionization is a distinctive characteristic of the Nordic SMEs rather than all SMEs. Leaving the United States out of the picture, unionization rates in the other LMEs are comparable to those of the countries in the middle of the continental SME range: Austria, Germany, and the Netherlands.

As table 5.2 shows, the continental SMEs are distinguished by the fact that collective bargaining coverage rates—the percentage of the labor force that is covered by collectively bargained agreements—in these countries exceed unionization rates by a wide margin. In Austria, Germany, the Netherlands, and Switzerland, the coverage rate was at least twice as high as the unionization rate in 2000.[4] Essentially, there are two reasons for the discrepancy between coverage rates and unionization rates. First, some governments engage in the extension of collectively negotiated agreements—in effect mandating that all firms, possibly all firms in a particular sector or region, adhere to the terms of the agreement in question. Secondly, and more generally, collective agreements in these countries typically stipulate that their terms apply to all employees of the firms that are party to the agreement, regardless of whether or not individual employees are union members. In large measure, collective bargaining coverage rates exceed unionization rates because employers are better organized than workers; that is, the percentage of firms that belong to employer associations is higher than the percentage of workers that belong to unions.

With the notable exception of Australia, with its distinctive system of industrial tribunals, the scope of collective bargaining in liberal market economies is basically determined by the ability of unions to organize the labor force.[5] This is also true for the Nordic countries. Whereas the Nordic SMEs are distinguished from the LMEs by higher unionization rates, the continental SMEs are distinguished from the LMEs by the extension of collectively bargained agreements to non-union workers. In both sets of social market economies, collective bargaining encompasses the wages and other employment terms of virtually all employees.[6]

Following the lead of Mancur Olson, a great many authors argue that encompassment makes unions more likely to exercise wage restraint.[7] Put simply, the argument runs as follows. Suppose that there is a single union in the economy, exclusively devoted to the interests of its members; that this union has the capacity to extract a wage increase that exceeds the rate of productivity growth; and that the firms with which the union bargains have the capacity to pass on these wages increases to consumers. If the union's membership is small relative to the labor force, it should take full advantage of its bargaining leverage, for the wage increase thus obtained only benefits its members, while the inflationary effect is shared by all worker-consumers in the economy. As encompassment increases, however, this hypothetical union should become increasingly concerned with the inflationary effects of its wage demands. If the union organizes the entire labor force, it does not stand to gain anything from wage increases that exceed productivity growth.

To the extent that collective bargaining coverage generates economy-wide wage increases, the logic of encompassment should be just as applicable to the Netherlands (23 percent unionization, 80 percent coverage) as it is to Denmark (74 percent unionization, 80 percent coverage). It should also be noted that this logic applies to employers as well as to workers and their unions. Like unions, individual employers would like to keep the lid on economy-wide wage increases while they themselves pay premium wages to attract the best workers. The larger the firm or the employer association is, the less readily it can ignore the inflationary consequences of its wage behavior.

Turning from the hypothetical to the real world, the number of unions and the extent to which they compete with each other for members can also be expected to shape their wage demands and behavior. This consideration does not lend itself so easily to summary measurements and it is not my intention to enter into a detailed discussion of cross-national variations in union structure. A brief comparison of Germany and the United Kingdom will serve to convey the scholarly consensus on this subject.

Unionization rates in Germany and the United Kingdom were roughly comparable in the 1990s, and the two cases resemble each other in that they both have unitary labor movements headed by a single umbrella organization—the Deutsche Gewerkschaftsbund (DGB) and the Trades Union Congress (TUC). Beyond these similarities, the two union movements are fundamentally different. In 1990, the DGB consisted of 16 member unions while the TUC had 76 member unions. (Subsequent mergers have reduced the number of member unions in both cases.) The largest DGB affiliate, the Metalworkers' Union (IG Metall), accounted for 34 percent of the total membership of the DGB unions, and the three largest affiliates together accounted for 59 percent of total membership. By contrast, the largest TUC affiliate accounted for 15 percent and the largest three affiliates for 34 percent of total membership.[8] Most importantly, the DGB affiliates are industrial unions with clearly defined jurisdictions, organizing workers based on the sector in which they work rather than on their skills or job descriptions. By contrast, the TUC consists of multi-sectoral craft unions and "general unions" as well as industrial unions, frequently organizing workers in the same sectors and, indeed, in the same workplaces.

Individual TUC affiliates have a strong organizational stake in being able to deliver better wages and other benefits for their members than other unions do. German unions have an interest in keeping up with wage developments in other sectors of the economy, but they do not compete with each other directly for membership. While the broad scope of collective bargaining provides German unions with the motive to moderate their wage demands, their high degree of concentration and the relative absence of jurisdictional overlaps gives them the capacity to pursue a more coordinated approach to wage bargaining. Broadly speaking, this generalization holds for union movements in all the social market economies.

Centralization constitutes another institutional variable that figures prominently in the comparative literature on collective bargaining systems and their implications for wage restraint. There are two ways that this variable might be conceived. First, we can think of centralization in terms of the level at which bargaining between unions and employers occurs. In the United States and other liberal market economies, unions commonly bargain over wages with individual companies. In the social market economies, by contrast, multi-employer bargaining is the norm. Typically, unions bargain with sector-wide employer associations in these economies. In Germany and Austria, sectoral bargaining occurs on a regional level, but in the other SMEs the scope of sectoral bargaining is nationwide. In some SMEs, the postwar era also featured multi-sectoral bargaining at the national level. In Sweden, commonly cited as the example *par excellence* of centralized bargaining, each round of wage bargaining between 1956 and 1983 began with an economy-wide settlement between the national federations of blue-collar unions (*Landsorganisationen*) and private sector employers (*Svenska Arbetsgivareföreningen*), defining the parameters for subsequent industry-level negotiations between affiliates of these organizations.

The other way to think about centralization is in terms of the authority that peak organizations wield over affiliated unions and employer associations as well as the authority that these affiliates wield over local organizations. Formally, German wage bargaining occurs at the regional level, but within any given sector, separate negotiations for different regions are closely coordinated on the employer side as well as on the union side. Informally, German unions and employer associations also coordinate their demands across sectors. Typically, this type of coordination takes the form of pattern bargaining, with wage agreements in the export-oriented engineering sector setting the ceiling for wage growth in other sectors.[9] Like concentration, centralization of bargaining and authority within unions and employer associations facilitates the coordination necessary for the exercise of wage restraint.

Generalizing across the advanced capitalist countries, more concentrated union movements and employer associations tend to be more centralized than less concentrated union movements and employer associations. Empirically, these institutional features of wage bargaining are also correlated with union density and collective bargaining coverage. Regressing various indicators of macro-economic performance on separate measures of labor encompassment, bargaining coverage and centralization, a recent OECD study finds very few robust and statistically significant effects.[10] This is perhaps to be expected when the total number of observations is small and the independent variables are correlated with each other. Using single measures or composite indices of labor encompassment and organizational cohesion, an extensive body of empirical research shows that these variables tend to be associated with lower rates of inflation as well as lower rates of unemployment.[11] Most importantly, this literature suggests that labor market institutions condition the effects of fiscal and monetary policies.

COORDINATED BARGAINING UNDER PRESSURE

If intensified international competition affects the macro-economic benefits of coordinated wage bargaining, it should enhance rather than diminish these benefits. Yet in some social market economies, notably Sweden, politicians embraced monetarism in the 1990s because they had become convinced that the wage bargaining system could no longer effectively deliver wage restraint. Is it perhaps the case that unions and employers in the social market economies have lost some of their coordinating capacities, even though coordinated wage bargaining remains efficient from an economic point of view?

Several developments motivate this question. De-unionization is one of these developments. As table 5.2 indicates, Finland and Belgium are the only OECD countries in which union density increased from 1980 to 2000. Over these two decades, Danish, Norwegian, and Swedish unions suffered only minor membership losses, but union density declined sharply in Austria, Germany, the Netherlands, and Switzerland. By the logic set out above, we would expect unions to become less concerned with the inflationary implications of their wage demands as their membership declines. It should be noted, however, that union density declines in the continental SMEs were typically smaller than union density declines in the LMEs. More importantly, de-unionization has been accompanied by corresponding declines in collective bargaining coverage in most LMEs, a trend that does not hold for the continental SMEs. The declines in bargaining coverage observed for Germany and Switzerland from 1980 to 2000 are much smaller than the declines in union density. Despite significant union membership losses, collective bargaining coverage held steady in Austria and actually increased in the Netherlands.

The Nordic countries are distinguished not only by high union density rates but also by the existence of separate unions for blue-collar and white-collar workers in most economic sectors. With the shift of employment from industry to services in the 1970s and 1980s, white-collar unions rapidly gained membership and became more important players in the wage-bargaining process. Arguably, competition between white-collar and blue-collar unions made it more difficult for the Nordic countries to keep overall wage growth consistent with the international competitiveness in this period. In a similar vein, a number of observers of wage bargaining in the Nordic countries argue that wage rivalries between private and public sector unions have rendered the exercise of wage restraint more problematic. In terms of the analytical categories set out above, the growth of separate white-collar unions represents a process of "de-concentration" or, in other words, a weakening of the organizational cohesion of labor. It must be underscored, however, that this represents a uniquely Nordic problem.[12] In other countries, union membership has become *more* concentrated since the early 1980s as unions have sought to offset membership losses through mergers. Also, it should be noted that blue-collar and white-collar unions have developed various informal mechanisms of coordination in the Nordic countries.

The issue of public sector wage militancy may pose a more general problem for social market economies. The public sector is not only sheltered against international competition, it also tends to be sheltered against domestic competition. By comparison to their private sector counterparts, conventional wisdom suggests, public sector employers are therefore more likely to accede to union wage demands, and public sector unions have less reason to worry that wage gains will translate into unemployment.[13] The theoretical rationale for this view of public sector unions is, however, not entirely clear and compelling. Unemployment induced by excessive wage growth may pose less of a constraint for public sector unions than for private sector unions, but as far as inflation is concerned the logic of encompassment applies equally to both kinds of unions. Furthermore, public sector unions have particularly strong reasons to worry about the partisan composition of the government. To the extent that the reelection of incumbent governments depends on the state of the economy as a whole, there are strong incentives for public sector unions to consider the economy-wide implications of their wage bargaining stance when parties that they support hold power. Surveying the OECD countries in the 1990s, what we observe is surely not a story of militant public sector unions engaged in "rent-seeking behavior" at the expense of unemployment in other economic sectors. In the context of fiscal austerity, public sector employment in many countries has grown very slowly or even contracted. The fragmentary evidence available on this score suggests that public sector wages have generally failed to keep up with private sector wages.

Decentralization represents another trend that has led a number of observers to suggest that wage-bargaining arrangements in the social market economies have become less conducive to coordinated wage restraint. Previously noted for its highly centralized system of wage bargaining, Sweden is the most commonly invoked example of decentralization. Very briefly, Sweden's export-oriented engineering employers became increasingly dissatisfied with the existing bargaining system from the mid-1970s onwards. Specifically, they resented the way the system ensured that the wages of workers in sheltered and less productive sectors would keep up with wages in the engineering sector, making it hard for these firms to recruit and retain qualified and motivated workers. In addition, engineering employers became convinced that centralized bargaining represented an obstacle to the wage differentiation required to pursue more flexible, quality-oriented production strategies. At the insistence of these employers, economy-wide peak-level negotiations were eventually scrapped.[14]

Pivoting on industry-level negotiations, the new Swedish bargaining system allows considerably more room for firm-level bargaining than the old system did, but Swedish decentralization stopped well short of individual firms bargaining independently with their unions (as radicals within the employers' federation advocated in the late 1980s). Following a decade of contention, Sweden ended up with a wage-bargaining system that is quite similar to the German system. And, in contrast to their Swedish counterparts, German employers have shown very little proclivity to engage in conflict with the unions over the institutional arrangements of wage bargaining.[15] The experience of other social market economies falls somewhere between Sweden's clear-cut and rather far-reaching decentralization of wage bargaining and Germany's institutional stability. In the Netherlands, the government and the peak organizations of labor and business retreated from direct intervention in the wage bargaining process in the 1970s, and firm-level bargaining has subsequently taken on more importance than elsewhere in northern Europe. (Philips and other Dutch multinationals are no longer part of multi-employer bargaining.) At the same time, however, informal coordination of wage bargaining by union and employer peak associations in the name of employment creation became an integral part of the new Dutch model.

To the extent that wage-bargaining decentralization has occurred in the social market economies, it has primarily involved a retreat from peak-level bargaining. In the liberal market economies, by contrast, peak organizations never played much of a role in wage bargaining, and decentralization has involved a shift from multi-employer to single-employer bargaining.[16] Arguably, the latter type of decentralization renders coordination far more difficult than the former type. So long as industrial unions are internally centralized and do not compete with each other for members, they are likely to be able to solve the collective action problems involved in the exercise of wage restraint.

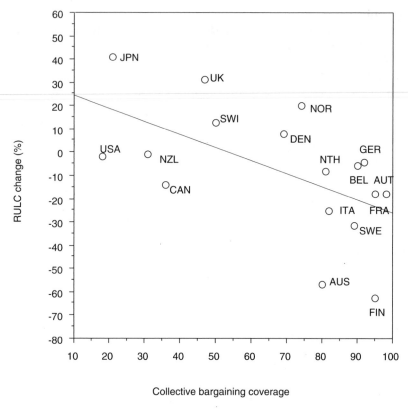

Collective bargaining coverage

Correlation: −.572
Sources: Table 5.2 and OECD, *Employment Outlook*, n. 69 (2004), 272.

Figure 5.1 Percentage change in relative unit labor costs (RULCs) in manufacturing 1990–99 vs. rate of collective bargaining coverage in 1994

In the 1990s, employee compensation (wages and employer-provided benefits) in the private sector tended to grow more rapidly in countries with higher rates of union density, but so did economy-wide productivity (real GDP per employed person). Taking into account not only productivity but also social security contributions and other payroll taxes, readily available OECD data on the evolution of relative unit labor costs (RULCs) in manufacturing industry provide a crude way to assess the implications of labor market institutions for competitiveness. Plotting changes in RULCs from 1990 to 2000 against union density in the mid-1990s, we do not find any pattern of consistent association between these variables. As figure 5.1 illustrates, however, there is a weak but quite consistent relationship between changes in RULC and levels of collective bargaining coverage. In general, the manufacturing competitiveness of countries with more extensive collective bargaining coverage tended to improve in the course of the 1990s.[17] Whether or the coordinating capacities of unions have diminished over time, the data on RULCs clearly contradict the proposition that collective bargaining (or unionization) has been an obstacle to competitive labor cost adjustments.

WAGE BARGAINING AND MONETARY POLICY

Many economists explain cross-national difference in macro-economic performance in terms of the degree of central bank independence, that is, the degree to which monetary policy is insulated from electoral and parliamentary politics. The basic argument in this literature holds that uncertainty about the future course of monetary policy leads to inflationary wage growth as unions seek to insure nominal wage increases against future price increases. Rendering the central bank more independent of political control increases the credibility of its assurances that monetary policy will remain tight and allows unions to settle for lower nominal wage increases.[18]

With the German Bundesbank generally considered to be the most autonomous central bank among the OECD countries, central bank independence and coordinated wage bargaining might be construed as alternative explanations of the strong performance of the German economy in the 1970s and 1980s. However, these explanations are not mutually exclusive. As several authors have recently argued, there may be an interaction effect between central bank independence and coordinated wage bargaining in the sense that the wage-moderating effects of each variable are enhanced by the presence of the other variable. Arguably, coordinated wage bargaining makes it easier for central banks to evaluate the implications of wage bargaining for monetary policy and renders unions and employers more responsive to central bank concerns. As Peter Hall and Robert Franzese put it,

> where wage bargaining is coordinated, the central bank may be able to influence the level of [wage] settlements and reduce inflation simply by signaling policy intentions so that monetary policy does not raise the level of unemployment. Where wage bargaining is uncoordinated, however, such that small bargaining units have no reason to expect a direct response to their settlement and disincentives to exercise general moderation lest others fail to do so, the central bank may have to apply tight monetary policies that induce substantial increases in unemployment before wage and price contracts will respond.[19]

Adapted from Hall and Franzese, table 5.3 sorts the OECD countries according to two criteria—more or less coordinated wage bargaining and more or less independent central banks—and then reports average inflation and unemployment rates over the 1955–90 period for each of the four groups of countries that emerge from this sorting.[20] Among the countries with less coordinated bargaining systems, those with independent central banks tended to have lower inflation rates and higher unemployment rates than those with dependent central banks. The same effects of central bank independence—lower inflation and higher unemployment—appear when the comparison is restricted to countries with more coordinated wage bargaining systems. The other way to read table 5.3 is to look for the effects of bargaining coordination while holding central bank independence constant. From this perspective, we find that among countries with dependent central banks, those with coordinated wage bargaining systems enjoyed less inflation and less unemployment than those with uncoordinated bargaining systems. Among countries with independent central banks, those with coordinated bargaining systems did decidedly better on the unemployment front than those with uncoordinated bargaining systems, but the inflation record of these two sets of countries was the same.

The key result that emerges from table 5.3 is that central bank independence invariably lowers the rate of inflation, but in the absence of coordinated wage bargaining this effect is associated with significantly higher unemployment. Coordinated wage bargaining lowers inflation as

Table 5.3 Average inflation and unemployment by central bank independence and coordination of wage bargaining, 1955–90

Coordination of wage bargaining	Central bank independence			
	Low		High	
Low	Inflation:	7.5	Inflation:	4.8
	Unemployment:	4.7	Unemployment:	6.1
	Misery:	12.2	Misery:	10.9
High	Inflation:	5.9	Inflation:	4.8
	Unemployment:	2.9	Unemployment:	3.1
	Misery:	8.8	Misery:	7.9

Country classifications:
Low CBI/low CWB: Australia, France, Ireland, Italy, New Zealand, United Kingdom.
High CBI/low CWB: Canada, United States.
Low CBI/high CWB: Belgium, Finland, Norway, Japan, Sweden.
High CBI/kigh CWB: Austria, Denmark, Germany, the Netherlands, Switzerland.
Source: Peter Hall and Robert Franzese, "Mixed Signals," *International Organization* 52 (1998), 517, 527, 530.

well as unemployment, but its effect on inflation rates is not as strong as that of central bank independence. Using the sum of inflation and unemployment as a composite measure of overall performance, commonly referred to as the "misery index," countries that combined central bank independence and bargaining coordination clearly performed best and those that lacked both characteristics performed worst over the 1955–90 period.

Using the same country classifications as in table 5.3, table 5.4 reports average inflation and unemployment rates for the 1990–99 period. (It does not make sense to replicate the exercise with more recent data since the European Central Bank took over monetary policy from most of the EU member states in 1999.) For this period, bargaining coordination is associated with both lower inflation and lower unemployment irrespective of central bank independence, while central bank independence is associated with lower unemployment in both coordinated and uncoordinated bargaining systems. Central bank independence is also associated with lower inflation in uncoordinated systems, but this is not true for coordinated systems. Countries that combine both features still have the best overall performance, and countries that lack both features still have the worst overall performance. Among the mixed cases, countries with coordinated bargaining have done marginally better than countries with independent central banks in this more recent period. Not surprisingly, perhaps, the significance of domestic monetary policy arrangements seems to have declined as the EU member states geared up for the introduction of the Euro. At the same time, table 5.4 confirms that coordinated wage bargaining remains an institutional asset for the social market economies.

Table 5.4 Average inflation and unemployment by central bank independence and coordination of wage bargaining, 1990–98

Coordination of wage bargaining	Central bank independence			
	Low		High	
Low	Inflation:	3.3	Inflation:	2.6
	Unemployment:	10.0	Unemployment:	7.7
	Misery:	13.3	Misery:	10.3
High	Inflation:	2.2	Inflation:	2.3
	Unemployment:	7.4	Unemployment:	5.8
	Misery:	9.6	Misery:	8.1

Country classifications: Same as table 5.3.
Sources: Table 4.1 and OECD, *Economic Outlook* 69 (2001), 246.

European Integration

To reiterate, the preceding discussion suggests that the social market economies could have engaged in macro-economic stimulation to achieve lower rates of unemployment in the 1990s. Why is it that SME governments have apparently pursued more restrictive macro-economic policies than LME governments? The insider-outsider perspective discussed in the previous chapter suggests one possible answer to this question: while unemployment tends to be more long-term and more concentrated, core segments of the labor force enjoy a higher degree of employment security in SMEs than in LMEs. At the same time, a more extensive social safety net implies that the consequences of unemployment for family income tend to be less severe in SMEs than in LMEs. Along these lines, Francine Blau and Lawrence Kahn speculate that the institutional arrangements characteristic of social market economies "reduce the resolve of the electorate to pursue policies that lower unemployment."[21] There is surely something to the claim that public welfare provision has cushioned the impact of unemployment and thereby mitigated the political disaffection associated with rising unemployment, but I do not believe that this argument alone constitutes a satisfactory answer to the question before us. Even employed workers benefit from falling unemployment, and European unions clearly do care about the rate of unemployment. There are many instances of incumbent governments being punished by West European voters for allowing unemployment to rise, and I am not aware of any evidence suggesting that this phenomenon is more prevalent in LMEs than in SMEs.

It is noteworthy that Ireland and the United Kingdom, the two LMEs that are members of the EU, pursued less expansionary aggregate demand management than other LMEs in the 1990s. This suggests that in explaining the orientation of macro-economic policy we need to take into account the experience of European integration and, specifically, the politics of European monetary cooperation. As commonly noted, the pursuit of economic and monetary union (EMU)—a single currency, with interest rates set by a supranational central bank—can largely be seen as a response by France and other countries to the deflationary bias of the German Bundesbank. France wanted more control over monetary policy—more room for fiscal expansion—but in order to get Germany to cooperate in the EMU project it had to accept a strong deflationary emphasis in preparation for the single currency as well as a European central bank modeled on the Bundesbank.

The deflationary bias of European monetary cooperation was exacerbated by the politics of German unification in the 1990s. The German government and the unions seriously overestimated the prospects for private investment in the East.[22] As a result, the government engaged in unfunded expenditure growth, and the unions pushed through inflationary wage demands. The Bundesbank responded by tightening monetary policy, and, via pegged exchange rates, the deflationary effects of this policy stance spread to other EU member states. In short, a number of circumstances conspired to force the social market economies of northern Europe, particularly the small trade-dependent states in Germany's immediate vicinity, to pursue restrictive macro-economic policies in the 1990s. The obvious question becomes, does the realization of EMU, now up and running, lock in the deflationary bias that characterized the preparatory phase? Thus far the new European Central Bank (ECB) has failed to ease the supply of money in the face of persistent unemployment, low inflation, and, recently, a sharp increase in the exchange rate vis-à-vis the U.S. dollar. Most observers agree that this stance reflects the ECB's desire to establish its credibility—that is, the credibility of its independence from political pressures—in the eyes of financial markets. As Robert Dunn puts it, "The fact that the ECB is an extremely young institution creates a bias towards tighter policies."[23]

Looking beyond the transition phase, the preceding discussion suggests that EMU might render wage restraint more difficult for the social market economies. Simply put, German unions represent a much smaller percentage of labor force in the new Euro economy than they did in the old deutsche mark economy and consequently have less reason to internalize the inflationary effects of their wage demands. In other words, the move to a single currency entails a de facto reduction of union encompassment. At the same time, the ability of the European Central Bank to discipline unions in any one of the EMU states (say, Germany) is more limited than that of the national central banks that it replaces, for the simple reason that the ECB targets the rate of inflation in the Euro area as a whole. Relative to national central banks, it will be more difficult for the European Central Bank to identify the sources of wage-push inflation and to engage in preemptive signaling of its policy intentions. By the logic established above, more inflationary union wage demands countered by tighter monetary policy might be expected to translate into higher rates of unemployment.[24]

Cognizant of this problem, EU leaders and some economic policy advisers have begun to advocate greater coordination of wage bargaining across the Euro zone. However, the institutional, political, linguistic, and cultural obstacles to the formation of an EMU-wide wage-bargaining system are formidable. More plausibly, for the near future, Germany might become the anchor in a more informal system of "pattern bargaining." In such a scenario, the European Central Bank would specifically target the German inflation rate, forcing German unions to exercise wage restraint, and competition in product markets would force unions in other countries to keep their wage settlements in line with German wage settlements.

Arguably, EMU enhances the capacity of national governments to pursue expansionary fiscal policies for the same basic reasons that it weakens the incentives for unions to engage in wage restraint. With a single currency, the exchange rate costs that governments engaged in deficit spending incurred in the 1980s and early 1990s no longer apply; so long as deficit spending does not translate into EMU-wide inflation, there is no mandate for the European Central Bank to respond by raising interest rates. Under the terms of the so-called Stability and Growth Pact, penalties may be imposed on countries with a government deficit exceeding 3 percent of GDP, but such penalties have to be decided by ministers of finance. During the recession of 2000–02, deficit spending exceeded the 3 percent ceiling in quite a few countries. In November 2003, the European Commission formally requested that the Ecofin Council fine Germany and France for continuing to violate the Stability and Growth Pact with no immediate plans to bring deficits into line, but the Ecofin Council did not adopt this proposal. Despite a subsequent court ruling upholding the European Commission's position, the Stability and Growth Pact effectively remains in abeyance.

The most obvious problem with EMU is that it imposes a common interest rate on economies that are growing at different rates. Less obviously, EMU threatens to undermine the positive interaction between central bank independence and coordinated wage bargaining. On the other side of the ledger, EMU seems to have created more room for expansionary fiscal policies. For the German government, EMU certainly imposes fewer constraints on fiscal policy than the Bundesbank did in the 1980s. The single currency thus (re-)introduces the possibility of government-union pacts, whereby unions agree to exercise wage restraint in return for fiscal stimulation. The capacity of unions to coordinate among themselves continues to matter in this context. At the same time, the dynamics of EMU create pressure on EU governments to coordinate fiscal measures to stimulate employment.

SUMMARY

Wage bargaining involves distributive conflicts between unions and employers, but also within unions and employers. The wage-bargaining arrangements characteristic of northern Europe's social market economies have traditionally facilitated coordinated wage restraint by enabling national union and employer organizations to manage their internal conflicts more effectively. The macro-economic benefits of co-ordinated wage bargaining do not appear to have diminished over time: quite the contrary, they have probably increased as globalization has progressed. To the extent that the capacity of unions and employers to co-ordinate their wage-bargaining behavior has diminished, this trend has been more pronounced in liberal than social market economies. European monetary integration poses new challenges, but coordinated bargaining remains possible and desirable for the social market economies.

CHAPTER 6

Participation, Security, Mobility, and Skills

This chapter explores institutional differences between social market economies and liberal market economies that pertain to micro-economic issues or, in other words, incentives and constraints facing individual firms. The chapter is organized around four topics. First, I will discuss employee participation in corporate decision-making, commonly referred to as "codetermination" (*Mitbestimmung* in German). Though the particular arrangements differ, government legislation provides for formalized employee participation in all the social market economies. On this score, the distinction between SMEs and LMEs is a categorical one rather than one of degree. In LMEs, individual firms have developed various schemes for employee participation, but there is no external regulatory framework for participatory practices.

The second topic covered in this chapter is employment security. As noted earlier, workers in social market economies typically enjoy a much higher level of employment security than do workers in liberal market economies. Government legislation, regulatory practices, and collective bargaining arrangements constrain the ability of firms to fire workers and render individual as well as collective dismissals more costly. Third, I will briefly discuss active labor market policies, which can partly be seen as a mobility-enhancing complement to the protectionist orientation of employment security provisions. As we shall see, this is an area in which there is a great deal of variation among SMEs. Traditionally, the Nordic SMEs have emphasized active labor market policy to a greater extent than the continental SMEs, but some continental SMEs have recently developed a more active approach to labor market policy as well. Finally, the fourth section explores the question of skill formation, which intersects with the other issues covered in this chapter in a number of ways. Here too we observe important differences among SMEs. In general, the continental SMEs are distinguished from LMEs by their emphasis on vocational training and the way that their vocational training systems are regulated cooperatively by employers, unions, and government officials. This is less true of the Nordic SMEs, which are first and foremost distinguished by high levels of public investment in education.

With regard to each of these topics, I will review the arguments that have been made for and against the social market model and try to adjudicate among these arguments based on the available evidence. Thus my discussion in this chapter focuses on the implications of social market arrangements for labor market dynamics and the ability of firms to meet the challenges of intensified international competition.

CODETERMINATION

Among the social market economies, Germany has the most elaborate legal framework for employee participation in corporate decision-making. Dating back to the early 1950s, German codetermination provides for two channels of employee participation: board representation and works councils. It is noteworthy that it was a Christian Democratic government, not a Social Democratic government, that introduced the legislation that resulted in this system. Initially, the unions were highly skeptical of codetermination, if not outright hostile to it, fearing that works councils directly elected by employees would provide management with an alternative interlocutor and thus a means to sidestep collective bargaining. Over time, however, the unions effectively came to dominate works council elections. Legislation introduced by Social Democratic governments in 1972 and 1976 extended and modified the system of codetermination in ways that corresponded to union demands.[1]

German joint stock companies have a two-tiered governance structure: an executive board (*Vorstand*) made up of top management and a supervisory board (*Aufsichtrat*). Codetermination pertains to the latter body, which wields extensive formal powers but meets rather infrequently and tends to defer to the executive board so long as things are running smoothly. By law, any company with more than 500 employees must set aside one third of the seats on its supervisory board for employee representatives, elected directly by the workforce or nominated by the relevant union. In coal and steel, companies with more than 1,000 employees must set aside half of the seats for employee representatives; in other sectors 2,000 employees triggers parity representation. However, managerial employees form a separate constituency, electing one of the "employee representatives" on the supervisory board. Furthermore, the law stipulates that the chairman of the supervisory board must be a shareholder representative; the chairman casts the deciding vote in case of a tie. These legal arrangements effectively preclude shareholder representatives being outvoted by employee representatives, but companies that desire a reputation for being well-run can hardly afford to alienate their (nonmanagerial) employee representatives on a permanent basis. The significance of codetermination at the level of supervisory boards is that it sensitizes top management and shareholder representatives to labor concerns and also provides labor representatives with information about the company.

Turning to works councils, German law requires this form of employee representation in all workplaces with more than five employees, provided that a majority of employees supports the establishment of a works council. The Works Constitution Act of 1972 also provides for enterprise-level works councils in companies with multiple workplaces. Employees elect works councilors in regularly scheduled elections at each workplace, and works councilors in turn elect representatives to the company-wide works council. In the early 1990s, the laws pertaining to works councils covered more than 80 percent of all private sector employees. By all accounts, however, many small firms never had effectively functioning works councils. In 1998, a commission sponsored by labor-affiliated foundations reported that the share of the private sector labor force represented by works councils had fallen from about 50 percent in the mid-1980s to 40 percent in the mid-1990s. The commission's report also noted a drop in the share of the labor force with employee representatives on supervisory boards, from 30.5 percent in the mid-1980s to 24.5 percent in the mid-1990s.[2] In the wake of this report, legislation introduced by the Schröder government makes it easier to establish works councils in small firms and reduces the size of companies required to pay for at least one full-time works councilor.[3]

German works councils do not formally bargain over wages and do not have the right to strike. However, they enjoy legally enforceable rights to veto management decisions in certain areas pertaining to the company's treatment of individual employees (recruitment, redeployment, and dismissal). More importantly, the works councils have "co-decision rights" in matters pertaining to daily work schedules, scheduling of holidays, the design of pay systems, piecework, work organization, company-provided training, and the "social plans" that firms must develop when they contemplate layoffs. Simply put, "co-decision" means that management must bargain with the works council and that it must do so in good faith. Beyond co-decision rights, German works councils have "information and consultation rights" in any other area where corporate decisions directly affect the workforce. Thus management must consult with works councils

about strategic decisions such as the location of a new plant or the introduction of new production technologies, but it may ignore the advice
offered by works councils in these matters.

With a few notable exceptions, the codetermination arrangements
of the other social market economies are broadly similar to those of
Germany. As legislated in the 1970s, the Swedish system of codetermination allows unions to appoint two members of the board of directors of
joint stock companies with more than twenty-five employees. In contrast
to Germany, Swedish unions never pushed for parity representation at the
board level, viewing this form of codetermination as a means of access to
information rather than direct influence over corporate decisions. The
Swedish approach to codetermination also eschewed the German model
of creating a separate mechanism for employee representation in codetermination matters, instead vesting codetermination rights in local
union organizations. The Codetermination Act of 1977 treated codetermination essentially as an extension of collective bargaining to new issues
and explicitly stipulated that unions retained the right to strike over these
issues. In the economic circumstances of the 1980s and 1990s, however,
local unions were not in a position to strike, and Swedish-style codetermination effectively evolved into collaborative problem-solving in the
context of voluntarily established joint management-union councils.[4] The
attempt by the Swedish labor movement to go beyond the German model
clearly failed, and Germany remains the showcase for employee representation in corporate decision-making, providing the most extensive
range of legally enforceable codetermination rights.

What, then, are the implications of codetermination for the ability of
SME firms to compete in world markets? Reviewing the empirical studies
in a recent volume, Wolfgang Streeck argues that works councils contribute to micro-economic efficiency in several ways.[5] According to
Streeck, codetermination improves the quality of decisions by improving
the flow of communication within companies. In his words, "as well-
resourced councils can ask detailed questions and offer counterpropos-
als, management must scrutinize their own projects more, making it more
likely that flaws are discovered early and that the range of alternatives is
enlarged." Streeck argues that codetermination also facilitates the implementation of decisions—above all, by making decisions more legitimate
in the eyes of workers—and points out that codetermination provides top
management with useful feedback on the performance of middle management. More specifically, the studies on which Streeck bases his assessment suggest that codetermination is associated with lower rates of
absenteeism, that it pressures firms to rationalize their human resource
policies and to invest in training, and that it helps firms handle worker
grievances, which often indicate organizational deficiencies. Finally, co-

determination provides for customized, flexible, locally negotiated implementation of regulatory laws pertaining to health and safety standards
and the like.

The main employer complaint against works councils seems to be that
their participation renders corporate decision-making more cumbersome
and time-consuming. Arguably, codetermination also makes it harder for
management to get rid of unproductive workers, but this constraint is
more a matter of employment protection legislation than codetermination. Leaving the issue of employment protection aside for the moment,
it is hard to imagine that the administrative costs associated with codetermination outweigh the benefits enumerated by Streeck.

Across the social market economies, employers have become increasingly outspoken in their criticisms of labor market rigidities and social
welfare arrangements since the 1980s, but codetermination has not been
the primary target of such criticisms. Swedish employers seem to have
grown increasingly fond of the flexibility that employee representation
within the firm affords them relative to the constraints of centralized wage
bargaining, high payroll taxes, and employment protection legislation.
German employers fought hard against legal changes pertaining to board
representation introduced by the Social Democrats in 1976, but they did
not object to the principle of board representation and never questioned
employee participation in the form of works councils. It is noteworthy,
however, that European employers uniformly and quite vigorously
resisted various efforts in the 1980s and 1990s to introduce European
works councils through legislation by the European Union. Reasonably
content with their own domestic arrangements, German and other SME
employers are apparently unwilling to support the extension of these
arrangements across the single market. Conceivably, German employers
consider codetermination to be an institutional advantage that they would
just as soon keep to themselves, but it seems more plausible to argue that
they gain leverage vis-à-vis their German works councils by having the
option to locate operations in countries without similar codetermination
laws.

It should also be noted that the federations of German employers
(Bundesvereinigung der Deutschen Arbeitgeberverbände) and German
industry (Bundesverband der Deutschen Industrie) very recently issued
a report proposing an overhaul of the board-representation component
of codetermination.[6] In a manner reminiscent of the European Union's
Works Councils Directive, this proposal would allow companies to negotiate alternative arrangements with local works councils, with one-third
representation being the default option in the absence of an agreement.
As in the 1970s, German employers are challenging the idea of parity
between shareholder and employee representatives while conceding that

some form of employee representation at the board level is beneficial. Though the particulars continue to be a subject of contestation between unions and employers, codetermination has survived the economic difficulties of the 1990s. Primarily relevant to large firms, codetermination remains a distinctive institutional feature of social market economies.

EMPLOYMENT SECURITY

Government legislation that restricts the ability of firms to fire or lay off workers figures prominently among the labor market rigidities that are commonly blamed for Europe's poor employment performance in the 1980s and 1990s. As part of the ongoing policy debate, researchers at the OECD have devised a series of comparable measures of employment protection. Table 6.1 presents country scores for 2003 on the OECD's composite employment protection index. This index encompasses not only legislative requirements but also court rulings and collective bargaining practices pertaining to temporary employment and collective as well as individual dismissals of regular employees. With an index score of 0.7, the United States stands out as the country in which employers enjoy the most unrestricted regulatory environment, while France, with an index score of 2.9, occupies the opposite end of the spectrum. In the late 1990s, Italian workers enjoyed even more employment protection than French workers, but the Italian government subsequently moved to curtail employment protection. In general, the social market economies of northern and central Europe provide less employment protection than southern European countries, but they provide significantly more employment protection than the liberal market economies.[7] Table 6.1 also presents average employment tenure rates in 1999. Not surprisingly, employment protection and employment tenure rates are closely correlated: in countries with high levels of employment protection, workers tend to work for the same employer for longer periods of time. (The correlation between average employment tenure rates in 1999 and employment protection scores for the late 1990s is .903.)

The substantive meaning of the index scores reported in table 6.1 might be illustrated by comparing employment protection in Germany, representing the upper end of the SME range, and the United States, representing the lower end of the LME range.[8] To begin with, the employment protection index contains several items pertaining to notification periods and administrative procedures for individual and collective dismissals. In Germany, the law stipulates that workers who have been employed for less than two years must be notified at least four weeks prior to dismissal; from this baseline the required notification period rises with

Table 6.1 Employment protection, 2003 and average employment tenure, 1999

	Employment protection (index scores)	Average employment tenure (years)
Nordic SMEs	**2.3**	**9.6**
Denmark	1.8	8.5
Finland	2.1	10.1
Norway	2.6	
Sweden	2.6	11.5
Continental SMEs	**2.2**	**9.7**
Austria	2.2	10.6*
Belgium	2.5	11.7
Germany	2.5	10.3
Netherlands	2.3	9.6
Switzerland	1.6	9.4
LMEs	**1.2**	**7.6**
Australia	1.5	6.9
Canada	1.1	8.1
Ireland	1.3	9.4
New Zealand	1.3	
United Kingdom	1.1	8.3
United States	0.7	6.7
France	2.9	11.2
Italy	2.4	12.1
Japan	1.8	11.3*

Sources: Employment protection: OECD, *Employment Outlook* (2004), 117. Tenure rates: OECD, *Employment Outlook* (1997), 138, and *Employment Outlook* (2002), 119.
Note: Figures marked with an asterisk refer to 1995.

employment tenure. Someone who has worked for a company for twenty years must be notified seven months prior to dismissal. The works council must be informed prior to notification and may contest individual dismissals in court, delaying the onset of the notification period. In the case of collective dismissals involving a significant number of employees, the firm is required to negotiate a "social plan" with the works council. In the United States, the law provides for a sixty-day notice period in the case of collective dismissals, but exceptions to this rule are allowed for a variety of reasons, and there are no legal requirements for advanced notification of individual dismissals.

While German law does not specify any severance pay requirements, collective bargaining agreements and social plans commonly provide for severance pay. In the United States as well, collective bargaining agreements typically include severance pay provisions, but this represents much less of a constraint on U.S. employers, since the percentage of the labor force covered by collective bargaining is much lower. In addition, German law provides a more expansive definition of "unfair dismissal" than U.S.

law. Whereas unfair dismissal is largely restricted to equal opportunity issues in the United States, German employers can be taken to court for failing to explore adequately whether or not the employee might be trained in some other capacity or for failing to take due account of the employee's social situation (seniority, age, family obligations, etc.).

Like other social market economies, Germany has significantly relaxed restrictions on temporary employment since the early 1990s. German law used to restrict fixed-term employment contracts to project-specific work, seasonal work, and temporary replacement of permanent workers. These restrictions have been removed, but it remains the case that German firms cannot employ workers on fixed-term contracts for more than twenty-four months. Similarly, restrictions on the practice of subcontracting for work with temporary employment agencies have been relaxed, but by American standards they remain considerable.

The constraints that German-style employment protection imposes on employers should not be exaggerated: in Germany and other social market economies, firms did shed a great deal of labor in the first half of the 1990s. As we shall see in chapter 7, disability insurance and early retirement provided mechanisms whereby firms could circumvent some of the constraints and avoid some of the costs imposed by employment protection. Still, there can be little doubt that the legal provisions and institutional practices associated with the social market model make it more difficult and expensive to get rid of workers. The conventional wisdom among economists holds that these costs represent an obstacle to labor mobility across firms and sectors and thereby reduce the efficiency of the economy as a whole, as workers are locked into the companies in which they are currently employed. To the extent that employment protection increases labor costs for employers, it may also reduce the overall level of demand for labor. Certainly, it seems plausible to suppose that employers operating under German-style employment protection will be reluctant to hire new workers during upturns of the business cycle and will instead, at least initially, seek to increase output through overtime employment of their existing labor force. By this logic, employment protection is a source of labor market dualism as well as inefficiency, protecting currently employed workers at the expense of the unemployed and new entrants into the labor force.[9]

On the other hand, the proponents of the social market model argue that employment security provides the basis for trust between management and workers, improving worker motivation and loyalty. While workers and unions are more willing to cooperate with management to improve productivity and quality, employers have an incentive to invest in worker training because workers can be expected to stay with the company. According to Streeck, the training efforts of German firms typically increase during economic downturns, when firms find themselves stuck with a certain number of redundant workers. Much like the Japanese system of lifetime employment, Streeck and others argue, German-style employment protection constrains the ability of firms to respond to changes in the marketplace by hiring and firing ("external flexibility"), but it facilitates the adoption of new technologies, organizational change, and redeployment of workers ("internal flexibility").[10]

The connection between employment protection and skill formation has recently been developed by Margarita Estevez-Abe, Torben Iversen, and David Soskice, who argue that the manufacturing success of Germany and other northern European countries presupposes workers with industry-specific skills. Relative to universal skills, provided by typical high school and college curricula, such skills are more vulnerable to economic downturns and structural economic shifts. Some degree of employment security is necessary, Estevez-Abe, Iversen, and Soskice argue, to ensure that individuals invest in industry-specific skills.[11]

The positive and negative effects of employment protection identified in the literature are not mutually exclusive. Ideally, what we would want to know is how these effects stack up against each other. However, the benefits of employment protection posited by proponents of the social market model are not readily measurable, and I am not aware of any attempt to assess these effects in a systematic fashion. Short of a comprehensive balance sheet, what do the aggregate data tell us about the alleged costs of employment protection? As figure 6.1 illustrates, plotting average unemployment rates for the 2000–03 period against the employment protection index scores for 2003 produces a weak positive association, but there is an awful lot of cross-national variation in unemployment that cannot be explained by cross-national variation in employment protection. Austria, Norway, and the Netherlands have managed to combine relatively high levels of employment protection with relatively low levels of unemployment. Most strikingly, the seven countries that score between 2.2 and 2.6 on the OECD's employment protection index cover the entire range of unemployment outcomes.

Controlling for other relevant variables, the OECD's reports on this topic fail to establish any robust statistical support for the proposition that employment protection is associated with higher rates of unemployment.[12] Moreover, these reports fail to confirm the supposition that deregulation of employment protection has translated into lower rates of unemployment. As noted by the most recent report, employment protection may make it more difficult for job seekers to enter employment, but this effect appears to be offset by the fact that employment protection reduces "inflows into unemployment" during economic downturns. Not surprisingly, the OECD does find a strong association between

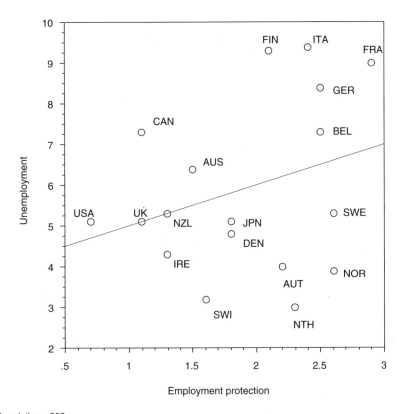

Correlation: .306
Sources: Tables 4.1 and 6.1.

Figure 6.1 Average unemployment rate in 2000–03 vs. employment protection in 2003

employment protection and the duration of unemployment. As employment protection increases, fewer workers become unemployed, fewer unemployed workers find new jobs, and, as a result, the average duration of unemployment increases. With respect to the implications of employment protection for different categories of workers, the OECD finds some support for the claim that employment protection adversely affects the employment prospects of women and youth, but these effects are quite tenuous, especially for youth. More decisively, the OECD's most recent report indicates that employment protection improves the relative employment prospects of unskilled workers. The latter finding should not come as a surprise, given that unskilled workers are more vulnerable to unemployment than skilled workers under laissez-faire conditions.

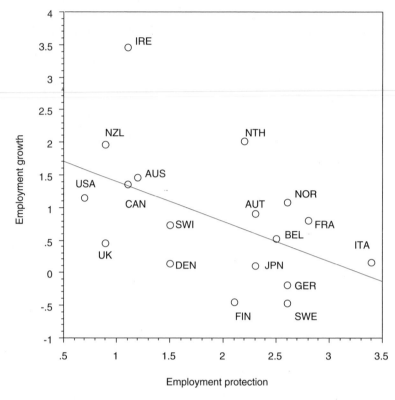

Correlation: −.495 (−.596 without Ireland and the Netherlands)
Sources: Tables 4.5 and 6.1.

Figure 6.2 Average annual growth of total employment in 1990–2002 vs. employment protection in the late 1990s

As figure 6.2 illustrates, the argument that employment protection has negative employment consequences works better for employment growth than for unemployment. Even if we ignore the Irish economic miracle of the 1990s, from 1990 to 2002 countries with lower levels of employment protection in the late 1990s tended to generate more new jobs than countries with higher levels of employment protection. Liberalization of employment protection standards can hardly be construed as the linchpin of the fight against unemployment, but the social market economies might well be able to improve their employment performance by relaxing such standards. If employment protection is indeed associated with efficiency gains at the firm level, as proponents of the social market model argue, there is an important policy trade-off to be negotiated here. For the time being, let me simply make two points pertaining to the relationship between employment protection and skill formation. First, the trade-off between micro-economic efficiency and employment growth might be mitigated, if not outright resolved, if the government guarantees the income stream necessary to induce individuals to invest in industry-specific skills rather than making it more difficult or costly for employers to fire workers. Secondly, it is also possible for the government to subsidize the acquisition of industry-specific skills.

ACTIVE LABOR MARKET POLICIES

It is tempting to view restrictions on the ability of employers to fire workers as an expression of the power of organized labor and of the political influence of parties representing the interests of workers. This interpretation of the politics of employment protection must be qualified. As already noted, employment protection has long been a prominent feature of labor market regulation across continental Europe and particularly in southern Europe—Spain and Portugal as well as France and Italy. From the perspective of northern Europe, especially Scandinavia, these countries have been and still remain distinguished by low levels of union density as well as politically divided and weak labor movements. Indeed, employment protection can at least partly be seen as part of an institutional regime created by traditional political elites, often inspired by Catholic social doctrine, to regulate conflict between employers and workers and to keep radical union organizers at bay. On the other hand, and more importantly for our present purposes, it should be noted that employment protection was not a prominent feature of the reformist agenda advanced by Scandinavian labor movements when they held political dominance. Cognizant of Sweden's export dependence and the need for economic restructuring in response to changes in world markets, Swedish union leaders and Social Democratic politicians very explicitly rejected the idea that the government could and should provide workers with security in their current jobs. The official goal of Swedish Social Democracy in the 1950s and 1960s was to provide for "security in the labor market," as distinct from "job security." This entailed generous unemployment compensation, to protect workers against the income losses associated with unemployment, but also active labor market policies, to improve the ability of workers to find new, better (higher-paying) jobs. As initially conceived, Sweden's active labor market policy primarily involved public employment services, retraining programs, and relocation subsidies.

In the context of severe industrial adjustment problems, the Swedish labor movement embraced employment protection in the 1970s, but this

Table 6.2 Government spending on active labor market policies, 1998–2002

	Spending in % of GDP	Active/passive spending ratio
Nordic SMEs	**1.3**	**1.0**
Denmark	1.7	0.5
Finland	1.0	0.5
Norway	0.8	1.7
Sweden	1.5	1.2
Continental SMEs	**1.1**	**0.7**
Austria	0.5	0.4
Belgium	1.3	0.6
Germany	1.2	0.6
Netherlands	1.8	1.0
Switzerland	0.5	0.7
LMEs	**0.5**	**0.7**
Australia	0.5	0.4
Canada	0.4	0.8
Ireland	1.1	1.6
New Zealand	0.6	0.5
United Kingdom	0.4	0.9
United States	0.2	0.2
France	1.3	0.8
Italy	0.6	0.8
Japan	0.3	0.6

Source: OECD, *Employment Outlook* (2004), 319–27.

Note: Ratio is of spending on active labor market policies to spending on unemployment compensation and early retirement schemes, in percent of GDP.

was essentially a defensive move. While employment regulation has become more restrictive, active labor market policy (ALMP) remains an important feature of the Swedish model, which other SMEs have emulated. As shown in table 6.2, Denmark, Finland, Sweden, Belgium, Germany, and the Netherlands all devoted, on average, at least 1 percent of their GDP to active labor market policies from 1998 to 2002 (as did France as well), with Denmark and the Netherlands being the biggest ALMP spenders. Distinguished by comparatively low unemployment rates, the remaining SMEs—Norway, Austria, and Switzerland—spent between 0.5 percent and 0.8 percent of their GDP on active labor market policies. By contrast, the LMEs have largely eschewed this type of government intervention in labor markets. Ireland stands out in table 6.2 as the LME that spends the most on active labor market policies relative to the size of its economy. For the same time period, table 6.2 also reports the ratio of spending on active labor market measures to spending on "passive" measures, that is, government spending on income support for the unemployed (unemployment compensation) and on early retirement schemes. By this measure, Norway, Ireland, Sweden, and the Netherlands stand out as the countries with the most active approach to labor market policy, devoting more resources to employability and employment promotion than to income support. The remaining SMEs do not appear to be significantly different from the remaining LMEs in their mix of active and passive measures.

Figure 6.3 plots spending on active labor market policies, relative to GDP, in the 1998–2002 period against the OECD employment protection index for the late 1990s. With the exception of Ireland, the LMEs form a distinct cluster, together with Switzerland, distinguished by low ALMP spending and low employment protection. Characterized by the opposite constellation of these variables (high/high), the other main cluster in figure 6.1 consists of France, Germany, Belgium, Sweden, Finland, and the Netherlands. Italy exemplifies the traditional southern European model (low/high) while Denmark best exemplifies the traditional Scandinavian model (high/low).

At least in part, the development of active labor market policies in the continental SMEs, and also in France, can be seen as an attempt to offset the negative employment consequences of employment protection. In this sense, active labor market policy and employment protection might be seen as offsetting but complementary features of the social market model. At the same time, the distinctive circumstances that triggered the expansion of active labor market policy in the Netherlands and Ireland in the 1990s should be noted. As we saw in chapter 4, the overall rate of unemployment fell sharply in the Netherlands and Ireland in the 1990s, yet long-term unemployment has proven quite persistent in both cases. As the number of claimants on the system of unemployment insurance declined, budgetary resources were freed up for selective measures to tackle the problem of getting the long-term unemployed back to work.

Do active labor market policies indeed counteract the negative employment consequences of employment protection or otherwise improve employment performance? The varied labor market measures encompassed by the aggregate spending data presented in table 6.2 can be grouped into three broad categories: first, public employment services intended to lower search costs, to help job seekers market themselves and, ideally, to produce a better match between workers and jobs; second, retraining programs primarily targeting unemployed workers (and sometimes workers at risk of losing their jobs); and, third, employment-promoting programs targeting special categories of workers—most commonly, youth and people with disabilities. In principle, these measures ought to be evaluated separately.[13] Such an undertaking would take us too far afield, but it is important to keep in mind that active labor market

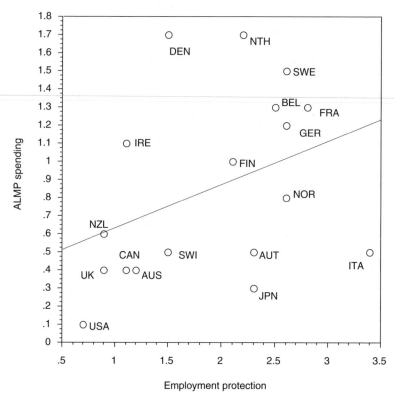

Correlation: .379
Sources: Tables 6.1 and 6.2.

Figure 6.3 Government spending on active labor market policies in percent of GDP 1998–2002 vs. employment protection score in the late 1990s

policy was never really meant to generate new jobs, at least not on any permanent basis.

The primary objectives of labor market policy are to shorten unemployment spells and, more broadly, to improve the efficiency of labor markets. By the same token, there are fundamental limits to the scope of active labor market policy. During employment crises, when there are very few jobs to be had, active labor market measures tend to lose their distinctive quality and to evolve into passive income support for the unemployed under a different label. In short, active labor policy does not by itself constitute an "employment strategy," and, beyond a certain point, the payoffs of government spending on active labor market policy are likely to diminish.

A commonly cited study by Stephen Nickell and Richard Layard finds that government spending on active labor market policy, measured as spending per unemployed in percent of GDP per member of the labor force, reduces the overall rate of unemployment.[14] Pooling data from twenty OECD countries over the 1980s and the first half of the 1990s, Nickell and Layard's analysis includes employment protection and a number of other institutional variables that might be expected to affect the rate of unemployment. Having replicated and extended Layard and Nickell's analysis, Francine Blau and Lawrence Kahn conclude that "high-unemployment countries use active labor market policies to undo some of the unemployment that would otherwise be caused by labor market institutions such as high taxes, union wage setting, and generous (unemployment) benefits."[15] Skeptics might well object that these studies suffer from a reverse-causality problem. Assuming that governments are faced with budgetary constraints, it seems likely that ALMP spending per unemployed will decline as the number of unemployed increases. Thus it could be that rising unemployment reduces ALMP spending rather than the other way around.

The problem of reverse causality is likely to bedevil most attempts to assess the effects of active labor market policies on unemployment, but the problem would seem to be less severe if we use the ratio of active to passive spending as our measure of ALMP effort and, more importantly, if we use the duration of unemployment as our dependent variable. In the short run, rising unemployment will reduce the active/passive ratio by boosting spending on income support for the unemployed, but over time high unemployment will exert downward pressure on passive as well as active spending per unemployed.

Against this background, table 6.3 reports the results of three simple (cross-sectional) regression exercises. First, I report the results of regressing the average rate of unemployment on employment protection and the active/passive ratio. The two independent variables have statistically significant effects of similar magnitude—but opposite signs: employment protection is associated with more unemployment while ALMP effort is associated with less unemployment. Controlling for the exceptional case of Ireland, we observe the same pattern in the second regression, with the rate of long-term unemployment (people who have been unemployed for more than six months as a percentage of the labor force) as the dependent variable. Finally, the dependent variable of the third regression is the percentage of the unemployed who have been unemployed for more than six months. With a very high incidence of long-term unemployment as well as a high active/passive ratio, the Irish case again proves to be quite exceptional, but if we control for this case, we observe not only a strong positive effect of employment protection (consistent with aforemen-

Table 6.3 Employment protection and active labor market policy as determinants of unemployment outcomes, OLS regression results

	Overall unemployment rate	Long-term unemployment rate	Incidence of long-term unemployment
Constant	5.154	.721	24.201
	(.0010)	(.3688)	(.0067)
Employment protection (late 90s)	.497	.930	.875
	(.0356)	(.0001)	(.0003)
Active/passive spending ratio	−.439	−.609	−.545
(1998–2002)	(.0593)	(.0083)	(.0219)
Ireland		.509	.702
		(.0230)	(.0053)
N	18	18	18
Adjusted R^2	.25	.61	.55

Sources: see tables 4.1, 4.2, 6.1 and 6.3.
Note: Standardized (beta) coefficients, with p-values (two-tailed tests) in parentheses. Long-term unemployment is defined as unemployment lasting more than 6 months. Incidence is measured as long-term unemployed as percent of unemployed.

tioned OECD findings), but also a strong negative effect of ALMP effort. The reverse-causality objection may well apply to the results of the first and second regressions, but it is less obviously relevant to the third. Also, it should be noted that these results refer to a time period in which unemployment was falling in most countries, leaving governments with a fair amount of discretion in determining the mix of active and passive labor market measures.

The regression results reported in table 6.3 do not prove that increasing ALMP spending improves employment performance. What they do show—quite compellingly, I think—is that shifting support for the unemployed from passive to active measures tends to reduce the duration of unemployment and possibly also the rate of unemployment. By adopting a more active approach to the problem of unemployment, SMEs have offset some of the negative consequences of employment protection.

TRAINING AND EDUCATION

Hardly anyone would dispute that investment in human capital is critical to economic efficiency and long-term prosperity. At the same time, skill formation represents a classic "collective goods problem" from the point of view of business. As noted in chapter 2, the problem is that companies want workers with strong skills, but in a free market economy there is no assurance that they will be able to reap the returns of investing in the skills of their workers. Other companies are likely to engage in poaching, offering better wages and benefits to their best workers. In this stylized situation, companies will only invest in narrow, firm-specific skills, which are of little or no value to other companies, and it is up to individuals whether or not to acquire broader skills. For working-class families without significant assets, financing investment in human capital can be very difficult.[16]

Consistent with this intuition, it became rather commonplace in the 1980s to argue that the difficulties experienced by American companies in the face of intensified foreign competition had something—perhaps a great deal—to do with the fact that Japanese and German workers were better trained than American workers. Even more so, British observers worried that their economy was falling into a "low-skills trap."[17] In retrospect, the problem may seem exaggerated, but it is important to keep in mind that the argument was never that the *entire* U.S.—or British—labor force was poorly trained by comparative standards. By all accounts, the American system of post-secondary education compares favorably to those of other countries: to the extent that the American economy has a skills problem, the problem has to do with the skills of high school graduates and, especially, high school dropouts. More sharply, Estevez-Abe, Iversen, and Soskice argue that the skills problem of liberal market economies pertains to a particular kind of skills, "industry-specific skills" that occupy the middle ground between the firm-specific skills that employers will always be willing to fund and the general skills provided by typical high school and college curricula.[18]

How have Japan and Germany resolved the collective goods problem of skill formation? As is commonly noted, "permanent employment" is the key to the Japanese solution. In the large enterprise sector, the wage premia associated with seniority are much higher in Japan than in other advanced capitalist countries, so workers have a strong incentive not to switch employers. Furthermore, large Japanese firms have traditionally recruited their "core workers" straight out of high school and, in effect, agreed not to hire workers away from each other. Under these conditions, it becomes rational for employers to invest not only in narrow, firm-specific skills but also in skills that would be of value to other employers.[19]

As Wolfgang Streeck argues, Japanese skill formation involves a degree of worker dependence on employers that is alien to the cultural and political norms of Western Europe.[20] The German solution to the skills problem is quite different, combining apprenticeships provided by firms with training in government-financed vocational schools. The workplace-based training provided by firms is monitored and certified by external agents—business associations, unions, and public authorities. Arguably, the skills that workers acquire through German-style vocational training are more marketable than the skills they may acquire through Japanese-style company training. In the German system, employers, apprentices, and taxpayers share the costs of training. While the government foots the bill for the in-school component of vocational training and also covers some of the administrative costs associated with apprenticeships, the earnings of unskilled workers exceed the earnings of apprentices by a factor of three or four. In return for training, young persons who take up an apprenticeship (typically for two or three years) thus sacrifice potential earnings in the short run. To some extent the apprentices perform unskilled tasks, but the system constrains the ability of employers to use the apprenticeships in this fashion, and there can be no doubt that taking on apprentices also entails a significant cost for employers. David Soskice argues persuasively that firms are willing to bear this cost because apprenticeships provide a means to recruit and screen workers.[21]

Trade unions and works councils play an important supporting role in the German system of vocational training. The system presupposes that unions are willing to exempt apprentices from collectively bargained wage rates. In return for their acceptance of this arrangement, unions need to be assured that apprenticeships really do deliver training in marketable skills. While German unions participate alongside chambers of commerce and other business associations in monitoring apprenticeship programs at the sectoral level, works councils ensure that individual firms do not abuse the system by using apprentices as a substitute for unskilled labor. Equally important, codetermination and industry-wide wage bargaining jointly curtail the ability of firms to use wage inducements to recruit workers trained by other firms.

Though it is difficult to quantify these benefits, most observers agree that polyvalent worker skills have been a crucial factor in the ability of German manufacturing firms to pursue competitive adjustment strategies based on sustained productivity and quality improvements. Because skilled workers require less supervision than unskilled workers, Christel Lane argues, the German system of vocational training also reduces indirect labor costs. According to Lane, the ratio of supervisors to production workers tends to be significantly lower in German than in French or British firms.[22]

In a slightly different vein, Lisa Lynch argues not only that American firms typically invest less in worker training than comparable European firms but also that the productivity gains yielded by a certain amount of training investment tends to be smaller in the United States. Using the nuclear power industry as an illustration, Lynch observes that workers in the U.S. nuclear industry, such as technicians, receive similar amounts of training compared to their European counterparts. . . . However, half of all formal technician training in the U.S. nuclear industry . . . is spent on teaching basic technical skills and in some cases remedial math and literacy skills, whereas Europeans use training hours for more advanced study of nuclear engineering and plant administration. This difference reflects the different level of preparedness that workers have coming into the industry.[23]

Clearly, employer-provided training must be seen as part of a larger institutional complex pertaining to human capital. It is important to emphasize that German young people pursuing the apprenticeship track are typically expected to spend about half their time on formal coursework in vocational schools.

For our present purposes, it is also important to note that apprenticeship-based vocational training is *not* a universal feature of northern Europe's social market economies. As the enrollment data presented in table 6.4 show, vocational training accounts for a significantly smaller share of upper-secondary education in the Nordic SMEs than in

Table 6.4 Percentage of upper-secondary students enrolled in vocational and technical programs, 2002

	All vocational and technical programs (%)	Combining school and workplace training (%)
Nordic SMEs	**54.5**	
Denmark	53.0	53.0
Finland	57.2	10.8
Norway	58.0	
Sweden	49.6	
Continental SMEs	**67.8**	
Austria	72.3	35.8
Belgium	69.7	2.5
Germany	63.0	50.8
Netherlands	69.2	23.5
Switzerland	64.6	58.6
LMEs		
Australia	63.0	
Canada	7.2	
Ireland	21.0	5.0
New Zealand	38.0	12.0
United Kingdom	72.1	
France	56.3	11.8
Italy	26.8	
Japan	24.9	

Sources: OECD, *Education at a Glance* (1997), 157, and *Education at a Glance* (2004), 292. *Note:* Figures for Ireland and New Zealand refer to 1995.

Table 6.5 Public and total spending on education as percent of GDP, 2001

	All levels		Primary/secondary	
	Public	Total	Public	Total
Nordic SMEs	**6.2%**	**6.5%**	**4.2%**	**4.2%**
Denmark	6.8	7.1	4.2	4.3
Finland	5.7	5.8	3.7	3.7
Norway	6.1	6.4	4.6	4.6
Sweden	6.3	6.5	4.3	4.3
Continental SMEs	**5.2**	**5.6**	**3.5**	**3.9**
Austria	5.6	5.8	3.8	3.9
Belgium	6.0	6.4	4.0	4.2
Germany	4.3	5.3	2.9	3.6
Netherlands	4.5	4.9	3.1	3.3
Switzerland	5.4		3.9	4.5
LMEs	**4.8**	**5.9**	**3.5**	**3.8**
Australia	4.5	6.0	3.6	4.3
Canada	4.9	6.1	3.1	3.4
Ireland	4.1	4.5	2.9	3.1
New Zealand	5.5		4.3	
United Kingdom	4.7	5.5	3.4	3.9
United States	5.1	7.3	3.8	4.1
France	5.6	6.0	4.0	4.2
Italy	4.9	5.3	3.6	3.7
Japan	3.5	4.6	2.7	2.9

Source: OECD, *Education at a Glance* (2004), 229–30.

the continental SMEs. Moreover, Finland and Belgium do vocational training without much reliance on apprenticeships. This appears to be true for Norway and Sweden as well, though we lack exact figures on the percentage of upper-secondary students engaged in workplace training for these countries. In the Swedish case, apprenticeship-based training declined as educational reforms in the 1950s and 1960s stressed the idea of comprehensive schooling for children of all classes (and both sexes) as a means to promote equality of opportunity. In-school vocational training was first separated from workplace training and subsequently brought into comprehensive secondary schools. Though placing less emphasis on vocational training than the continental SMEs, Denmark has retained an apprenticeship approach to vocational training.

Eschewing apprenticeship-based vocational training in the name of educational equality, the Nordic SMEs stand out in table 6.5 as the country group with the highest levels of public investment in education, measured by education spending as a percentage of GDP. Total education spending in the United States exceeds that of the Nordic SMEs, but the public component of total spending is significantly smaller in the

United States. Similarly, total education spending in Australia and Canada is comparable to Nordic SME levels, but public spending falls short of that in the Nordic SMEs. On average, the Nordic SMEs devote more of their GDP to education than either the LMEs or the continental SMEs. Comparing group averages, we find that the LMEs spend more on education than the continental SMEs, but it is immediately apparent that this difference is entirely due to higher levels of private spending on tertiary education. When we look only at spending on primary and secondary education, high levels of total spending as well as public spending still distinguish the Nordic SMEs, and there appears to be no meaningful differences between LMEs and continental SMEs. The United States and Canada no longer stand out as big spenders when we restrict ourselves to primary and secondary education. Also, it should be noted that the data presented in table 6.5 do not include the costs of vocational training borne by employers in the continental SMEs.

Do the cross-national differences in education spending, particularly public education spending, shown in table 6.5 matter for the quality of labor available to employers in these economies? Measuring and explaining educational achievement across countries involves a great many complicated issues, well beyond the scope of this study, but even a cursory look at the results of the International Adult Literacy Survey carried out from 1994 to 1998 is quite instructive. For the countries covered in this book that were included in this survey, table 6.6 reports mean test scores along with the scores of test takers in the 5th percentile and the ratio of test scores in the 95th percentile to the scores in the 5th percentile.

Among the countries represented in table 6.6, the Nordic countries clearly stand out as group, distinguished not only by higher average adult literacy but also by a narrower spread around the mean. Comparing average test scores for the remaining countries, Germany and the Netherlands outperform all the liberal market economies, but both Belgium and Switzerland fall short of Canada, and Switzerland also falls short of Australia, New Zealand, and the United States. On average, adult literacy is higher in the continental SMEs than the LMEs. More decisively, adult literacy tends to be more evenly distributed in the continental SMEs than the LMEs. (This statement would be absolute, except that Switzerland narrowly falls below New Zealand in the rankings.) At least as far as literacy is concerned, the quality of "unskilled labor" is clearly higher in SMEs than LMEs.

Figure 6.4 shows that cross-national differences in the spread of literacy test scores are closely correlated with cross-national differences in wage inequality among full-time employees. (Plotting Gini coefficients for disposable household income against 95–5 test score ratios yields an almost identical picture.) As Evelyne Huber and John Stephens suggest,

Table 6.6 Literacy test scores for population aged 16–65, 1994–98

	Mean	5th percentile	Ratio of 95th to 5th percentile
Nordic SMEs	**294**	**208**	**1.76**
Denmark	289	214	1.65
Finland	288	195	1.86
Norway	294	207	1.75
Sweden	304	216	1.79
Continental SMEs	**280**	**181**	**2.00**
Belgium	277	163	2.20
Germany	285	208	1.73
Netherlands	286	202	1.76
Switzerland	271	151	2.31
LMEs	**271**	**146**	**2.49**
Australia	274	146	2.46
Canada	280	145	2.57
Ireland	263	151	2.34
New Zealand	272	158	2.29
United Kingdom	267	145	2.48
United States	272	133	2.79

Note. The figures are averages for three separate literacy tests, each scored on a 500-point scale. The Swiss figures are unweighted averages for three language groups. The Belgian figures refer to Flanders only.

Source. OECD, *Literacy in the Information Age* (2000), 135–36.

the correlation between these variables might be seen as an expression of the role of family circumstances in the educational process. In Huber and Stephens's words, "When the environmental conditions of the lower-status families are more similar to the mean—i.e., when there is more social equality—they are more likely to acquire skills similar to the mean."[24] However, the distribution of cognitive skills might also be considered a cause (rather than an effect) of the distribution of earnings in the labor market. Adopting the latter perspective, a recent paper by Francine Blau and Lawrence Kahn estimates that differences in the distribution of literacy test scores account for 5–15 percent of the differences in levels of wage inequality between the United States and a number of other OECD countries.[25]

It is tempting to attribute the uneven distribution of literacy skills in the United States to the high proportion of adult Americans for whom English is a second language and, by extension, to explain the contrast between LMEs and SMEs in terms of the latter being small and ethnically homogeneous countries. Foreign-born inhabitants do indeed represent a larger percentage of the total population in the United States (11.1 percent) than in Denmark (6.0 percent), Finland (2.8 percent), and Norway (6.9 percent). However, the relative size of immigrant populations in Sweden (11.5 percent), Austria (11.0 percent), Belgium (8.2

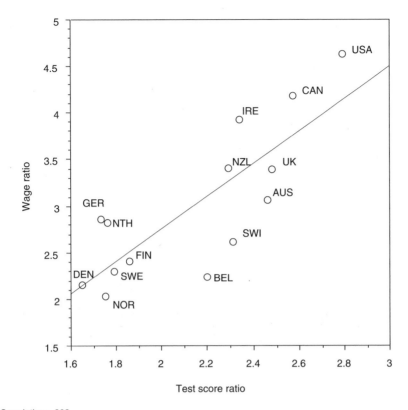

Correlation: .808
Sources: Tables 3.4 and 6.4.

Figure 6.4 Most recent 90–10 wage ratio vs. 95–5 test score ratio

percent), Germany (8.9 percent), and the Netherlands (10.4 percent) is roughly comparable to that of the United States. Also, it is noteworthy that Australia, Canada, New Zealand, and Switzerland all have more evenly distributed literacy skills than the United States despite their immigrant populations being much larger (23.1 percent, 18.2 percent, 19.5 percent, and 19.7 percent, respectively).[26] Arguably, the composition of immigrant populations must be taken into account to appreciate the impact of immigration on the distribution of literacy skills. Setting this issue aside, figures 6.5 and 6.6 offer compelling evidence that public spending on primary and secondary education also matters a great deal.

To begin with, figure 6.5 plots 95–5 test score ratios (from the 1994–98 International Adult Literacy Survey) against public spending on primary and secondary education in 1995, with spending again measured in

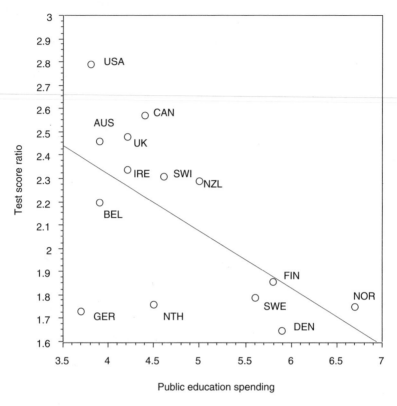

Correlation: −.610 (−.789 without Germany)
Sources: Tables 6.5 and 6.6.

Figure 6.5 95–5 literacy test score ratio 1994–98 vs. public spending on primary and secondary education in percent of GDP in 1995

percent of GDP. Germany constitutes a major outlier in this figure. Ignoring the German case, we observe a remarkably strong and consistent association between high levels of public education spending and more equally distributed literacy skills. In the German case, literacy skills are more equally distributed than what we would expect based on public education spending alone. Arguably, German's outlier status in this regard is a reflection of the egalitarianism of the East German educational system as well as the West German emphasis on employer-financed vocational training. For its part, figure 6.6 plots test scores in the 5th percentile against public spending on primary and secondary education. Again, the German case emerges as quite exceptional, but we still observe a consistent and rather strong association between these variables. Taken

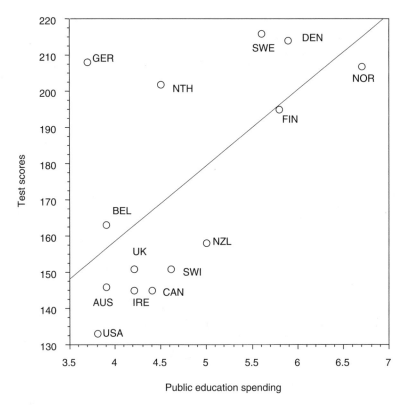

Correlation: .630 (.813 without Germany)
Sources: Tables 6.5 and 6.6.

Figure 6.6 Fifth percentile literacy test scores 1994–98 vs. public spending on primary and secondary education in percent of GDP, 1995

together, figures 6.5 and 6.6 suggest that public investment in basic education compresses the distribution of cognitive abilities and that it does so primarily by raising cognitive abilities at the lower end of the distribution.

The continental SMEs and the Nordic SMEs represent two quite distinct approaches to education and training (with Denmark and Belgium as hybrid cases). Typified by Germany, the continental approach emphasizes vocational training and integrates in-school and workplace training. Firms bear a significant share of the costs associated with this system. By contrast, the Nordic SMEs place greater emphasis on general education and public funding and rely primarily on schools, rather than firms, to provide vocational training. With or without apprenticeship-based vocational training, SMEs are characterized by a more compressed distribution of educational achievement and higher standards at the lower end of the skill hierarchy than LMEs. Arguably, the latter feature makes it easier for SME firms, relative to LME firms, to achieve productive growth with unskilled workers. Especially in the Nordic countries, high levels of public investment in basic education would appear to have played an important supporting role, enabling firms to cope with wage-equalization pressures generated by strong unions and centralized wage bargaining.

There is no reason to suppose that globalization renders the supply of well-trained workers less beneficial to business. Quite the contrary, intensified competition among high-wage countries makes this feature of the social market model even more attractive. To the extent that the dynamics of the advanced capitalist economies have changed in ways that undermine the institutional advantages enjoyed by SME firms, this has to do with the rise of services as the engine of employment growth and the specifics of the German approach to vocational training. Some German firms in the service sector do provide apprenticeships, but there can be no doubt that the German-style vocational training caters primarily to the needs of manufacturing industries. While manufacturing competitiveness still remains critical to the prosperity of advanced capitalist economies, incremental productivity growth in low-skill services represents a major constraint on growth. The liberal market economies do not appear to have performed particularly well in the latter respect over the last decade: rather, their advantage in the service sector stems from the ability of firms to pay very low wages to unskilled workers. Sustained productivity growth in low-skill services presupposes high-quality public education, and on this count the social markets are better positioned than the liberal market economies.

SUMMARY

Including employee representation in corporate governance, codetermination remains an entrenched feature that serves the social market economies well. The evidence presented above suggests that employment protection constitutes an important reason for the long-term nature of unemployment in SMEs and also, more tentatively, that employment protection represents an obstacle to employment growth. With regard to unemployment, active labor market policies have partly offset the negative consequences of employment protection. Active labor market policy cannot be the solution to the problem of sluggish employment growth, but it is an important complement to any progressive strategy to tackle this problem. While the rise of services as the engine of employment growth requires Germany and other SMEs to shift resources from apprenticeship-based vocational training to general education, vocational training remains an institutional asset for German manufacturing firms. Perhaps most importantly, the preceding discussion suggests that public investment in education is critical to reconciling egalitarianism with the imperatives of competitiveness and growth.

CHAPTER 7

Welfare States, Redistribution, and Economic Growth

Across Western Europe, the thirty or so years following World War II witnessed a very rapid expansion of government spending on various social programs. Political parties of the left, with more or less close ties to labor movements, played a critical role in enacting the reforms that laid the foundations for the postwar welfare state, but Christian Democrats, liberals, and conservatives quickly embraced these reforms. The welfarist consensus of the postwar era began to fray in the 1970s. Over the last two decades, it has become increasingly common to hear Europeans say, "We can no longer afford the welfare state." The market-liberal view that generous welfare programs represent shackles on capitalist dynamism and exert downward pressure on long-term growth rates feeds such doubts, suggesting that the welfare state is itself the source of the economic stagnation that renders the welfare state unaffordable. The specter of globalization also feeds popular doubts about the viability of the welfare state. Especially on the left of the political spectrum, it has become commonplace to argue that capital's growing ability to move across borders in pursuit of profits forces governments to cut taxes and spending. The policy prescriptions associated with this line of argument are different from those associated with the conservative critique of the welfare state, but the underlying premises of these two views are strikingly similar. Under conditions of international openness, both posit a fundamental conflict between public welfare provision and market-driven economic growth.

This chapter explores the consequences of the welfare state for income distribution as well as economic growth. In the next chapter, I will address the question of whether or not welfare states are in decline, surveying recent social spending trends and welfare-related reforms and providing a preliminary assessment of the implications of these changes as well as of the political and economic forces behind them. In exploring the consequences of the welfare state in its heyday, the present chapter again adopts a comparative approach. As I document below, there are big differences among the advanced capitalist countries with respect to the level of social spending and the generosity of social benefits but also with respect to terms of eligibility and the importance of services relative to transfer payments. What then can we learn about the effects of public welfare provision from a comparative analysis of the advanced capitalist countries?

The evidence presented below calls into question arguments advanced by Vito Tanzi and Ludger Schuknecht, economists working for the IMF and the European Central Bank, in their recent book on *Public Spending in the Twentieth Century*. Tanzi and Schuknecht begin by asserting their conviction that the growth of government was essentially a good thing, but only up to a certain point, roughly approximated by 1960 levels of government spending relative to GDP. The expansion of government activities improved the quality of life by reducing risks and by redistributing educational opportunities and income; it may even have contributed to a higher average standard of living through the provision of public goods. From 1960 onwards, however, "progress in improving the social and economic objectives slowed down considerably or even reversed in spite of continuous large expansion in public spending in many countries."[1]

Tanzi and Schuknecht raise but do not resolve the central analytical issue confronting market-liberal critics of the welfare state: why is it that countries with large welfare states performed comparatively well on a range of both economic and social indicators prior to the mid-1970s? Why didn't the disincentives and distortions that allegedly explain their poor economic performance in the 1980s and 1990s manifest themselves earlier? Tanzi and Schuknecht assert that "marginal tax rates of 50 percent or more on income or 20 percent on sales are likely to cause significant distortions," but they do not provide any empirical support for their specification of this "tipping point," where the societal losses associated with government spending supposedly outweigh the gains.[2] Also, Tanzi and Schuknecht do not provide any empirical support for their claim that the redistributive effects of government spending have diminished over time, to the point of being essentially negligible. Finally, their effort to show that big government is associated with slow growth is questionable.[3]

To anticipate, my own analysis provides strong support for the claim that the public provision of social welfare redistributes income in favor of the poor, and in favor of low-income earners more generally, and very little support for the claim that it dampens economic growth. Social spending actually appears to have promoted economic growth in the 1960s and 1970s. For the last two decades, there is no clear association between levels of social spending and growth of GDP per capita, but the evidence indicates that reliance on payroll taxes to finance the welfare state has been associated with sluggish employment growth.

THE SIZE OF THE WELFARE STATE

Let us begin by considering cross-national differences in the degree of "welfare effort" or, in other words, the amount of economic resources devoted to public welfare provision. For each of our eighteen countries, table 7.1 reports on public social spending, measured in percent of GDP, in 1980 and 2001. Several limitations of this measure should be noted at the outset. First, the figures presented in table 7.1 only include spending on government services that fall under a fairly strict definition of "social programs." In particular, they do not include any spending related to education. While it is surely desirable to separate education and social policy, it is also clear that education spending often does have an important social policy component. Second, it should be noted that social policy purposes can be served by tax credits as well as government expenditures. To cite the most obvious example, the figures in table 7.1 capture public support for children when it takes the form of family allowances but not when it takes the form of tax deductions for dependents. Finally, the figures in table 7.1 do not take into account cross-national differences in the taxation of income that individuals receive from social insurance schemes and other social programs.

Keeping these limitations in mind, table 7.1 shows a remarkable range of variation in how much OECD countries spend on government-run social programs. In 1980, such programs accounted for 26–29 percent of GDP in Denmark, Sweden, and the Netherlands. At the opposite end of the spectrum, government-run social programs only accounted for 10.2 percent of Japan's GDP in 1980. Alongside Japan, the welfare state "laggards" of 1980 were Australia, Canada, the United States, and Switzerland. From 1980 to 2001, social spending declined relative to GDP in Denmark, the Netherlands, and Ireland, but the contraction of the Danish welfare state was rather small. Measured in this fashion, the size of the Swedish welfare state was the same in 2001 as it had been in 1980. In all other countries, we observe some increase in social spending relative to GDP over the 1980s and 1990s, but Sweden and Denmark were still the biggest social spenders in 2001. While Australia, Canada, and

Table 7.1 Total public spending on social programs in
percent of GDP, 1980 and 2001

	1980	2001
Nordic SMEs	**22.9%**	**25.6%**
Denmark	28.7	27.7
Finland	17.5	23.9
Norway	17.9	23.1
Sweden	27.6	27.5
Continental SMEs	**22.0**	**24.8**
Austria	22.5	25.5
Belgium	24.1	25.9
Germany	23.0	26.3
Netherlands	26.3	20.3
Switzerland	14.1	25.9
LMEs	**14.9**	**17.0**
Australia	11.3	17.6
Canada	14.0	17.4
Ireland	17.0	13.1
New Zealand	16.6	18.0
United Kingdom	17.3	21.5
United States	13.1	14.6
France	21.1	27.2
Italy	18.4	23.9
Japan	10.2	16.6

Source: OECD Social Expenditure Database, http://www.oecd.
org/els/social/expenditure, November 2004.
Note: The figures refer to total spending minus spending on
active labor market programs, as defined by the OECD.

Switzerland had moved up, Ireland had joined the United States and
Japan at the bottom of the OECD league by 2001.

In 1980, the average share of GDP devoted to public welfare provisions
was smaller for continental SMEs than for the Nordic SMEs, but if we
exclude Switzerland the difference between these two groups of countries
becomes negligible. From 1980 to 2001, the Swiss welfare state nearly
doubled in size—primarily on account of the expansion of public pensions—and by 2001 Switzerland was no longer an outlier among the continental SMEs. On average, in 2001 the Nordic SMEs still spent marginally
more of their resources on public welfare programs than did the continental SMEs. As for 1980, however, the differences between Nordic and
continental SMEs are small by comparison to the differences between all
SMEs and the LMEs.

The figures in table 7.1 are problematic from the point of view of inter-
preting and comparing changes over time. Measuring social spending in
percent of GDP provides a good way to compare welfare effort across

countries at any given point in time, but any observed change over time might be due either to a change in welfare spending or to a change in the denominator, in this case GDP. We cannot say how much of the reduction in the size of the Dutch and Irish welfare states shown in table 7.1 reflects spending cuts and how much reflects the acceleration of economic growth that these countries experienced. Conversely, some of the comparatively rapid growth of the Swiss welfare state from 1980 to 2001 might be attributed to comparatively slow economic growth. (The next chapter will consider alternative measures of change in welfare effort.)

WELFARE STATE REGIMES

From the scholarly literature of the last two decades we learn that welfare states differ not only in terms of size, reflecting average levels and duration of benefits, but also in terms of eligibility principles, the mix of cash benefits and services, and the determination of benefit levels for individual recipients. The single most important contribution in this tradition, Gösta Esping-Andersen's *The Three Worlds of Welfare Capitalism*, distinguishes three fundamentally different types of welfare states: the Social Democratic type of the Nordic countries, the Christian Democratic type of continental Europe, and the liberal type characteristic of the United States, other former British colonies and, to some extent, the United Kingdom itself as well.[4] More broadly, the comparative welfare state literature identifies several overlapping dimensions of cross-national variation that warrant our attention.[5]

Transfers vs. Services

To begin with, welfare states differ in terms of the importance of transfer payments relative to services or, in other words, the balance between benefits in cash and benefits in kind. As the first two columns of table 7.2 illustrate, this dimension of welfare state variation clearly differentiates the Nordic welfare states from their continental counterparts. For 1980, the first column shows the share of total social spending represented by "social security transfer expenditures" while the second column reports on public employment in education, health, and various other welfare services, expressed as a percentage of the working-age population.[6]

The contrast between the Nordic and continental welfare states that emerges from these figures is most clearly illustrated by reference to Sweden and the Netherlands. As we saw in table 7.1, in 1980 these two countries devoted nearly the same amount of their GDP to social programs. In the Netherlands, virtually all social spending took the form of

Table 7.2 Dimensions of cross-national welfare state variation, circa 1980

	Transfer spending[1]	Welfare-related government employment[2]	Means-tested social assistance[3]	Population coverage[4]	Benefits differentiation[5]
Nordic SMEs	**62.7**	**16**	**2.8**	**90**	**81**
Denmark	59.4	18		87	99
Finland	51.4	9	1.1	88	72
Norway	75.3	15	2.9	95	69
Sweden	64.7	20	4.4	90	82
Continental SMEs	**87.2**	**5**	**5.7**	**79**	**58**
Austria	81.5	4	4.7	72	52
Belgium	86.8	6	2.4	67	79
Germany	83.7	4	8.2	72	56
Netherlands	97.7	4	6.5	87	57
Switzerland	86.1	5	6.9	96	48
LMEs	**75.2**	**7**	**35.3**	**71**	**53**
Australia	70.8	7	67.5		
Canada	76.9	7	16.0	93	48
Ireland	69.9		22.3	60	77
New Zealand	80.6		57.3		
United Kingdom	68.2	8	16.7	76	64
United States	84.6	5	31.8	54	22
France	90.0	7	6.8	70	55
Italy	76.1	5	20.7	59	52
Japan	99.0	3	4.0	63	32

Definitions and sources:
[1] Spending on social security transfers in percent of total social spending. Table 7.1, and Evelyne Huber and John Stephens, *Development and Crisis of the Welfare State* (Chicago: University of Chicago Press, 2001), table A.3.
[2] Public health, education, and welfare employment as a percentage of the working-age population. Huber and Stephens, 88–89.
[3] Spending on means-tested social assistance spending as a percentage of total spending on cash benefits. Calculations based on data in Ian Gough et al., "Social Assistance in OECD Countries," *Journal of European Social Policy* 7, no. 1 (1997), 25, 27, and Huber and Stephens, 352–53.
[4] Percentage of the population aged 16–64 eligible for sickness, unemployment, and pension benefits (averaged across the three programs): Gøsta Esping-Andersen, *Three Worlds of Welfare Capitalism* (Princeton: Princeton University Press, 1990), 70.
[5] Average guaranteed basic benefit for sickness, unemployment, and pensions as a percentage of the legal maximum benefit (based on net after-tax benefits): Esping-Andersen, 70.

cash payments to households (including reimbursements of incurred health care costs). In Sweden, by contrast, transfer payments accounted for less than two-thirds of total spending. By the same token, the Netherlands and Sweden occupy opposite ends of the OECD spectrum in terms of the relative size of welfare-related public services: 4 percent of the Dutch working-age population was employed in such services in 1980, as compared to 20 percent of the Swedish working-age population.

The Dutch welfare state in particular and the continental welfare states more generally are essentially "social transfer states," while the Nordic welfare states tend to be more service-oriented. In terms of the relative importance of transfer payments in the public provision of social welfare, the liberal market economies occupy an intermediary position between the Nordic SMEs and the continental SMEs. Though the LMEs tend to spend less of their GDP on public welfare provision, they typically devote more resources to welfare-related public services than the continental SMEs do.

The prominence of government-provided services within the public welfare mix of the Nordic countries reflects the postwar political dominance of Social Democratic parties with close ties to the labor movement. By the 1930s, these parties had effectively abandoned any ambitions to nationalize industry. As they instead turned their attention to the construction of the welfare state, some of their socialist tradition took on a new meaning. At least in part, these parties conceived the welfare state in terms of satisfying basic societal needs outside the market economy, with the definition of "basic societal needs" left deliberately vague, open to piecemeal expansion. As Harold Wilensky points out, however, the absence of direct government involvement in the provision of social services does not necessarily imply that market forces govern the provision of such services. Nonprofit organizations play a particularly important role in the continental SMEs.[7]

Means-testing

A second dimension on which welfare states differ concerns the extent to which eligibility for welfare benefits involves some form of means-testing or, in other words, the extent to which welfare programs are targeted to the poor. As the third column of table 7.2 documents, the Nordic welfare states tend to rely less heavily on means-testing than the welfare states of continental Europe, but means-testing is first and foremost a distinguishing feature of liberal welfare states. In 1980, means-tested benefits accounted for 16 percent of total social spending in the LME that relied least heavily on means-testing (Canada), which is nearly twice the corresponding figure for the SME that relied most heavily on means-testing (Germany).

In part, the relatively heavy reliance of the liberal market economies on means-testing can be seen as a result of their relatively low level of overall spending on social welfare. Arguably, means-tested social assistance constitutes the minimalist core of the modern welfare state—even the least welfare-oriented societies must somehow take care of the indigent—and it is the extent to which they have gone beyond this minimalist core that distinguishes the social market economies from the liberal market economies. Yet there is more to the contrast here than this argument suggests: the liberal welfare states devote a larger portion of total spending to antipoverty programs that entail means-testing in all countries, but also rely on means-testing in areas where the entitlement principle has come to prevail in most of Western Europe. The distinction between means-tested social assistance and welfare programs based on some form of entitlement is more tenuous in LMEs than SMEs. This is most obviously the case for Australia and New Zealand, where an individual's assets and income figure into the determination of his or her eligibility for public pensions, unemployment, and health insurance.

The obvious argument in favor of means-testing is that targeting public resources on the truly needy is the most efficient way to reduce poverty and possibly to redistribute income more generally. With means-testing, a smaller amount of government spending is needed to achieve a certain reduction of poverty. On the other hand, critics of the liberal approach to public welfare provision commonly argue that means-tested programs entail stigmatization, bureaucratic red tape, and arbitrariness. As a result, many of the truly needy never get the benefits to which they are entitled.[8] The politics of the welfare state must also be considered here. For obvious reasons, welfare programs that target the poor tend to enjoy less political support than welfare programs that benefit the middle class as well. Means-tested programs may be more efficient in the sense that a given amount of government spending is associated with a greater reduction of poverty, but at the same time this approach to poverty reduction generates taxpayer resistance to increased spending. Social programs that provide benefits to people who are not truly needy also tend to provide more generous benefits to the poor.[9]

Citizenship vs. Social Insurance

A third dimension of variation among welfare states concerns the entitlement principles behind social programs that do not entail means-testing. Broadly speaking, we can distinguish two entitlement principles other than demonstrated need: social citizenship and social insurance. The former principle holds that benefits should be provided to all citizens (or residents). In the social insurance model, by contrast, eligibility derives from prior contributions: people must contribute to public pension and unemployment schemes in order to collect benefits, and the amount of benefits they can collect is often tied to the amount of contributions they have made. (Typically, contributions take the form of payroll taxes.) The distinction between social citizenship and social insurance overlaps with the distinction between benefits in kind and benefits in cash, for the citizenship principle underpins virtually all forms of service-based public welfare provision. However, the opposite identity does not hold: transfer programs may be based on the citizenship principle as well as the social insurance principle. Citizenship-based transfer programs include, most notably, family allowances and basic flat-rate pensions.

For transfer programs, the fourth column of table 7.2 reports on the percentage of the population between the ages of 16 and 64 who are eligible for sickness, unemployment, and pension benefits (averaging separate percentages for the three programs). The more prominent the principle of citizenship is, the greater the welfare state's population coverage should be. Alongside the data on the relative importance of public services (column 1), the figures strongly support Esping-Andersen's claim that universalism is the outstanding characteristic of the Nordic welfare states. In all the Nordic countries, these basic transfer programs cover roughly 90 percent of the population (as compared to 54 percent for the United States). The continental SMEs divide into two camps: while the Swiss and Dutch welfare states are just as universalistic as the Nordic welfare states, the population coverage in Austria, Belgium, and Germany is at least 15 percentage points lower. With the notable exception of Canada, the gap between the Nordic countries and the liberal market economies is greater still on this score.

Benefits Differentiation

The distinction between social citizenship and social insurance relates closely to the distinction between flat-rate benefits and income-differentiated benefits. As noted above, social insurance schemes commonly provide for individuals to receive different benefit levels based on prior contributions or, in other words, based on their income before they retired or before they became sick or unemployed. In principle, universalistic welfare programs based on the principle of social citizenship could also accommodate benefit differentiation, but in practice such programs typically provide for flat-rate benefits. That said, it must also be noted that not all social insurance programs are alike: stipulations regarding minimum and maximum benefits very much affect the degree to which benefits are differentiated.

In a rough way, the last column of table 7.2 measures the degree of benefits differentiation in sickness, unemployment, and pension schemes by relating the standard benefit of the average production worker to the maximum benefit stipulated by the rules of each program (again averaging separate percentages for the three programs). The country groups line up according to the same pattern that we observed with respect to the population coverage of these welfare programs: the benefit structure of the Nordic welfare states is most egalitarian, and the continental SMEs in turn have a more egalitarian benefit structure than the liberal market economies. Looking at individual countries, however, there is some indication of a trade-off between broad social insurance coverage and egalitarian benefits in the data presented in the last two columns of table 7.2.

The story of Swedish pension reform is instructive in this regard. Corresponding to the egalitarian ideology of the Swedish labor movement, the pension reform introduced by the Swedish Social Democrats in the immediate postwar period was based on the British model of social citizenship and flat-rate benefits. As inflation eroded the value of public pension benefits in the 1940s and 1950s, the labor movement became dissatisfied with this reform. The problem was not simply that the benefits provided by the public pension system were inadequate: equally important, the blue-collar unions resented the fact that employers provided supplementary pension schemes to their white-collar staff. Blue-collar workers in the public sector also enjoyed better pension coverage than their private sector counterparts.

Over time, the Swedish labor movement came to recognize that it had to abandon the principle of flat-rate benefits in order to redress the problem of inequality of pension coverage or, in other words, to establish an equal right to old-age income security. Creating a mandatory public system of employment-based, income-differentiated pensions to supplement the existing flat-rate pension, the pension reform of 1959 was designed to crowd out private pension schemes and to give white-collar employees a strong material stake in the expansion of the welfare state. Raising flat-rate pensions to a level that would achieve these objectives was simply not feasible. The traditional flat-rate egalitarianism of the labor movement was thus displaced by a new approach, emphasizing equality of pension rights (or status) within a comprehensive public system.[10]

Family Policy and Women's Employment

Public support for children and families correlates closely with the overall size of the welfare state and essentially pits the social market economies against the liberal market economies: characterized by comprehensive and generous welfare states, the social market economies provide a lot more support for children and families than the liberal market economies. However, things get more complicated once we ask how family policy relates to women's participation in the labor market. Public support for children and families may be organized so as to encourage or facilitate labor force participation by women with young children, but it may also be organized to encourage mothers to stay home with their children.

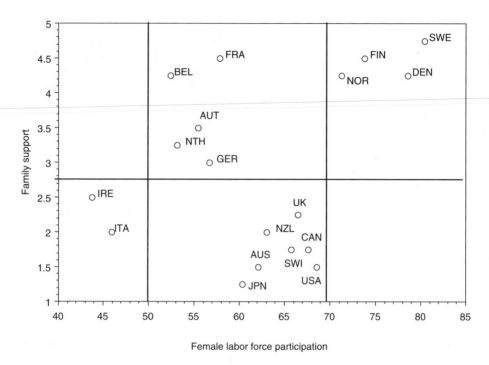

Sources: Alan Siaroff, "Work, Welfare, and Gender Equality," in *Gendering Welfare States*, ed. Diane Sainesbury (London: Sage, 1994), 92, and OECD, *Historical Statistics* (2001), 39.

Figure 7.1 Public support for families vs. female labor force participation, 1990

Figure 7.1 relates these cross-cutting issues. The variable on the vertical axis is an index of family support developed by Alan Siaroff that takes into account parental leave provisions and public daycare facilities as well as the size of family allowances. The variable on the horizontal axis is the labor force participation rate of women in 1990. The clustering of countries broadly corresponds to the overall mapping of advanced capitalist political economies employed in this book. The Nordic countries are clearly distinguished by their combination of high levels of public family support and high levels of labor force participation by women. At the opposite end of the spectrum, Ireland and Italy constitute an equally distinct cluster, combining low levels of family support with low levels of female labor force participation. Leaving Ireland aside, the LMEs and the continental SMEs alike occupy an intermediate position in terms of female labor force participation. Along with France and leaving out Switzerland, the continental SMEs provide more generous support for children and families than do the LMEs.

Since the 1960s, family policy in the Nordic countries has been systematically geared toward encouraging or enabling mothers to work. Alongside family allowances, these welfare states provide subsidized public daycare to virtually all families in which the adults work as well as parental leave insurance schemes that enable parents to take extended time off from their jobs when a child is born with nearly complete income maintenance. On the other side of the equation, the huge increase of female employment that occurred in the Nordic countries in the 1960s and 1970s primarily took the form of women entering into welfare-related public sector employment: education, child care, health, and elderly care. By 1985, government employment accounted for 33.0 percent of total employment and 55.2 percent of female employment in Sweden, with women constituting 67.1 percent of the public sector labor force.

In the social market economies of continental Europe, by contrast, positive measures to facilitate the combination of employment and child-rearing have largely been missing. In the absence of public daycare, generous family allowances may well have encouraged women to exit the labor force during their child-rearing years. At the same time, the heavy reliance on transfers as the mechanism of public welfare provision meant that the postwar expansion of the welfare state did not generate as many job opportunities for women in the continental SMEs as it did in the Nordic SMEs. In West Germany, the public sector's share of total employment was 16.1 percent and its share of female employment 19.8 percent in 1983, with women constituting 39.4 percent of the public sector labor force. The German figures are comparable to those for the United States, where in 1985 government employment accounted for 15.8 percent of total employment and 17.7 percent of female employment, and women constituted 46.6 percent of the public sector labor force.[11]

THE REDISTRIBUTIVE IMPACT OF WELFARE STATES

The scope of the following analysis of the redistributive effects of the welfare state is limited in a twofold sense. First, my analysis pertains strictly to the distribution of income and does not take into account the effects of public services, offered free of charge or at highly subsidized prices, on the distribution of consumption or, in other words, on the living conditions of people at different positions in the social hierarchy. Second, this analysis conceives redistribution as the difference between the distribution of "market income"—income before taxes and transfers—and the distribution of "disposable income"—income after taxes and transfers—and does not take into account the effects that welfare-related govern-

Table 7.3 Inequality and redistribution among working-age households, late 1990s

| | Year | Gini coefficients | | Redistribution (% change) |
		Market income	Disposable income	
Nordic SMEs		**35.2**	**23.6**	**32.9**
Denmark	1997	34.5	23.7	31.3
Finland	2000	35.2	23.3	33.8
Norway	2000	33.7	23.6	30.0
Sweden	2000	37.5	23.8	36.5
Continental SMEs		**34.8**	**25.6**	**25.7**
Belgium	1997	37.8	23.7	37.3
Germany	2000	34.2	24.0	29.8
Netherlands	1999	33.9	25.1	26.0
Switzerland	1992	33.2	29.7	9.7
LMEs		**41.8**	**32.4**	**22.6**
Australia	1994	39.6	29.3	26.0
Canada	1998	39.0	29.8	23.6
United Kingdom	1999	45.0	34.1	24.2
United States	2000	43.6	36.3	16.7

Source: Luxembourg Income Study, calculations of Gini coefficients by Lane Kenworthy.
Note: Figures based on "household equivalent income," with square root of persons living in household as equivalence scale (see chapter 3, note 3). Working-age households defined as households headed by individuals aged 25–59.

ment activities have on the distribution of market income (so-called second-order effects).

For purposes of cross-national comparison, it is desirable to exclude the retired population when comparing the distribution of market income and the distribution of disposable income. In countries with generous public pension plans, individuals have little incentive to save for their retirement and employers also have little incentive to offer supplementary private pension benefits to their employees. As a result, many retired people have little or no income prior to receiving their public pension. Studies of income distribution that include the retired population yield very high levels of "pre-government" inequality and poverty and, in a sense, overstate the redistributive effects of public policy in these countries.

Based on the most recent data available from the Luxembourg Income Study, table 7.3 provides Gini coefficients for the distribution of market income and disposable income among households headed by individuals aged 25–59 (see chapter 3 for an explanation of the meaning of Gini coefficients). Except for Switzerland and Australia, the figures refer to the late 1990s. The measure of redistribution in the last column expresses the difference between pre- and post-government Gini coefficients as a

Table 7.4 Redistributive effects of taxes and income transfers (% change in Gini coefficient, working-age households), late 1990s

	Taxes	Transfers
Nordic SMEs	**1.6**	**31.9**
Denmark	−0.6	32.5
Finland	4.3	30.9
Norway	5.0	26.3
Sweden	−2.4	38.0
Continental SMEs	**7.1**	**20.5**
Belgium	9.5	30.7
Germany	10.2	21.8
Netherlands	6.5	20.8
Switzerland	2.1	8.6
LMEs	**6.5**	**17.1**
Australia	7.8	19.7
Canada	6.9	17.9
United Kingdom	1.6	23.0
United States	9.6	7.9
France		25.0
Italy		8.7

Note: See table 7.3 for years, definitions, and source.

percentage of pre-government Gini coefficients. In other words, the last column reports the percentage reduction of income inequality brought about by taxes and income transfers. By this measure, Belgium and Sweden stand out as the countries in which governments redistribute the most, while Switzerland and the United States are the countries in which governments redistribute the least. (Note that Switzerland's standing may well have changed as a result of its expansion of social spending in the 1990s.) In Germany and the Netherlands, government redistribution is marginally greater than in Australia, Canada, and the United Kingdom, but the large extent of variation among continental SMEs makes it difficult to generalize about differences between LMEs and continental SMEs. As a group, the Nordic welfare states clearly stand out as the most redistributive welfare states. Again, it is important to note that the measure presented in table 7.3 fails to capture the redistributive effects of public services, that is, welfare benefits that individuals or households consume directly. As noted earlier, the Nordic welfare states are distinguished by their service orientation. If we could measure inequality in terms of consumption rather than income, their egalitarian cast would be still more pronounced.

Table 7.4 separates the redistributive effects of taxes and transfers. The first column reports the percentage change in Gini coefficients that we observe as we move from gross to net (post-tax) market income, while the second column reports the percentage change in Gini coefficients that we observe as we move from net market income to disposable (post-transfer) income. In this table, the United States stands out as the only country in which taxation has a larger redistributive effect, among working-age households, than do social programs that provide cash benefits to individuals or households. In general, the bulk of the redistribution produced by welfare states occurs through the provision of benefits rather than through taxation. This is especially true for the Nordic countries. Indeed, taxation in Denmark and Sweden actually has a regressive effect on the distribution of household income (the Gini coefficient for net market income being greater than the Gini coefficient for gross market income). With the Luxembourg Income Study providing data on net (but not gross) market income for France and Italy, figures for these countries are included in the second column of table 7.4. While the French welfare state is more redistributive than any of the liberal welfare states, Italy emerges, along with Switzerland and the United States, as a country with very little redistribution through income transfers. As figure 7.2 illustrates, government spending on transfer programs that are not targeted to the elderly provides a very good predictor of redistribution through transfers shown in table 7.4. Looking at this figure, it does not appear to be the case that welfare states that engage in extensive means-testing are more efficient in the sense of achieving a larger redistributive effect for a given amount of spending.

In all countries, poverty alleviation figures prominently as a goal of social policy. Do the cross-national differences in redistribution documented above translate into similar differences in poverty alleviation? Or is it perhaps the case that liberal welfare states, by relying on means-testing, perform relatively better in this regard? In cross-national research, it is commonplace to define the poor as people who live in households with an income lower than 40 percent of the median household income. For the United States, this threshold yields a poverty rate that roughly corresponds to the official poverty line, based on objective indicators of living conditions. Organized like table 7.3, table 7.5 reproduces the estimates of poverty rates before and after taxes and government transfers that Lane Kenworthy derives from the Luxembourg Income Study. In contrast to tables 7.3 and 7.4, these figures refer to the entire population—all households, not just households headed by working-age adults. With two exceptions, the figures refer to some year between 1989 and 1992: the exceptions are Ireland (1987) and Switzerland (1982).

When poverty is measured in terms of income before taxes and transfers, the United States is very much near the average. Once we take into account the effects of taxation and transfers, however, the United States stands out as the country with the highest poverty rate, by far—nearly

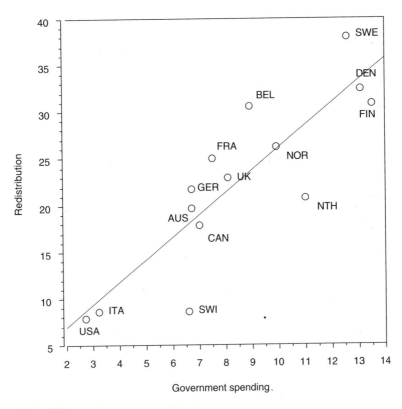

Correlation: .862
Note: Swiss figures refer to 1992 (redistribution) and 1990 (spending).
Sources: Tables 7.1 and 7.4.

Figure 7.2 Redistributive effect of income transfers (working age households) in late 1990s vs. government spending on transfer programs not targeted to the elderly in percent of GDP in 1995.

twice as high as the next highest poverty rate. In 1991, taxes and transfers reduced the percentage of Americans living in "poor" households (as defined above) from 21.0 percent to 11.7 percent. Put differently, taxes and transfers brought 44.3 percent of the poor out of poverty. At the opposite end of the spectrum, in Belgium taxes and transfers brought 90.8 percent of the poor out of poverty. Even excluding the United States, the average poverty reduction produced by taxation and public income support in the LMEs is smaller than the average for the continental SMEs, and the difference is quite considerable if we in turn exclude Switzerland from the average for the continental SMEs. (Again, I suspect that Switzerland improved its poverty alleviation record in the course of the

Table 7.5 Relative poverty (below 40% of median household income) and poverty reduction, circa 1990

	Year	Poverty rate		Poverty Reduction (% change)
		Before taxes/transfers	After taxes/transfers	
Nordic SMEs		**15.9%**	**2.8%**	**81.3%**
Denmark	1992	23.9	3.5	85.4
Finland	1991	9.8	2.3	76.5
Norway	1991	9.3	1.7	81.7
Sweden	1992	20.6	3.8	81.6
Continental SMEs		**17.8**	**3.3**	**79.8**
Belgium	1992	23.9	2.2	90.8
Germany	1989	14.1	2.4	83.0
Netherlands	1991	20.5	4.3	79.0
Switzerland	1982	12.8	4.3	66.4
LMEs		**23.1**	**6.7**	**69.9**
Australia	1989	21.3	6.4	70.0
Canada	1991	21.6	5.6	74.1
Ireland	1987	25.8	4.7	81.8
United Kingdom	1991	25.7	5.3	79.4
United States	1991	21.0	11.7	44.3
France	1989	27.5	4.8	82.5
Italy	1991	21.8	5.0	77.1

Source: Lane Kenworthy, "Do Social-Welfare Policies Reduce Poverty?" *Social Forces* 77, no. 3 (1999), 1130.

1980s and 1990s.) Indeed, the remaining continental SMEs—Belgium, Germany, and the Netherlands—do just as well as the Nordic SMEs in alleviating poverty through cash transfers.

Plotting poverty reduction against government spending on .social transfers as a percentage of GDP, figure 7.3 illustrates the exceptional nature of the American case and also shows that there is a fairly close association between the size of the welfare state and its effects on the incidence of poverty. Again, it does not appear to be the case that welfare states that rely more heavily on means-testing are more redistributive. The multiple regression results reported in table 7.6 confirm this point. In the first regression, the dependent variable is redistribution among working-age households through transfers (last column of table 7.3); in the second and third regressions, the dependent variable is poverty reduction among all households (last column of table 7.5). As explanatory variables, each regression includes means-tested social assistance as a percentage of total transfer spending as well as transfer spending in percent of GDP. Transfer spending that is not targeted on the elderly has a strong positive effect on redistribution among working-age households, and total transfer spending similarly has a strong positive effect on poverty reduction for

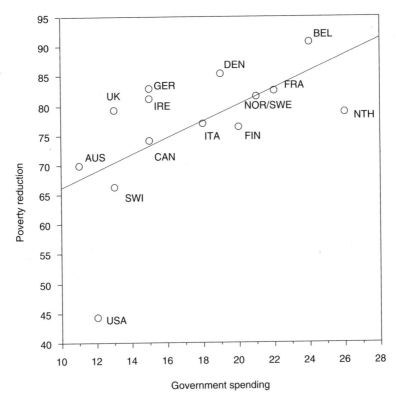

Correlation: .600
Note: Swiss figures refer to 1982 (poverty reduction) and 1980 (spending).
Sources: Tables 7.1 and 7.5.

Figure 7.3 Poverty reduction in the early 1990s vs. government spending on income transfers in percent of GDP in 1991

the population as a whole. For redistribution, we observe no discernable effect of means-testing. With poverty reduction as the dependent variable, we do observe a positive effect of means-testing that is nearly significant by conventional criteria, but this effect disappears once we control for the American case. From a comparative perspective, there is good reason to doubt the commonsensical notion that increased reliance on means-testing ensures that the poor will derive more benefits from the welfare state.

The public provision of social welfare affects not only the incidence of poverty in the aggregate but also the exposure of different categories of people to poverty. The issue of child poverty is particularly salient in this context. Based on the most recent LIS data available, table 7.7 shows the

Table 7.6 Determinants of redistribution and poverty reduction, OLS regression results

	Redistribution	Poverty reduction	
Constant	2.480	38.456	60.381
	(.4781)	(.0118)	(.0001)
Non-elderly transfers in % of GDP	.909		
	(.0001)		
All transfers in % of GDP		.843	.425
		(.0087)	(.0461)
Means-testing	.026	.396	.092
	(.8495)	(.1673)	(.6146)
USA			−.683
			(.0008)
N	14	15	15
Adjusted R²	.78	.37	.76

Sources: see tables 7.1, 7.2, 7.4, and 7.5.
Note: Standardized (beta) coefficients, with p-values (two-tailed tests) in parentheses. Data on non-elderly transfers refer to 1995 (1990 for Switzerland), data on total transfer spending to 1991 (1980 for Switzerland). Means-testing is measured as means-tested social assistance in percent of total spending on income transfers in 1992.

Table 7.7 Aggregate and child poverty rates after taxes and transfers, late 1990s

	Year	Entire population	Children
Nordic SMEs		**3.2**	**1.8**
Denmark	1992	3.8	2.4
Finland	2000	2.1	1.3
Norway	2000	2.9	1.6
Sweden	2000	3.8	1.8
Continental SMEs		**4.7**	**5.7**
Austria	1997	4.4	6.5
Belgium	1997	3.3	3.2
Germany	2000	4.7	5.8
Netherlands	1999	4.6	5.8
Switzerland	1992	6.7	7.1
LMEs		**6.8**	**8.1**
Australia	1994	7.1	8.0
Canada	2000	6.5	7.7
Ireland	1996	4.0	5.0
United Kingdom	1999	5.8	5.5
United States	2000	10.8	14.1
France	1994	3.4	2.9
Italy	2000	7.3	10.5

Source: Luxembourg Income Study, http://www.lisproject.org/ keyfigures/povertytable.htm, October 2004.
Note: poverty rate set at 40% of median disposable household income.

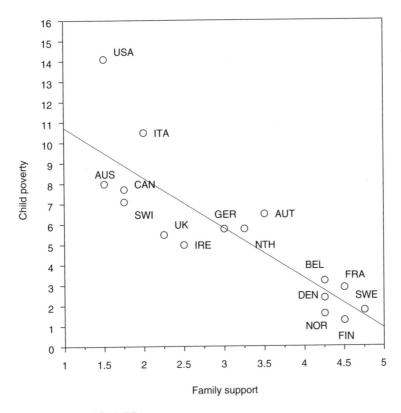

Sources: Figure 7.1 and Table 7.7.

Figure 7.4 Child poverty in the late 1990s vs. public family support (Siaroff index) in the early 1990s

percentage of the entire population and also the percentage of the population below the age of sixteen living in households earning less than 40 percent of the median household income after taxes and transfers. The Nordic countries are distinguished by child poverty rates that are significantly lower than overall poverty rates. Though the differences are less pronounced, child poverty rates are also lower than overall poverty rates in Belgium, the United Kingdom, and France. On the other hand, children are significantly more likely to live in poor households than the population at large in most LMEs and continental SMEs. Italy and the United States stand out as the countries with the most serious child poverty problems.

As figure 7.4 illustrates, child poverty rates (after taxes and transfers) correlate quite closely with Siaroff's index of public support for children and families. Once again, cross-national evidence indicates that the public provision of social welfare has a very significant redistributive impact. Tanzi and Schuknecht's claim that rolling back the welfare state would benefit all citizens more or less equally seems highly dubious in light of this evidence.

THE WELFARE STATE AND ECONOMIC GROWTH

In Europe, conservative critics of the welfare state typically argue that too much of social spending goes to people who are not truly in need of public support. In the United States, it is more commonplace to hear conservatives argue that the public provision of social welfare breeds a culture of dependence among the poor.[12] Somewhat at odds with each other, these alternative tacks of conservative criticism reflect different patterns of welfare state development. However, both arguments represent something of a sideshow: what unites conservatives on both sides of the Atlantic is the claim that the public provision of social welfare is detrimental to the efficient operation of capitalist economies and, over the long run, reduces average living standards. This claim constitutes the core of the market-liberal critique of the welfare state and involves important issues with which we must contend.

Couched in terms of cross-national comparison, the essential insight behind the market-liberal critique of the welfare state is that we should not be content to compare countries in terms of the distribution of income around the median (or mean); we should also compare median incomes. Put differently, the poverty data presented in tables 7.5 and 7.7 are of only limited interest because they refer to relative rather than absolute poverty. Consider two hypothetical countries with identical distributions of market income, each with a median household income of $20,000 and a pre-government poverty rate of 20 percent.[13] While country A engages in redistribution from the rich to the poor that brings the poverty rate down to 10 percent, country B does not engage in any such redistribution, so the post-government poverty rate remains 20 percent. In a direct (or static) sense, the poor are better off in country A as a result of redistribution by the government. But suppose that redistribution by the government has the additional effect of reducing the rate of economic growth so that, fifteen years later, the median income of country A is $25,000 as compared to a median income of $30,000 in country B. Relative to the median income in their own country, the poor in country A are still better off than the poor in country B, but since the median income in country B is now much higher, the poor in country B may well be better off than the poor in country A in an absolute sense.

Several different arguments, deeply rooted in neoclassical economics, have been invoked to support the claim that the public provision of social welfare has detrimental consequences for economic growth over the long run.[14] To begin with, it is commonplace for critics of the welfare state to argue that high marginal income taxes represent a serious work disincentive. As marginal tax rates rise, so the argument runs, leisure time becomes more valuable (relative to the remuneration one receives for an additional hour of work), something that is especially true for the best-paid, and presumably the most educated and productive, segments of the labor force. This motivation problem is not simply a matter of the number of hours that people are willing to work: income tax rates may also affect how hard people are willing to work and, most serious of all, their propensity to invest in education or other forms of skill acquisition.

A second line of argument holds that the benefits provided by the welfare state also represent a disincentive to work. In contrast to the work disincentives generated by progressive taxation, this type of disincentive operates primarily at the lower end of the skill hierarchy. Most commonly, the argument here is couched in terms of the need to make sure that the level of income support provided by means-tested social assistance falls well short of the going rate of pay for unskilled work. The same logic also applies to unemployment insurance: to the extent that it provides high levels of income maintenance, unemployed workers have little or no incentive to seek jobs that pay less than what they used to earn. Generous welfare provision might thus translate into higher rates of unemployment or, more accurately, lower rates of employment among people of working age. The non-employment induced by public income support represents an under-utilization of resources, which we would expect to translate into slower economic growth.

Alongside these arguments about work (dis-)incentives, critics of the welfare state commonly argue that there are deadweight costs associated with high overall taxes and that progressive income taxes and capital gains taxation tend to lower the rate of savings and investment in the economy. Finally, the market-liberal critique of the welfare state holds that public monopolies in the provision of social services are a source of economic inefficiency. In the absence of competition, public agencies charged with the provision of health care and other services have little incentive to improve productivity and to respond to changes in consumer demand.

In the tradition of comparative political economy, on the other hand, it is commonplace to note that the countries that experienced the most rapid expansion of the welfare state in the postwar era were also distinguished by a high degree of trade dependence or, in other words, by a high degree of exposure to international competition.[15] This observation does not invalidate any of the specific arguments recounted above, but it does suggest that the implications of public welfare provision for economic efficiency and growth are more complicated than the market-liberal critique of the welfare state suggests. Partly to explain the historical association between trade openness and social spending, an extensive body of literature points out ways that social spending may enhance efficiency and growth. One strand of this alternative approach emphasizes that a great deal of social spending can be seen as a form of investment in human capital, as suggested by Esping-Andersen's concept of a "social investment strategy."[16] This line of argument works best if the welfare state is conceived broadly, so as to include public education and training programs, but it may also hold for health care and income support programs that improve the economic conditions of children and thereby enhance their ability to take advantage of educational opportunities. Moreover, it can be argued that a well-constructed social safety net serves to maintain the employability of unemployed adults.

In a different vein, some scholars question the market-liberal assumption that work effort is essentially a function of individual economic incentives. Perceptions of fairness may also affect worker motivation. At the level of firms, George Akerlof and Janet Yellen argue that wage compression may yield more harmonious labor relations and greater employee effort.[17] To the extent that such a logic also operates at a societal level, social programs that redistribute income or promote a sense of economic security among workers may indirectly contribute to labor productivity.

The fact that health care costs rose far more rapidly in the United States than in any West European country in the 1980s suggests another counterargument to the market-liberal critique of the welfare state. In the realm of social insurance and certain kinds of social services, public monopolies may provide for more effective cost containment, benefiting the economy as a whole.[18] Yet another argument to the effect that the welfare state promotes efficiency and growth proceeds from the observation that social benefits provided by employers represent an obstacle to labor mobility. At least in Scandinavia, the expansion of social insurance under public auspices has often been justified on the grounds that if such benefits are provided by the government rather than companies, workers will be more willing to move between firms, providing for a more efficient allocation of labor. This line of argument may seem dubious given that labor mobility is higher in the United States than Western Europe, despite the fact that employer-provided benefits are far more prominent in the United States. Clearly, it would be foolish to suppose that the organization of social insurance is the sole or even primary determinant of labor mobility. The argument suggested here simply holds that the public provision of social welfare has some positive effect on labor mobility and, by implication, that the labor mobility gap between the United States and Western Europe would be greater had West European countries not developed public social insurance schemes.

Finally, Peter Katzenstein's more political interpretation of the historical association between economic openness and the size of the public sector deserves to be noted here.[19] Katzenstein accepts the conventional view that openness promotes efficiency by exposing firms to worldwide competition and, in the case of small countries, by enabling consumers to gain the benefits of economies of scale, but he also points out that continuous economic restructuring in response to global market forces has a negative impact on the economic well-being of certain segments of the labor force, notably unskilled workers. Referring to the welfare state as a mechanism of "domestic compensation," Katzenstein suggests that welfare benefits might be seen as side-payments to the losers in economic modernization driven by world markets, financed out of the collective gains from trade. The public provision of social welfare, in other words, may be an important political lubricant, facilitating societal acceptance of economic change—in particular, the phase-out of employment in industries exposed to competition from low-wage countries.

The arguments advanced by these alternative traditions of thought on the relationship between the welfare state and economic growth are not mutually exclusive. It is perfectly possible, for example, that income support programs financed by progressive income taxes are a source of work disincentives and, at the same time, facilitate societal acceptance of economic restructuring. The welfare state, being a complex thing, may well have contradictory effects on economic growth. From this perspective, the question becomes whether, on balance, one set of effects prevails over the other.

Figure 7.5 plots GDP per capita, expressed in U.S. dollars, at purchasing power parities, against total social spending in percent of GDP in 2001. The two smallest welfare states, Ireland and the United States, are among the three most affluent countries in the OECD world. On the other hand, Norway is a very affluent country with a relatively large welfare state, and New Zealand is a poor country with a relatively small welfare state. Most important, the remaining fourteen countries fall within a rather narrow range of GDP per capita, between $25,000 and $31,000, despite a great deal of variation in the size of the welfare state. Among these fourteen countries, there is no consistent association whatsoever between economic affluence and size of the welfare state.

Obviously, cross-national differences in levels of economic development are determined by a host of factors, many of which—for instance, natural resource endowments—have nothing to do with the welfare state. Both sides in the debate about the economic impact of the public welfare pro-

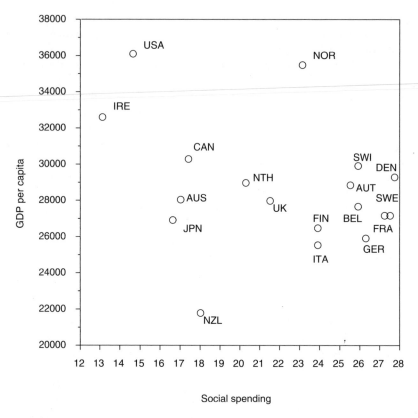

Sources: Tables 1.1 and 7.1.

Figure 7.5 GDP per capita (US$ at purchasing power parities) in 2002 vs. social spending in percent of GDP in 2001

vision are making arguments about marginal effects, that is, about additions to or subtractions from some "given" growth potential. To test such arguments, it is more appropriate to look at rates of economic growth rather than levels of economic development. In other words, we should ask whether levels of social spending correlate, positively or negatively, with growth of GDP per capita on a cross-national basis. In trying to answer this, we should ideally control for any other variables that might affect the rate of growth. In addition, it would be desirable to decompose economic growth so as to be able to discern more precisely how taxation and social spending affect different components of economic growth: the supply of labor and capital and the productivity (efficient use) of these "factors of production."

As noted by Tony Atkinson in a recent literature review, empirical studies of the relationship between social spending and economic growth in the OECD countries have yielded very different conclusions.[20] Of the ten studies reviewed by Atkinson, four find that social spending has been associated with more rapid rates of growth, while another four find the opposite to be the case; the remaining two studies fail to find any consistent (statistically significant) association between these variables. As Atkinson points out, these discrepancies have to do with the time periods covered, the countries included, and the particular measures of social spending and control variables used by the different studies.

For each of the four decades between 1960 and 2000, table 7.8 reports the results of regressing average annual per capita GDP growth on social spending as a percentage of GDP at the beginning of each decade. The regressions reported here include initial levels of GDP per capita, which are meant to capture a variety of "catch-up effects," and dummy variables for the countries that proved to be the biggest outliers in any particular decade.[21] The purpose of this admittedly crude exercise is not to settle the debate on the economic consequences of the welfare state but rather to illustrate the simple point that such consequences probably vary over time.

Controlling for levels of economic development, the regression results reported in table 7.8 suggest that countries with larger welfare states enjoyed more rapid economic growth in the 1960s and 1970s. The coefficients for initial levels of social spending do not quite clear the conventional threshold for statistical significance, but they come rather close, and, with only 18 observations, a more forgiving standard might be warranted. For the 1980s and 1990s, we obtain much smaller coefficients for initial levels of social spending (negative for the 1980s, positive again for the 1990s), and the coefficients are not in the least statistically significant.[22] Certainly, this simple regression exercise does not provide any support for the market-liberal view that social spending hampers economic growth. For the 1960s and 1970s, the opposite view—that social spending enhances economic efficiency and growth—seems more plausible. Again, however, the main point that I want to make here is that the effects of social spending, and the taxation that funds it, seem to have changed over time.

Table 7.8 suggests that the growth-enhancing effects of social spending diminished or that the growth-inhibiting effects of spending and taxation increased from the 1960s and 1970s to the 1980s and 1990s. Why might this be so? Tanzi and Schuknecht would presumably see in these findings a "tipping point" that most welfare states reached in the late 1970s or early 1980s. From this point of view, however, it is surely puzzling that we still do not observe any consistent negative association between size of the welfare state and economic growth since 1980.

Table 7.8 Determinants of real annual growth of GDP per capita by decade, OLS regression results

	1960–70	1970–80	1980–90	1990–2000
Constant	2.470	2.664	1.837	2.819
	(.057)	(.007)	(.006)	(.001)
Initial level of social spending in percent of GDP	.259	.350	−.027	.029
	(.123)	(.123)	(.879)	(.769)
Initial level of GDP per capita	−.020	−.422	−.031	−.262
	(.899)	(.039)	(.867)	(.026)
Japan	.952	.377	.618	
	(.000)	(.100)	(.003)	
Norway		.448		.254
		(.029)		(.020)
Ireland			.586	.797
			(.006)	(.000)
N	18	18	18	18
adjusted R²	.73	.44	.59	.85

Note: Standardized (beta) coefficients, with p-values (two-tailed tests) in parentheses; initial levels of GDP per capita in thousands of U.S. dollars (at 1990 prices and exchange rates for 1960–70, 1970–80, 1980–90; at 1995 prices and exchange rates for 1990–2000). GDP data from OECD, *National Accounts*; social spending data for 1960–80 from dataset compiled by Duane Swank, http://www.marquette.edu/polisci/Swank, June 2002, for 1980–2000 from OECD source (see table 7.1).

Two other types of argument may be advanced to explain why the balance between growth-enhancing and growth-inhibiting effects of the welfare state has changed. On the one hand, one might argue that the dynamics of economic growth have changed in some fashion that makes social spending less growth-conducive, presumably as a result of globalization. On the other hand, one might argue that the nature of social spending has changed in ways that make it less growth-conducive. Most obviously, support for the elderly has come to assume a significantly larger share of total social spending in most countries over the last two or three decades. While there are many good reasons why the government should provide income support and social services to the elderly population, the thesis that public provision of social welfare enhances the productive potential of the economy does not apply to this component of the welfare state.

Setting the implications of globalization aside for the next chapter, let us briefly dwell on the point that welfare states have increasingly become support systems for the elderly. Table 7.9 shows how the share of total spending devoted to old-age pensions has changed since 1980. As commonly recognized, the elderly are the chief beneficiaries of public spending on health care and other social services as well. Thus the figures in

Table 7.9 Public spending on old-age pensions as a
percentage of total public social spending, 1980 and 2001

	1980	2001	Change
Nordic SMEs	**28.7**	**31.5**	**2.8**
Denmark	28.2	30.0	1.8
Finland	29.7	33.1	3.4
Norway	28.5	29.4	0.9
Sweden	28.3	33.5	5.2
Continental SMEs	**34.9**	**39.4**	**4.5**
Austria	38.2	42.0	3.8
Belgium	25.3	33.6	8.3
Germany	43.5	44.5	1.0
Netherlands	27.0	31.3	4.3
Switzerland	40.4	45.6	5.2
LMEs	**31.7**	**29.2**	**−2.5**
Australia	28.3	26.7	−1.6
Canada	22.1	27.6	5.5
Ireland	26.5	20.6	−5.9
New Zealand	41.6	26.1	−15.5
United Kingdom	31.8	37.8	6.0
United States	39.7	36.3	−3.4
France	36.5	39.0	2.5
Italy	40.2	47.3	7.1
Japan	29.4	44.0	14.6

Source: Table 7.1.

table 7.9 understate the general trend for spending on the elderly to assume a larger share of total social spending. For our present purposes, the most important feature of table 7.9 is that the trend for spending on the elderly to assume a larger share of total social spending has been particularly pronounced in the social market economies, especially the continental SMEs. From 1980 to 2001, the share of total social spending devoted to old-age pensions actually declined in Australia, Ireland, New Zealand, and the United States.

The growth of spending on the elderly reflects the maturation of public pension schemes introduced in the 1960s and 1970s, but the fundamental force behind this trend is, of course, population ageing, which will continue to put pressure on public welfare systems for many years to come. Under the assumption that public policies in effect in 1996 are unchanged, the OECD estimates that population ageing between 2000 and 2030 will produce an increase of public pension spending corresponding to 3.9 percent of GDP and an increase of public health spending corresponding to 1.7 percent of GDP.[23] Under conditions of fiscal constraint, this pressure will squeeze other, more productive social policy programs. The challenge posed by population ageing is particularly acute for the social market economies because they provide more generous public benefits to the elderly but also because these countries have a more unfavorable age structure. In 1990, people above the age of 64 accounted for 16 percent of the total population in the United Kingdom and 13 percent in the United States, but only 11 percent in Australia, Canada, Ireland, and New Zealand. By contrast, the share of the total population above the age of 64 averaged 16 percent in the social market economies, ranging between 13 percent in Finland and the Netherlands and 18 percent in Sweden.[24]

A recent article by Lane Kenworthy cleverly integrates comparisons of average incomes and distributive outcomes.[25] Using data from the Luxembourg Income Survey for the late 1980s and early 1990s, Kenworthy measures poverty by absolute as well as relative standards—not simply as the percentage of the population of a country living in households with an income of less than 40 percent of the median household income in that particular country, but also as the percentage of the population living in households with less than 40 percent of the median household income *in the United States* (with purchasing power parities again used to convert foreign incomes into U.S. dollars). Table 7.10 reproduces Kenworthy's estimates of absolute poverty rates.

With the United States being used as the standard of absolute poverty, U.S. relative and absolute poverty rates are by definition the same. Comparing table 7.10 to table 7.5, we observe significant discrepancies between the two poverty measures for many of the other countries. Once we take into account cross-national differences in median household income, the United States no longer stands out as the country with the highest incidence of post-government poverty. That dubious distinction belongs to Ireland prior to its economic miracle in the 1990s. By Kenworthy's absolute poverty measure, several other countries also register post-government poverty rates that are higher than the U.S. rate. Indeed, the United States does better relative to every other country except Norway and Switzerland when we switch from a relative to an absolute poverty standard. However, there is another striking feature of table 7.10: by absolute standards, the post-government poverty rate in every one of the social market economies of northern Europe remains significantly lower than the U.S. rate. As a group, the liberal market economies actually do worse relative to the social market economies when we apply an absolute rather than a relative poverty standard. Moreover, Kenworthy's analysis shows that the association between the reduction of poverty brought about by taxation and government transfers and the size of the welfare state, measured by social spending in percent of GDP, remains as we switch from a relative to an absolute poverty standard.

Table 7.10 Absolute poverty rates and poverty reduction, circa 1990

		Poverty rate		Poverty reduction (% change)
	Year	Before taxes/transfers	After taxes/transfers	
Nordic SMEs		**17.8**	**4.3**	**75.9**
Denmark	1992	26.4	5.9	77.7
Finland	1991	11.9	3.7	68.9
Norway	1991	9.2	1.7	81.5
Sweden	1992	23.7	5.8	75.5
Continental SMEs		**19.2**	**5.4**	**72.2**
Belgium	1992	26.8	6.0	77.6
Germany	1989	15.2	4.3	71.7
Netherlands	1991	22.1	7.3	67.0
Switzerland	1982	12.5	3.8	69.6
LMEs		**27.1**	**15.3**	**46.5**
Australia	1989	23.3	11.9	48.9
Canada	1991	22.5	6.5	71.1
Ireland	1987	39.2	29.4	25.0
United Kingdom	1991	29.6	16.8	43.2
United States	1991	21.0	11.7	44.3
France	1989	36.1	9.8	72.9
Italy	1991	30.7	14.3	53.4

Source: see table 7.5.

Note: The poverty rate is defined as the percentage of the population living in households with a combined income below 40% of the median U.S. household income (at purchasing power parities).

Arguably, the fact that government spending on social programs alleviates absolute as well as relative poverty does not bear directly on the debate set out above. From the perspective of this debate, the relationship between government spending and pre-government rates of absolute poverty is more pertinent. As figure 7.6 illustrates, there is no consistent association between these variables. Figure 7.6 flatly contradicts the market-liberal notion of a vicious circle whereby government efforts to alleviate poverty themselves generate poverty.

THE WELFARE STATE AND EMPLOYMENT

Related to the question of ageing and pension costs, a number of scholars have recently focused attention on the role played by disability insurance and early retirement schemes in facilitating exit from the labor market in France and Italy as well as in the continental SMEs. The Dutch "disability crisis" of the 1980s represents the most extreme example of the syndrome that Esping-Andersen aptly refers to as "welfare without

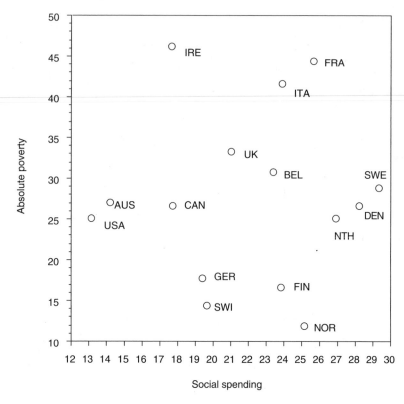

Sources: Tables 7.1 and 7.10.

Figure 7.6 Absolute pre-government poverty rates 1987–92 vs. social spending in percent of GDP, 1990

work."[26] In contrast to many other small European countries, the Netherlands eschewed the option of responding to the oil price shocks of 1973–74 and 1979 by engaging in domestic reflation and instead adopted a hard currency stance in the mid-1970s. As a result of these macroeconomic policy choices, unemployment increased sharply in the late 1970s and the early 1980s. However, Dutch unemployment would have increased even more sharply had it not been for the fact that the industry boards responsible for the administration of social insurance, made up primarily of employer and union representatives, adopted increasingly lenient eligibility standards for disability benefits. "Disability" in effect came to be defined as the incapacity of an individual to find a job similar to the one he or she held prior to an illness or injury. By 1986, there were more people drawing disability benefits than people with paying jobs among the Dutch population between the ages of 55 and 64, and by 1992 disability claimants accounted for 7.7 percent of the entire population between the ages of 15 and 64.[27] For a decade or so, the disability system provided a safety valve, enabling the Netherlands to pursue restrictive macro-economic policies while maintaining its tradition of cooperative labor relations.

Early retirement has served a similar function in Germany and other continental countries. The German pension reform of 1972 provided for the possibility of "flexible retirement" at the age of 63 without any reduction of pension benefits, and subsequent legislation provided for full pension benefits at the age of 60 for anyone who had been unemployed for more than 12 months. From the mid-1970s onwards, it became commonplace for companies to buy the acquiescence of their works councils in workforce reductions by topping off the unemployment benefits of older workers until such time that they became eligible for pension benefits under this provision. As the government extended the duration of unemployment insurance from 12 to 32 months in 1987, it became possible for German workers to exit the labor force by this route at the age of 57.[28]

The Dutch overhauled their disability insurance system in the 1990s, changing the administrative structure, requiring medical certification for eligibility, and cutting the benefits provided to the disabled. Though labor force participation among 55- to 64-year-olds remains low by comparative standards, it increased substantially from 1990 to 2000, from 45.8 percent to 50.8 percent for men and from 16.9 percent to 26.4 percent for women.[29] By contrast, German unification and the employment crisis that followed rendered early retirement an even more prominent feature of the German model in the 1990s. In 1992, only 18 percent of East Germans aged 55 to 65 were employed, while 53 percent collected early retirement benefits. Both employment and unemployment had risen considerably by 1996, but retirees still accounted for nearly half of this age group of erstwhile East Germans, as compared to a fifth of West Germans.[30] For Germany as a whole, the labor force participation rate of men aged 55 to 64 fell from 57.7 percent in 1990 to 55.2 percent in 2000, while labor force participation among men aged 25 to 54 increased from 91.2 percent to 95.8 percent over the same period.[31]

In Germany and elsewhere, early retirement and disability pensions have cushioned the impact of mass unemployment and changes in the structure of labor demand on elderly workers with poor skills or some form of disability. At the same time, such schemes have enabled employers to shed labor or to substitute more productive workers for less productive workers without protracted conflicts with their unions and works councils. In a sense, the welfare state has made labor flexibility—shedding or upgrading labor—possible within a legal framework that restricts the ability of firms to fire workers unilaterally, benefiting both firms and younger workers. It should also be noted that governments have had their own reasons to use social insurance schemes in this manner. In the German case, shifting the fiscal pressure associated with slower growth and higher unemployment from unemployment insurance, means-tested social assistance, and other social programs that are wholly or partially financed within the government budget to self-financed insurance schemes was central to the government's budget consolidation strategy in the 1980s and 1990s.

When all is said and done, the Dutch have been able to reverse the syndrome of "welfare without work" because they have been able to generate robust employment growth. As Wolfgang Streeck argues, any celebration of Germany's "success" in keeping wage inequality down and productivity growth up in the 1980s and 1990s must be tempered by recognizing Germany's "low activity problem" and the fiscal burden that it entails.[32] In the first instance, however, Germany's growing reliance on early retirement must surely be seen as a manifestation of its employment problem and not its underlying cause. More important for our present purposes, "welfare without work" is a syndrome pertaining to the continental welfare states in particular rather than all generous welfare states. The Nordic welfare states have traditionally been geared toward promoting labor force participation among older people as well as women. Having experienced a deep employment crisis in the 1990s, Sweden still has a higher employment rate among 55- to 64-year-olds than any of the liberal market economies. In 2000, 65.1 percent of Swedes in this age group were gainfully employed, as compared to 57.7 percent of Americans.[33]

That said, one might still wonder whether public provision of social welfare is somehow responsible for the poor employment performance of most of the social market economies in the 1980s and 1990s. In terms of growth of GDP per capita, as we have seen, countries with large welfare states (social market economies) seem to have performed, on average, just as well as countries with small welfare states (liberal market economies) over the last two decades, but the same cannot be said for employment growth. Plotting annual employment growth from 1990 to 2002 against average social spending in percent of GDP over the 1990–2001 period, we clearly observe a negative association between these variables. As figure 7.7 illustrates, Japan represents a major outlier in this respect, with virtually no employment growth despite a very small welfare state. The Japanese case notwithstanding, the association between high levels of social spending and slow employment growth is quite strong and consistent.

Combining figure 7.7 with evidence presented in the previous section, we might conclude that extensive public welfare provisions promote

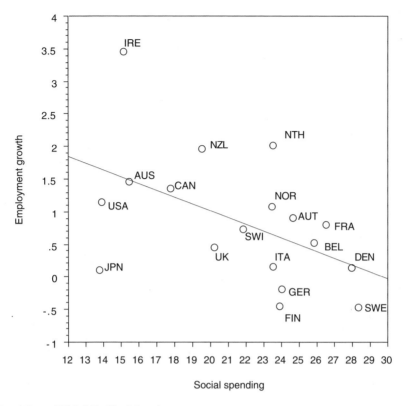

Correlation: −.501 (−.648 without Japan)
Sources: Tables 4.5 and 7.1.

Figure 7.7 Average annual growth of employment 1990–2002 vs. social spending in percent of GDP 1990–2001

reliance on productivity growth rather than employment growth as the engine of GDP growth. As suggested earlier, the welfare state might have this effect by boosting the productive potential of the labor force. In addition, public welfare provisions might discourage employment-intensive growth either by restricting the supply of labor or by imposing costs on employers and reducing their propensity to hire new workers. What can we learn from cross-national comparison about these causal mechanisms?

Along with the exit options provided by early retirement and disability insurance, the generosity of unemployment insurance is particularly germane to the question of labor supply. More so than early retirement and disability provisions, this dimension of cross-national policy variation lends itself to quantitative measurement. The logic of neoclassical economics and attendant critiques of the welfare state would lead us to expect

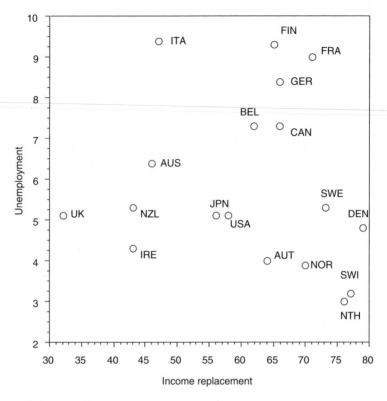

Sources: Tables 4.1 and 8.4.

Figure 7.8 Average rate of unemployment 2000–03 vs. net income replacement of unemployment insurance (percent) in 1999

the countries with the most generous unemployment compensation to have the highest rates of unemployment. The basic intuition at work here makes a great deal of sense: the generosity of unemployment benefits must surely affect the propensity of unemployed workers to accept the jobs available to them.

Several cross-national studies do indeed find that high unemployment benefits tend to be associated with higher rates of unemployment over the long run.[34] As figure 7.8 illustrates, however, this association is not immediately apparent if we plot unemployment rates against the net income replacement provided by unemployment insurance. In fact, there appears to be no consistent association at all between these variables: exactly half of our eighteen countries provide unemployment benefits in excess of 65 percent of previous income, and these nine countries encompass the entire range of unemployment outcomes. More decisively

176

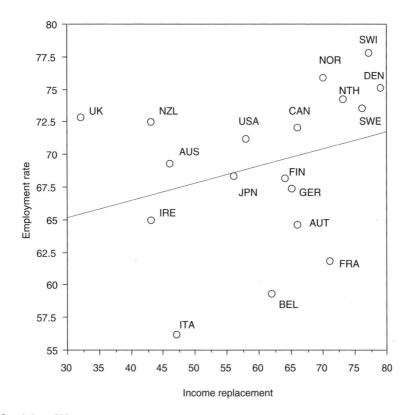

Correlation: .303
Sources: Tables 4.4 and 8.4.

Figure 7.9 Employment rate in 2003 vs. net income replacement of unemployment insurance (percent) in 1999

perhaps, figure 7.9 shows that higher levels of income support for the unemployed are not generally associated with lower rates of employment (employed as a percentage of the working-age population). To the contrary, figure 7.9 suggests that generous unemployment benefits may boost the rate of employment. Finding that this positive association between unemployment benefits and employment rates persists when we control for a variety of other factors that affect the employment rate, Stephen Nickell argues that high unemployment benefits make participation in the labor market more attractive.[35]

It should be noted that income replacement does not fully capture the generosity of unemployment insurance: we would also want to know what share of the labor force is covered by unemployment insurance and how long these benefits can be collected. The absence of any cross-national association between unemployment and the income replacement provided by unemployment insurance partly reflects the fact that some of the countries that provide generous income replacement restrict the duration of unemployment insurance benefits or at least make benefits contingent on recipients actively searching for employment. This is most notably true of the Nordic countries, which also spend large amounts of public monies on retraining and other active labor market programs designed to move unemployed workers back into employment. Along with Switzerland and the Netherlands, in figure 7.9 Denmark, Norway, and Sweden form a distinctive cluster, combining high employment rates with high levels of unemployment compensation.

The studies that do find that unemployment and income replacement are associated cross-nationally control for benefit duration and spending on active labor market policy. From this one might conclude that, everything else being equal, reducing the level of income replacement in unemployment insurance would indeed reduce the rate of unemployment. Alternatively, one might conclude that unemployment benefit generosity is not the key to the employment consequences of public policies vis-à-vis the unemployed and, more specifically, that the work disincentives that generosity entails can be and typically have been offset by the rules governing unemployment insurance and by positive measures to promote the employability of unemployed workers. In Nickell's judicious assessment, generous levels of unemployment benefit "do not appear to have serious implications for average levels of unemployment" so long as they "are accompanied by pressure on the unemployed to take jobs by, for example, fixing the duration of benefit and providing resources to raise the ability/willingness of the unemployed to take jobs."[36]

Turning to the demand side of the labor market, Fritz Scharpf argues persuasively that the structure of taxation has more important implications for employment than the level of taxation.[37] Scharpf distinguishes between, on the one hand, corporate and personal income taxes and, on the other hand, payroll and consumption taxes. Comparing OECD countries in the late 1990s, Scharpf finds that high payroll and consumption taxes tend to be associated with lower employment rates in the private sector and that this association is particularly strong for employment rates in service sectors characterized by low productivity and low wages (wholesale and retail trade, restaurants and hotels). In Scharpf's words,

> Consumption taxes reduce demand for all products, but they fall most heavily on services whose low productivity makes them vulnerable to automation on the one hand, and to self-service . . . or tax evasion on the other. Similarly, social security contributions are usually . . . raised as a proportional tax on total wages, with a cap at medium wage levels. Hence they fall heavily

on low-wage jobs, while the burden on highly productive jobs is relatively smaller. By contrast, personal income taxes are not collected on wages below a basic-income exemption, and since their rates are generally progressive, taxes on income elements that exceed the exemption begin at lower rates. Thus, the burden of income taxes on the cost of low-wage jobs tends to be minimal, and while they may have some effect on investments and on the ability of firms to attract high-wage professionals from low-tax countries, their negative impact on business employment is much weaker than is true of consumption taxes and social contributions.[38]

Across our eighteen countries, there is no consistent association between levels of income or consumption tax and overall employment growth from 1990 to 2002. Plotting annual employment growth against combined payroll and consumption taxes in the mid-1990s also does not yield any clear pattern of association. As figure 7.10 illustrates, however, such a pattern does emerge when we plot annual employment growth against levels of payroll taxation. Denmark and the Netherlands stand out as exceptional cases in this figure. Despite very low payroll taxes, Danish employment growth was relatively sluggish in the 1990s. On the other hand, the Dutch achieved rapid employment growth despite very high payroll taxes. Disregarding these two cases, we observe a strong negative association between employment growth and payroll taxes in figure 7.10.

Along with the evidence presented by Scharpf, figure 7.10 suggests that the social market economies of northern Europe might be able to boost employment growth by shifting the financing of public welfare provision from payroll taxes to income taxes. Since the latter form of taxation tends to be more progressive than the former, such a shift would render the welfare state more redistributive. Yet this prescription raises a political problem in that income taxes are more visible and more likely to generate resentment among voters than payroll taxes.[39] Moreover, unions and other supporters of the welfare state might resist such a shift to the extent that they believe that social programs financed by earmarked contributions are less vulnerable to cuts in a fiscal squeeze.

SUMMARY

The preceding analysis shows that the postwar expansion of the welfare state had a major impact on the distribution of income in the advanced capitalist countries. On a cross-national basis, welfare state largesse is closely associated with a more egalitarian distribution of disposable income and with a lower incidence of absolute as well as relative poverty. Overall redistribution and poverty alleviation typically go hand in hand. The redistributive effects of the more encompassing welfare states operate

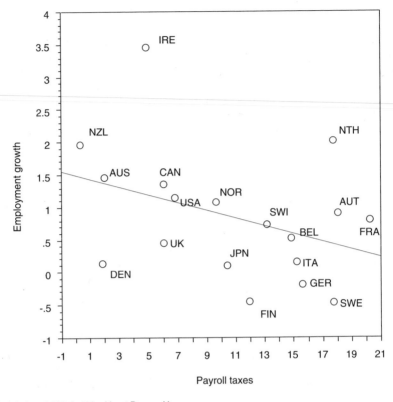

Correlation: −.382 (−.482 without Denmark)
Sources: Table 4.5 and Fritz Scharpf and Vivien Schmidt, eds., *Welfare and Work in the Open Economy* (Oxford: Oxford University Press, 2000), 363.

Figure 7.10 Average annual growth of employment 1990–2002 vs. payroll taxes in percent of GDP in 1997

primarily through the provision of benefits—services as well as cash payments. To the extent that they displace private mechanisms, even income-differentiated social insurance schemes have important redistributive effects. On the other hand, programs that specifically target the poor do not seem to enhance the redistributive impact of social spending. Such programs generally lack the broad-based political support necessary to sustain generous benefits.

We have also seen that cross-national comparison provides precious little support for the proposition that welfare state expansion undercuts economic growth and average living standards. For the 1960s and 1970s, the evidence is more consistent with the view that the public provision of social welfare strengthens the economy and improves its performance.

For the 1980s and 1990s, the evidence is more mixed: the growth-inhibiting and growth-enhancing effects of the welfare state seem to cancel each other out as far as GDP per capita is concerned. While high payroll taxes seem to have held back employment growth in the 1990s, there is little evidence to support the proposition that income support for the unemployed seriously restricts the supply of labor.

I do not wish to imply that all is well with Europe's large welfare states, nor do I wish to deny that certain taxes and social programs entail work disincentives or distort the efficient allocation of resources. Let me close with three basic points pertaining to disincentives and distortions. First, social policy should not be evaluated solely in terms of its effects on efficiency, growth, and employment. Its essentially social, redistributive objectives must always be kept in mind. To the extent that these objectives are met, some efficiency losses are acceptable. Second, the effects of social policy should be gauged against the outcomes produced by actually existing capitalist economies rather than an idealized "free market economy" in which the allocation of resources is perfectly efficient. Social policy is by no means the only source of distortions and inefficiencies in existing capitalist economies. Third, it is not very useful to think of this set of public policy problems in terms of "small vs. big government," as economists like Tanzi and Schuknecht are wont to do. The negative effects of social policy on efficiency and growth have more to do with the design of social programs than with aggregate levels of social spending.

CHAPTER 8

Welfare States in Retrenchment

Since the 1970s, conservative political parties and other political representatives of business interests have become increasingly outspoken in their criticisms of the welfare state. The strong rhetoric of Thatcherism and Reaganism represents the most obvious manifestation of this development, but more subtle versions of the new "anti-welfarism" appeared in virtually all of the OECD countries in the 1980s. As part of their efforts to restore sound public finances, even governments dominated by Social Democrats and other parties with strong traditional commitments to social protection and redistribution have in recent years cut back on some welfare entitlements and otherwise sought to curtail the growth of social expenditures.

It is commonplace to interpret these developments as a response to globalization, particularly the internationalization of capital markets and the dramatic increase of capital mobility that occurred over the last two decades. Across the OECD world, conventional wisdom holds that governments must reduce the tax burden and the work disincentives associated with generous public provisions of social welfare in order to be able to attract capital and to maintain (or regain) competitiveness in the global economy of the twenty-first century. By this logic, globalization can be expected to generate a "race to the bottom," with the social market economies being forced to scale down their generous welfare states and move toward the market-liberal model of a minimalist, partly privatized, social safety net.

Contesting this conventional wisdom, most scholarly studies stress the resilience of welfare states in the face of globalization and the ascendancy of market-liberal political rhetoric. These studies point out that recent social policy reforms have primarily involved cost savings at the margins—for example, less generous cost-of-living adjustments in the calculation of welfare benefits—and that the core components of postwar welfare states, such as public health care and public pension programs, remain intact and, indeed, continue to enjoy strong support in public opinion polls. Against the convergence implied by the globalization thesis, the scholarly literature also stresses the continued diversity of welfare states and the path-dependent nature of recent reform initiatives.[1]

This chapter provides a general overview of recent changes in the public provision of social welfare in the OECD countries and attempts to capture the common dynamics at work behind these changes. Let me emphasize at the outset that my goal is not to undertake a complete inventory of welfare-related changes in any particular country, let alone a careful assessment of the social and economic implications of specific reform initiatives. (In particular, the following discussion shies away from the highly technical issues involved in reforms of taxation and public pension systems.) The evidence presented below belies the idea that welfare states have entered an era of long-term decline, let alone that they are on the verge of imminent collapse, but it also calls into question the more sanguine versions of the resilience thesis. Major changes in the public provision of social welfare have indeed taken place, and many of these changes have been of a regressive nature. Commonly used in the existing literature, the term "welfare state retrenchment," itself ambiguous, seems to capture recent developments quite well. Most distinctively, perhaps, the following analysis yields some evidence of cross-national convergence among welfare states. I argue that this convergence does not derive from globalization, at least not in the way that simple-minded versions of the globalization thesis posit, and that the process of welfare state retrenchment cannot be understood simply in terms of the imperatives of economic efficiency. Politics are of central importance to the trajectories of contemporary welfare states.

AGGREGATE SOCIAL SPENDING TRENDS

As we saw in table 7.1, data on aggregate social spending, measured in percentage of GDP, clearly belie the notion of a general decline of the welfare state across the OECD countries. In only four of our eighteen countries did total social spending account for a smaller share of GDP in 2001 than in 1980. In only two cases, the Netherlands and Ireland, can we speak of a significant reduction in the size of the welfare state relative to GDP. On the other hand, we observe substantial increases of the share of GDP devoted to social spending in quite a few countries. In Finland,

Norway, Switzerland, Australia, France, Italy, and Japan, the share of GDP devoted to social spending increased by more than five percentage points; in the United Kingdom, it increased by more than four points; and in Austria, Germany, and Canada, it increased by at least three points. The British experience is particularly noteworthy: despite seventeen consecutive years of government by conservatives committed to rolling back the welfare state, social spending increased from 17.6 percent of GDP in 1980 to 24.4 percent in 1998.

As noted earlier, however, it is problematic to assess changes in welfare effort based on social spending expressed as a percentage of GDP. Suppose that we have two countries that devote the same share of GDP to social spending in a given year and that the amount of money spent on social programs grows by an annual rate of 5 percent in both countries (in real, inflation-adjusted terms). If real GDP grows by an annual rate of 5 percent in country A and 2 percent in country B, over a ten-year period social spending as a percentage of GDP will remain unchanged in country A but will increase significantly in country B. We would not necessarily want to conclude, based on this evidence, that country B has increased its welfare effort relative to country A.

Looking at growth rates of social spending per capita provides a more meaningful basis for comparing changes in welfare effort in this hypothetical but quite realistic example. Social spending per capita can readily be calculated by multiplying GDP per capita by the fraction of GDP devoted to social spending. Using GDP per capita in constant prices yields an inflation-adjusted growth rate of social spending per capita. Table 8.1 reports the results of this exercise for each of the last three decades of the twentieth century.

In contrast to the steady growth of social spending suggested by the data on social spending in percentage of GDP, we observe a very sharp deceleration of social spending growth on a per capita basis from the 1970s to the 1980s in virtually all of the OECD countries. In only two countries, Finland and Italy, did the average annual growth rate of social spending per capita in the 1980s exceed that of the preceding decade. The reduction of the growth rate was quite modest in Norway and Canada, but the growth rate of the 1980s was less than half that of the 1970s in Denmark, Sweden, Austria, Belgium, Germany, the Netherlands, and Japan and very nearly half that of the 1970s in Switzerland, Australia, Ireland, and New Zealand. From the 1980s to the 1990s, the rate of social spending growth decelerated sharply in the four countries in which it had held up in the 1980s (Finland, Norway, Canada, and Italy). The rate of spending growth recovered somewhat in Germany, Australia, the United States, and Japan and held steady in Austria from the 1980s to the 1990s, but the deceleration of spending growth continued in Denmark, Sweden,

Table 8.1 Average annual growth of total social spending per
capita, 1970–2000

	1970–80	1980–90	1990–2000
Nordic SMEs	**5.8**	**3.7**	**1.5**
Denmark	5.9	1.8	1.6
Finland	5.5	5.7	1.6
Norway	5.2	4.9	2.1
Sweden	6.6	2.2	0.7
Continental SMEs	**4.9**	**2.3**	**2.1**
Austria	5.2	2.5	2.5
Belgium	5.2	2.4	1.7
Germany	4.3	1.5	3.1
Netherlands	3.6	1.5	−0.4
Switzerland	6.1	3.8	3.6
LMEs	**5.5**	**3.3**	**2.6**
Australia	6.3	3.8	5.0
Canada	4.7	4.2	1.0
Ireland	6.8	3.4	3.3
New Zealand	6.9	3.5	0.2
United Kingdom	4.5	3.3	3.1
United States	3.9	1.8	2.8
France	4.9	3.7	1.8
Italy	4.1	4.4	1.6
Japan	12.3	4.1	4.8

Sources: Calculated with data from OECD Social Expenditure
Database (see table 7.1) and OECD, *National Accounts* (various
years).

Note: Figures refer to real (inflation-adjusted) social spending
per capita.

Belgium, the Netherlands, Switzerland, Ireland, New Zealand, the United
Kingdom, and France. In every one of the countries included in table 8.1,
the average annual growth rate of social spending per capita in the 1990s
was more than one percentage point lower than the growth rate of the
1970s. In thirteen out of eighteen countries, the 1990s growth rate was
less than half the 1970s growth rate.

It is important to keep in mind that the deceleration of social spending growth shown in table 8.1 coincides with a very substantial increase
of the share of the population that depends on public welfare provisions
to maintain a decent standard of living or, alternatively, to maintain their
relative position in the distribution of income. To begin with, in all of
these countries the elderly accounted for a larger percentage of the population in 2000 than it did in 1970. As documented in previous chapters,
moreover, unemployment increased sharply in most of these countries at
some point between 1975 and 1995, and in many countries wage inequality grew in the 1980s and 1990s. Measured on a per capita basis, social

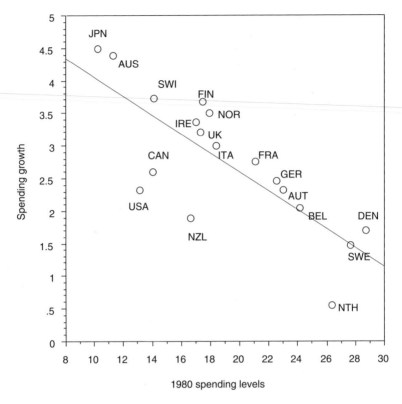

Source: Tables 7.1 and 8.1.

Figure 8.1 Average annual growth of social spending per capital 1980–2000 vs. social spending in percent of GDP, 1980

spending has continued to grow, but it seems implausible to argue that it has kept up with growing societal needs for public support. As the ranks of the elderly, the unemployed, and the working poor increased, maintaining the level of public welfare provision achieved in the 1970s would have required more rapid growth of social spending per capita.

The figures presented in table 8.1 do not appear to provide any support for the supposition that welfare state retrenchment (or stagnation) has been most pronounced in the liberal market economies. To the contrary, figure 8.1 shows that there is a strong negative correlation between size of the welfare state (in percent of GDP) in 1980 and subsequent growth of social spending per capita. In general, large welfare states have grown more slowly than small welfare states. To some degree, the OECD countries have converged with respect to aggregate social spending. This convergence might partly be explained in terms of what Peter Flora refers to as "growth to limits."[2] Arguably, the larger welfare states, notably Denmark, Sweden, Belgium, and the Netherlands, effectively provided a tightly meshed social safety net in 1980 and simply didn't need to grow in order to meet new welfare needs in the 1980s and 1990s. Alternatively, the association between size and growth shown in figure 8.1 might reflect political resistance to further tax increases in the larger welfare states.

As previous research has shown, the politically acceptable rate of taxation varies across countries, depending both on the form of taxation and the types of benefits provided by the government. With respect to forms of taxation, the standard argument, noted earlier, is that income taxes tend to generate more resistance than indirect taxes, such as payroll and value-added taxes.[3] With respect to types of benefits, the standard argument is that means-tested welfare programs tend to generate more taxpayer resistance than broad entitlement programs based on universalistic principles—as illustrated, for example, by the privileged status of Social Security in the politics of welfare retrenchment in the United States.[4] Still, it seems reasonable to suppose that, all else being equal, the potential for tax fatigue increases with the tax burden.

ALTERNATIVE INDICATORS OF RETRENCHMENT

An alternative way to approach the question of assessing changes in the public provision of social welfare is to identify specific societal needs that are addressed through social spending and then to ask to what extent the public sector's role in the satisfaction of these needs has changed. In this spirit, table 8.2 provides data on public health expenditures as a percentage of total health expenditures in 1980 and 1997. In eleven out of eighteen countries, we see some evidence of privatization of health care over this time period. This holds for all the Nordic countries and the majority of liberal market economies as well as France, Italy, and the Netherlands. As figure 8.2 illustrates, the data presented in table 8.2 again point to a degree of convergence among the OECD countries. There is clearly a catch-up component of this convergence, as public spending has expanded in countries that had less public involvement in the provision of health care in the 1970s. Again, however, the "growth to limits" thesis fails to explain why we observe a rather extensive privatization of health spending in countries where government finance already accounted for the bulk of health care costs in the 1970s (most notably Norway, Sweden, and Italy).

The privatization of health care is partly a matter of increased co-payments within public health care systems, both in systems based on health insurance and systems based on direct delivery of services, and

Table 8.2 Public health expenditures in percent of total
health expenditures, 1980–97

	1980	2001	Change
Nordic SMEs	**89**	**81**	**−8**
Denmark	85	84	−1
Finland	79	76	−3
Norway	98	82	−16
Sweden	93	83	−10
Continental SMEs	**74**	**76**	**+2**
Austria	69	73	+4
Belgium	83	88	+5
Germany	75	77	+2
Netherlands	75	73	−2
Switzerland	68	70	+2
LMEs	**73**	**70**	**−3**
Australia	63	67	+4
Canada	75	70	−5
Ireland	82	77	−5
New Zealand	84	77	−7
United Kingdom	89	85	−4
United States	42	46	+4
France	79	74	−5
Italy	81	70	−11
Japan	71	80	+9

Source: Adapted from Evelyne Huber and John Stephens, *Development and Crisis of the Welfare State* (Chicago: University of Chicago Press, 2001), table A.8.

partly a matter of the growth of supplementary private medical insurance. In the British case, Conservative tax policies subsidized the growth of private medical insurance in the 1980s. To the extent that it reflects the growth of private insurance, privatization does not necessarily entail a deterioration of the benefits provided by public health care. Indeed, one might suspect that in countries with strong public health care systems that adequately provide for basic needs, private health spending is primarily a matter of satisfying "frivolous" health care needs, such as cosmetic surgery. As societal norms change, however, it is far from obvious where to draw the line between frivolous and basic services. And, at least to some extent, the resort to private insurance by well-to-do households might be seen as a response to deterioration in the quality of public health care. Waiting lines certainly became a common complaint about public health services in the United Kingdom, Sweden, and other countries in the 1980s. Though I do not wish to exaggerate the extent to which this logic is currently unfolding, the political implications of privatization are clear and, from a progressive perspective, quite ominous: to the extent that the

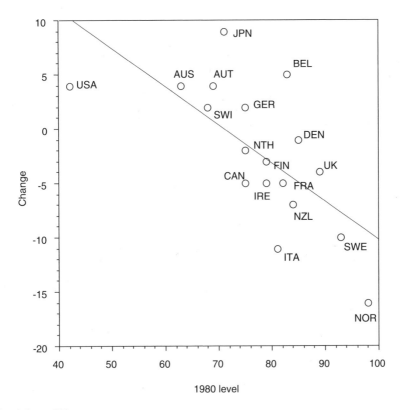

Correlation: −.682
Source: Table 8.2.

Figure 8.2 Change in government's share of total health expenditures 1980–97 vs. government's share of total health expenditures, 1980

well-to-do opt out of public welfare systems, their willingness to pay the taxes that support such systems is bound to diminish.

The size of the public sector labor force provides an indirect indicator of the extent of welfare state retrenchment. Unfortunately, the OECD's *Historical Statistics* only provides information on government employment as a percentage of total employment through the mid-1990s. As with social spending expressed in percent of GDP, the metric of this time series suffers from an obvious denominator problem. During a general employment contraction like that experienced by many countries in the early 1990s, the public sector's share of total employment may increase even though the public sector labor force shrinks. Since the OECD's *Labour Force Statistics* reports the total number of people employed, however, the denominator problem can be avoided by converting the government's

Table 8.3 Percentage change in government employment
from peak to most recent observation

	Peak year	% change
Nordic SMEs		
Denmark	1997	
Finland	1991	−1.5
Norway*	1995	
Sweden	1990	−15.5
Continental SMEs		
Austria*	1995	
Belgium	1992	−7.9
Germany	1992	−9.0
Netherlands*	1990	−2.8
Switzerland*	1995	
LMEs		
Australia*	1987	−11.1
Canada	1995	−0.4
Ireland	1987	−5.3
United Kingdom*	1988	−30.2
United States	1994	−5.2
France	1997	
Italy	1992	−7.3
Japan	1996	−0.6

Source: OECD, *Historical Statistics* (various years).
Note: Most recent observation is 1997 unless marked by an asterisk, in which case it is 1995.

share of total employment into thousands of government employees. Table 8.3 reports percentage changes in the number of government employees from its all-time peak to the most recent available observation (1995 or 1997). In twelve out of seventeen countries, we observe a decline in the number of people employed by the government since its all-time peak, and in several countries this decline has been quite pronounced. In the United Kingdom, the public sector labor force declined by a whopping 30 percent from 1988 to 1997.

The figures in table 8.3 refer to all forms of government employment other than employment in state-owned enterprises. Thus the figures include tax inspectors, police officers, and postal workers, as well as people employed in the production of welfare-related services. In the absence of any comparative dataset that allows us to track changes in different types of government employment, suffice it to note that employment in Britain's National Health Service fell by 7.7 percent from 1985 to 1994, while employment in Sweden's public health care system fell by 12 percent from 1992 to 1998.[5] In neither the United Kingdom nor Sweden was welfare-related employment specifically targeted for cutbacks in the 1980s or 1990s. Rather, cuts in welfare-related employment were part of a broader effort to reduce the size of the public sector labor force. This point holds more generally for public spending: as a percentage of total government outlays, social spending increased in the majority of countries, including all the liberal market economies, in the first half of the 1990s.

Productivity growth in the public sector may have partly offset the consequences of employment cuts for the range and quality of public services. For instance, changes in medical technology have drastically reduced the length of hospital stays associated with various kinds of surgery. It is difficult to believe, however, that employment cuts on the scale registered not only in the United Kingdom and Sweden, but also Australia, Germany, Belgium, and Italy have not been associated with some deterioration in the quality of public services. Moreover, privatization and market-oriented public sector reforms have contributed to inegalitarian labor market trends. In most countries, public employers led the way in eliminating discriminatory employment practices during the 1960s and 1970s, and the distribution of wages in the public sector has traditionally been more compressed than the distribution of wages in the private sector.[6] Though fragmentary, the available evidence indicates that, alongside privatization of public services, the 1990s marked a new trend toward increased differentiation of pay and other employment conditions within the public sector in many countries.

Yet another way to assess changes in the public provision of welfare is to look at the level of income replacement provided by various transfer programs. For two major transfer programs, unemployment compensation and sick-pay insurance, table 8.4 tracks changes in net (post-tax) income replacement from 1985 to 1999. For unemployment compensation, we observe cuts in net income replacement rates in fifteen out of seventeen countries. In particular, Ireland, Denmark, the Netherlands, Belgium, Sweden, New Zealand, and the United States significantly reduced the generosity of unemployment benefits over this period. For sick-pay insurance, cuts can also be observed in twelve out of seventeen countries, with the largest cuts occurring in Ireland, Denmark, Finland, New Zealand, and the Netherlands.

A handful of countries began to cut replacement rates provided by unemployment and sick-pay insurance prior to 1985, but earlier cuts were typically quite modest. However, table 8.4 fails to capture the very drastic cuts undertaken by Conservative British governments in the first half of the 1980s. In the United Kingdom, net income replacement for unemployment insurance and sick-pay insurance alike fell from 63 percent in 1975 to 35 percent in 1985. Also, it should be noted that the figures in table 8.4 only tell us about the benefits that fully insured individuals

Table 8.4 Net income replacement rates of unemployment compensation and sick pay insurance, 1985–99

	Unemployment compensation			Sick pay insurance		
	1985	1999	Change	1985	1999	Change
Nordic SMEs	**76**	**68**	**−8**	**89**	**80**	**−9**
Denmark	79	64	−15	79	64	−15
Finland	71	65	−6	89	74	−15
Norway	71	70	−1	100	100	0
Sweden	83	73	−10	91	83	−8
Continental SMEs	**74**	**69**	**−5**	**84**	**82**	**−2**
Austria	65	64	−1	77	80	+3
Belgium	73	62	−11	77	80	+3
Germany	67	66	−1	100	94	−6
Netherlands	88	76	−12	86	76	−10
Switzerland	78	77	−1	82	81	−1
LMEs	**55**	**48**	**−7**	**54**	**46**	**−8**
Australia	43	46	+3	45	46	+1
Canada	69	66	−3	69	66	−3
Ireland	65	43	−22	65	43	−22
New Zealand	52	43	−9	55	43	−12
United Kingdom	35	32	−3	36	32	−4
United States	67	58	−9			
France	73	71	−3	62	61	−1
Italy				81	75	−6
Japan	55	56	+1	55	56	+1

Source: Adapted from James Allan and Lyle Scruggs, "Political Partisanship and Welfare State Reform in Advanced Industrial Societies," *American Journal of Political Science* 48 (3): 500.

Note: Net replacement is defined as the average net income replacement for (a) a fully insured single worker earning the average production worker (APW) wage and (b) a fully insured couple with a single APW wage and two children.

receive under these social insurance programs: they do not tell us about the share of the labor that is covered by these programs, nor the duration of benefits. It seems quite likely that retrenchment has occurred on these dimensions as well, if only because of the growth of temporary and part-time employment in many countries. Plotting changes in unemployment replacement rates from 1985 to 1999 against 1985 levels, we again observe some degree of convergence among the OECD countries, as figure 8.3 illustrates. Though this pattern is less pronounced than for the growth of social spending per capita and for the share of public health expenditures in total health expenditures, it is generally the case that countries with more generous unemployment compensation provisions have cut back more than countries with less generous provisions.

The drastic reduction of unemployment insurance benefits in the United Kingdom in the 1980s clearly entailed a reduction of income support for the unemployed. Equally important, however, cumulative cuts

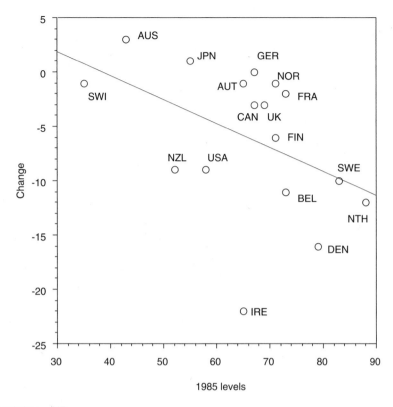

Correlation: −.447
Source: Table 8.4.

Figure 8.3 Change in unemployment compensation 1985–99 vs. level of unemployment compensation in 1985

of unemployment benefits were part of a shift in the nature of public income support for the unemployed. In the course of the 1980s, British unemployment compensation became less of a universal entitlement than it had previously been, and unemployed people increasingly came to rely on means-tested social assistance (the so-called Supplementary Benefit) for income support.[7] Successive governments headed by Margaret Thatcher engineered a similar shift in the orientation of housing policy. While the government stopped subsidizing public housing ("council estates" run by local authorities), it increased rent subsidies paid out to poor households. In the end, the enduring legacy of Thatcherite social policy reforms is not so much that benefits to the poor were cut in the 1980s, though that clearly did happen, but rather that the terms on which benefits were disbursed were changed. Overall, the share of means-tested assistance in total social spending increased in the United Kingdom from 19.5 percent in 1980 to 28.4 percent in 1993.[8]

Though we lack systematic cross-national data on this, it appears to be the case that the relative importance of means-tested welfare benefits increased in many other countries in the 1980s and 1990s. In part, this is simply a result of the growing number of low-income households that qualify for such benefits; in part, it would seem to reflect a conscious effort by government officials to increase the "efficiency" of social spending in alleviating poverty. As suggested in the previous chapter, increased reliance on means-testing represents a problematic solution to rising inequality and poverty from a political point of view. In the short run and in a narrow, technical sense, targeting social spending on the poor may well produce a larger poverty-reduction effect for any given amount of social spending. But over the long run and in a broader, political sense, targeting benefits on the poor is likely to weaken middle-class support for the welfare state and reduce the generosity of the welfare state.

CONSEQUENCES FOR REDISTRIBUTION

Have welfare states become less redistributive as a result of the deceleration of total spending growth and the benefit cuts documented above? Table 8.5 addresses this question based on data from the Luxembourg Income Study. While the first column reports on changes in the combined redistributive of taxes and income transfers from the mid-1980s to the mid-1990s, the second column reports on the redistributive effects of income transfers. As in chapter 7 (tables 7.3 and 7.4), total redistribution is here defined as the difference between Gini coefficients for disposable income and gross (pre-tax) market income expressed as a percentage of gross market income, and redistribution through transfers is defined as the difference between Gini coefficients for disposable income and net (post-tax) market income expressed as a percentage of net market income. Again, the data used to calculate Gini coefficients are restricted to working-age households (that is, households headed by individuals aged 25 to 59).

The evidence presented in table 8.5 is quite mixed. In Norway, the reduction of the Gini coefficient produced by taxes and transfers increased from 21.7 percent in 1986 to 30.0 percent in 2000. At the opposite end of the spectrum, the reduction of the Gini coefficient produced by taxes and transfers in the Netherlands declined from 33.9 percent in 1987 to 26.0 percent in 1999. In both these cases, the change in redistribution through transfers alone was significantly greater than the change in total redistribution, suggesting that Norwegian taxation

Table 8.5 Change in redistribution among working-age
households from the mid-1980s to the late 1990s

	Taxes and transfers	Transfers
Nordic SMEs		
Denmark (1987–97)	+2.4	+3.8
Finland (1987–00)	+0.2	+6.1
Norway (1986–00)	+8.3	+10.9
Sweden (1987–00)	–1.2	–1.2
Continental SMEs		
Belgium (1988–97)		–1.5
Germany (1984–00)	+4.6	+3.6
Netherlands (1987–99)	–7.9	–11.3
Switzerland (1982–92)	+2.1	+3.7
LMEs		
Australia (1985–94)	+3.2	+2.6
Canada (1987–98)	+2.9	+2.5
United Kingdom (1986–99)	–4.3	–4.1
United States (1986–00)	–0.8	–1.8
France (1984–94)		+4.7
Italy (1986–00)		–3.1

Definitions and Sources: See tables 7.3 and 7.4.

became less redistributive while Dutch taxation became more redistributive over this period. In the United Kingdom, both taxes and income transfers became less redistributive from 1986 to 1999, though the reduction of redistribution was not nearly as large as in the Netherlands. We also observe some reduction of redistribution in Sweden, the United States, Belgium, and Italy. On the other hand, we observe significant increases in redistribution through transfers for Denmark, Finland, Germany, Switzerland, Australia, Canada, and France. In Denmark, Finland, and Switzerland, these increases were partly offset by less redistribution through taxation. Taxes as well as transfers became more redistributive in Germany, Australia, and Canada.

The very large reduction of redistribution through transfers that has occurred in the Netherlands reflects the shrinkage of the Dutch welfare state over the last fifteen years. As documented above, the Netherlands is the only country in which real social spending per capita declined in the 1990s. In addition, it deserves to be recalled that the Netherlands is the only country in which inequality in market income among working-age households actually declined in the 1980s and 1990s. With the latter observation in mind, figure 8.4 plots changes in redistribution through income transfers against percentage changes in Gini coefficients for net

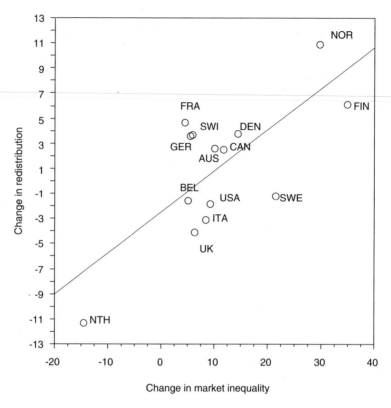

Correlation: −.727
Source: See tables 3.2 and 7.3.

Figure 8.4 Change in redistribution through transfers vs. percentage change in Gini coefficient for net market income, working-age households, mid-1980s to late 1980s

market income among working-age households over the country-specific time periods indicated in table 8.5. These variables turn out to be positively associated with each other. It is immediately clear from Figure 8.4 that the Dutch, Norwegian, and Finnish data points influence this association to a very large degree, but most of the data points in the middle of the scatterplot conform to the regression line defined by these extreme cases. With the notable exception of Sweden, increasing market inequality appears to have rendered welfare states more redistributive. (Sweden is exceptional in that redistribution through transfers declined despite a comparatively large increase of market inequality.) As unemployment and inequality have grown, an increasing number of low-income households have become eligible for unemployment and other social benefits and have come to depend on such programs for a larger share of their total income. Even though the benefits provided by the welfare state are no longer as generous as they once were, their redistributive effects have increased in the context of inegalitarian labor market trends.[9]

As we saw in chapter 3, the distribution of disposable income has become more inegalitarian in all OECD countries except the Netherlands (and arguably Ireland) since the early 1980s. Welfare states have failed to keep up with the rise of inequality generated by market forces, but most welfare states have nevertheless compensated for rising market inequality. Even in Sweden and other countries where this compensation did not occur, the welfare state continues to play an important redistributive role.

PRESSURES AND POLITICS OF RETRENCHMENT

The deceleration of social spending growth that began in the second half of the 1970s coincided with a major slowdown of economic growth across the OECD world. The implications of slow economic growth for the public provision of social welfare are straightforward. During an economic downturn, rising unemployment and declining real wages at the bottom of the income distribution generate more government spending as more people claim unemployment insurance benefits and qualify for means-tested supplementary income support and housing subsidies. On the other hand, the revenue base of the welfare state shrinks as fewer people work and average real incomes stagnate or decline. Unless governments can finance new spending by borrowing, taxes must be raised or benefits cut. Though self-interested individuals should be willing to pay higher taxes to insure themselves against unemployment under these circumstances, income stagnation makes tax increases less acceptable. Workers who enjoy some degree of protection against unemployment by virtue of skills or seniority are most likely to look for tax relief as compensation for income losses or foregone income gains.[10] In the short run, an economic slowdown boosts social spending, but persistent slow growth is likely to generate electoral support for cuts in social benefits.

The argument here is not that the welfare state expansion sooner or later runs into some inherent tax fatigue barrier. The point is rather that the level of taxation becomes a contentious political issue under conditions of slow growth, regardless of the initial level of taxation. This said, the experience of German unification illustrates that it is still possible, under some circumstances, to convince voters to accept higher levels of taxation in the name of national solidarity. Also, the argument that slow growth generates tax resistance hinges on the proposition that a sizable segment of the population is not directly threatened by unemployment. Relative to liberal market economies, social market economies provide more extensive protection of "insiders" against job loss and should therefore be particularly susceptible to the logic of slow growth generating tax resistance.[11] This may explain, at least in part, why social spending has tended to grow more slowly in the social market economies, especially the continental SMEs, over the last two decades.

The pressures on the welfare state generated by slow growth are, of course, closely linked to the pressures of population ageing. Over the long run, sustained employment and productivity growth are necessary preconditions for the political viability of the generous pension provisions introduced during the era of postwar growth. Though many countries have cut pensions and other benefits to the elderly over the last two decades, such cuts have been quite minor by comparison to cuts in support to the unemployed, the working poor, and their children.[12] The political logic at work here is not hard to understand, for the elderly are better organized and more likely to vote than the unemployed and the working poor. In the face of fiscal constraints, spending on elderly has, to some extent, squeezed out other forms of social spending. As suggested in chapter 7, the contribution of social spending to economic growth has diminished as a result of this trend, which has been most pronounced in Europe's social market economies because their provisions for the elderly are more generous and because the elderly account for a larger share of their population.

What, then, does globalization add to this picture of welfare states strained by demographic pressures and constrained by slow growth? The most recent and comprehensive investigation of this question is Duane Swank's book *Global Capital, Political Institutions, and Policy Change in Developed Welfare States*. Pooling observations from our eighteen countries over the 1965–93 period and controlling for a range of other relevant variables, Swank finds that higher levels of international trade are associated with higher rather than lower levels of welfare spending. This finding confirms the historical association between international trade and size of government noted by Katzenstein and a number of other scholars (see chapter 7). More surprisingly, perhaps, Swank finds no evidence to support the proposition that capital mobility has constrained welfare state expansion across these eighteen countries. To the contrary, Swank's regression results indicate that more liberal rules governing cross-border capital movements and borrowing on international capital markets are associated with greater social welfare effort, while his other three indicators of "global capital" (total cross-border capital flows, foreign direct investment, and interest rate differentials) do not have any statistically significant association with social welfare effort.[13]

Proponents of the globalization thesis might retort that Swank's analysis is already dated or that the consequences of globalization have yet to play themselves out fully. Another possible objection is that Swank's analysis focuses on cross-national variation in social welfare effort rather than common trends across the OECD countries. It may well be that globalization has been a source of downward pressure on the public provision of social welfare in all these countries. So long as this pressure does not disproportionately affect large, generous welfare states, it would not be captured by the kind of analysis undertaken by Swank and most other studies of comparative welfare state development.[14] The one conclusion that we can safely draw from these analyses is that the evidence available to date does not support the proposition that globalization has generated a "race to the bottom" with regard to the public provision of social welfare. Along the lines suggested above, other considerations must be invoked to account for the partial convergence of advanced welfare states that we observe for the 1980s and 1990s.

As we saw in chapter 7, there are good reasons to believe that some social programs actually contribute to labor productivity and competitiveness, and there is no clear-cut evidence in support of the claim that high levels of social spending dampen economic growth. To the extent that public welfare provisions promote—or at least do not undercut—productivity and competitiveness, there is no reason to expect productive capital to exit countries with large, generous welfare provisions as barriers to capital mobility are removed. The absence of any strong negative effects of globalization on social welfare efforts can thus be interpreted as support of the arguments and evidence presented in chapter 7.

That said, it should be noted that Swank does find that globalization exerts downward pressure of social welfare effort in interaction with fiscal deficits. The integration of world financial markets probably makes it cheaper for governments to borrow money when economic conditions are favorable, but it also constrains their ability to use deficit spending as an instrument of counter-cyclical management. In Swank's words, "The principal piece of evidence that supports a general role for globalization concerns the internationally generated pressure national policy makers face under conditions of notable fiscal imbalance . . . ; it is in this context—where national policy makers experience increasingly large interest rate premiums and other adverse conditions that international capital markets impose . . .—that higher levels of international capital mobility have a negative impact on the welfare state."[15]

To the extent that capital mobility poses a problem for the public provision of social welfare, the problem primarily has to do with financial capital, debt, and currency markets, rather than with corporate decisions about where to locate production. Put differently, globalization does not make social spending less rational from the point of view of the "real economy," but it makes it more imperative that social spending (as well as any other government spending) be directly financed with tax revenues. The implications of globalization thus bring us back to the problem of slow growth and tax fatigue. The conventional globalization argument implies that the link between economic growth and welfare state expansion has been severed: even under favorable macro-economic conditions, the welfare state must shrink in the new era of capital mobility. More plausibly, I think, the effect of globalization is to *reinforce* the link between economic growth and welfare state expansion.

I argued in chapter 5 that the creation of a single currency potentially provides the member states of the European Union with more room for fiscal expansion. However, there can be no doubt that the short-term effect of the agreement to form a single currency area was to constrain government spending, reinforcing the constraints imposed by global financial markets. The fiscal implications of European integration, a distinctively regional form of economic interdependence, add to our understanding of why larger welfare states did not grow as quickly as smaller welfare states in the 1990s.

It should be noted here that the direct social policy implications of European integration have been and will likely remain quite limited and certainly do not account for any of the major welfare-related reforms undertaken by various member states of the European Union in the 1980s and 1990s.[16] In the late 1980s and early 1990s, there was a lot of talk within the European Union about the need to agree on common minimum social policy standards to curtail the potential for a race to the bottom as firms and investors increasingly operated on a European-wide basis. Over the last decade, however, the only legislation coming out of the EU in this area pertains to working hours, parental leave provisions, employee representation inside companies, and employment conditions for temporary employees. None of these measures touch directly on social programs that involve significant spending by the member states.

As interpreted by the European Court of Justice in the 1970s, EU law provides for cross-border portability of social insurance benefits (retirement benefits earned in one country can be collected while residing in another) and also prohibits gender discrimination in the design of social programs (e.g., the retirement age of men and women must be the same). More importantly, EU law stipulates that the member states must not discriminate on the basis of nationality. If a country provides some benefits to all its citizens, it must provide the same benefits to any and all EU citizens residing in the country. This poses a potential political problem to the extent that foreigners might be perceived as "poaching" on citizen entitlements, and this circumstance might encourage governments to move to insurance-based social programs in which benefits are a function of how much one has paid into the program (i.e., years of employment). However, the insurance principle is already widespread, and there is little indication that the poaching problem has animated the politics of welfare state retrenchment thus far.

In a different vein, welfare state retrenchment might be seen as a manifestation of common political trends in the OECD countries. Much of the literature on comparative welfare state development emphasizes that trade unions and the labor-affiliated parties of the left played an important role in promoting the postwar expansion of social programs, especially public services and more redistributive programs. Indeed, the OECD-wide deceleration of social spending growth coincided with a sharp decline of government participation by parties of the left between 1975 and 1985. Generalizing across the OECD countries, left parties' share of cabinet portfolios fell sharply over this period while their share of legislative seats remained constant.[17] This suggests that centrist parties, which had previously governed in coalition with Social Democrats, moved to the right, preferring to form coalition governments with conservatives.

However we assess the lasting consequences of their efforts to "roll back the state" in the 1980s, it is clear that conservatives committed to the market-liberal model as the solution to all economic and social problems ultimately failed to sustain their political ascendancy. In the course of the 1990s, left parties scored an impressive series of electoral victories and regained much of the political power they had lost in the previous decade. It is equally clear, however, that left parties retreated from their commitment to welfare state expansion in the 1990s, accommodating themselves to new economic and political conditions.

Arguably, the rightward policy drift of the left or, perhaps more accurately, the new "centrism" of the left reflects a decline of union membership and of the capacity of unions to mobilize workers politically. Yet it would surely be a mistake to identify the fate of the welfare state too closely with the fate of the unionized industrial working class. It is certainly not the case that the core constituencies of the welfare state have shrunk over the last two decades. Quite the contrary, economic insecurity has been on the rise in all the OECD countries, in the sense of income volatility as well as employment insecurity, and has reached ever deeper into the ranks of the middle class as a result of globalization and related changes in economic structure.[18] With rising inequality, the percentage of voters who stand to gain from redistributive policies has increased as well. And, again, the ranks of the elderly have steadily increased in relation to the population as a whole. In short, societal demand for the public provision of social welfare has increased rather than diminished. The political problem is that, with the exception of the elderly, the main beneficiaries of such policies are less well-organized and amenable to mobilization today than they were twenty or thirty years ago.

SUMMARY

There are two ways to look at the evidence on welfare state retrenchment in the OECD countries. On the one hand, we might say that welfare states have held up reasonably well under conditions of austerity and that they have counteracted the rise of inequality. On the other hand, we might say that welfare states have failed to keep up with inegalitarian market forces and that the public provision of social welfare has become less generous in most (if not all) countries. Both statements being true, the debate about the extent of welfare state retrenchment largely becomes a question of whether the proverbial glass is half full or half empty.

In a sense, the evidence on convergence among OECD welfare states is more decisive. Again, this convergence does not seem to derive from some abstract, overarching logic of globalization. More concretely, the preceding discussion suggests that larger, more generous welfare states have been more constrained by the combination of slow growth, a rise in welfare claimants, political resistance to tax increases, and the fiscal constraints imposed by globalization in general and European integration in particular. Also, it should be underscored that cross-national convergence is not simply about constraints. As illustrated most clearly by the data on health expenditures, the other side to the story of convergence is the continued expansion of some of the smaller, less generous welfare states in certain areas of social welfare provision.

I hasten to add that most of the welfare-related changes that have taken place over the last twenty years have been of an incremental character or, at most, have involved the overhaul of specific social programs. The United Kingdom and New Zealand are the only cases in which we can speak of a coherent effort to restructure the welfare state as a whole—and even in these cases "dismantling" is clearly not the appropriate characterization. To the extent that overarching structural changes can be observed in other countries—for instance, a shift to means-tested social assistance—these changes have not been a result of political design but rather a result of changes in the way existing social programs function under new economic and social circumstances. In general, the historical distinctions among Nordic, continental European, and Anglo-American welfare states remain valid.

In many countries, especially the Nordic countries, cost containment has clearly been the primary motivation for cuts in social benefits. While we do observe the restoration of some cuts as economic conditions improved in the late 1990s, however, it is noteworthy that recent improvements in public welfare provisions have generally been more cautious and piecemeal than the cuts that preceded them. This observation illustrates my main reservation about the literature that emphasizes the resilience of welfare states. Given the comprehensive nature of the Swedish welfare state and the huge increase of unemployment benefits claimants in the 1991–93 period, it is easy to justify the decision to cut the income replacement provided by unemployment insurance from 90 percent to 80 percent as a necessary measure, with relatively minor implications for the welfare of the unemployed. But it would be a mistake to assess each change in the public provision of social welfare in isolation. Welfare state retrenchment must be seen as a cumulative and fundamentally political process. As suggested above, some of the changes that have occurred over the last twenty years—partial privatization of health care, marketization of public services, and transition to means-tested income support—have long-term political implications that render the mobilization of public support for the welfare state more difficult. I do not wish to imply that the political dynamics involved here are irreversible. My point is that defenders of the welfare state need to take these dynamics into account as they articulate solutions to immediate social policy problems.

CHAPTER 9

Directions for Progressive Reform

I begin this chapter by addressing the significance of the growth of financial markets in Europe since the 1980s. I argue that this development does not necessarily undermine the viability of the social market model. Second, I will revisit the question of the trade-off between equality and efficiency and try to articulate some reasons why such a trade-off does not appear in aggregate cross-national data. Third, I will propose a progressive approach to reforming social market economies that addresses the problem of employment growth. Finally, I will briefly address the implications of my analysis for progressive reform in liberal market economies.

THE END OF ORGANIZED CAPITALISM?

Building on ideas that feature prominently in the comparative political economy literature, I argued in chapter 2 that the social market economies of northern and central Europe are part of a larger universe of organized or coordinated capitalism. In the language of the Varieties of Capitalism school, the social market economies represent a variant of "coordinated market economies"; in the language of Wolfgang Streeck, they are part of the universe of "non-liberal capitalism."[1] In comparison to Anglo-American capitalism, this other type of capitalism involves more cooperative relations among firms in a variety of spheres. Again, the existing literature suggests that the structure of corporate finance, ownership, and governance is the key to this contrast between these two varieties of capitalism. In Japan, France, and Italy as well as the SMEs that have been the focus of my attention, stock markets have traditionally played a less prominent role, ownership has been more concentrated, and banks have played a more important role in corporate affairs than in the LMEs. Long-term stakeholders have dominated over more footloose shareholders.

The merits of bank-based systems of corporate finance relative to market-based systems and of insider systems of corporate governance relative to outsider systems have long been and still remain a subject of debate among scholars as well as newspaper columnists.[2] Critics typically charge that insider systems of corporate governance are incestuous and that insiders derive benefits that lead them to accept lower rates of return on capital rather than seeking to maximize shareholder value. Also, it is often suggested that banks are by nature conservative and that bank involvement in corporate finance and governance will stymie innovation and growth. On the other hand, proponents of organized capitalism argue that markets do not provide for effective control of corporate management. Monitoring management entails costs, and in an American-style system, with large equity markets and dispersed ownership of companies, individual shareholders do not have sufficient incentive to bear these costs. Instead, they will free-ride on the monitoring efforts of other shareholders or simply exit from firms that do not perform according to their expectations. In the coordinated market economies, banks and owners have more resources (better information access, for example) as well as a greater incentive to monitor management effectively, all of which enhances micro-economic efficiency. A slightly different line of argument holds that reliance on bank finance or strategic owners enables companies to undertake investments in training, production organization, and new products that will only pay off over a long period of time. By this logic, the implications of corporate finance and governance should not be assessed in terms of aggregate economic growth rates: the point is rather that different arrangements generate qualitatively different production strategies.[3]

This is certainly not the place to try to settle this debate about the economic implications of alternative systems of corporate finance and governance. Suffice it to say that much of the comparative political economy literature suggests that the existence of "patient capital" was a necessary precondition, along with strong labor movements, for the emergence of the labor market institutions and welfare state arrangements characteristic of Europe's social market economies in the postwar era. From this perspective, a number of recent European developments seem to call into question the long-term viability of the social market model.[4]

As European stock markets boomed in the 1990s, households shifted their savings from bank deposits to mutual funds and other market-based financial instruments. Also, the member states of the European Union removed legal obstacles to foreign ownership of corporate shares as part of the Single Market Program adopted in 1985, allowing American institutional investors to enter European corporate equity markets on a large scale. As large companies have grown and become more multinational in their orientation, they have increasingly come to rely on international bond markets for long- as well as short-term borrowing. A number of large European corporations also listed their shares on American stock exchanges in the 1990s.

The years leading up to the introduction of the Euro saw a huge boom of mergers and acquisitions in Europe. In 1999, deals involving European firms added up to a record $1.5 trillion, more than the combined value of all mergers and acquisitions from 1990 to 1994. Mergers between firms from the same country still accounted for a majority of mergers in the late 1990s, but cross-border mergers certainly became more common. Though the vast majority of mergers and acquisitions were friendly, a handful of hostile takeovers made big headlines and accounted for roughly a quarter of the total value of European mergers and acquisitions in 1999.[5] Perhaps most importantly, equity-based ties between companies declined in the 1990s. Relative to market capitalization in the European Union, not including the United Kingdom, corporate cross-shareholdings fell from about 18 percent in 1995 to less than 12 percent in 1999, according to the *Economist*.[6] Since the late 1980s, German banks have apparently become convinced that domestic equity holdings represent a constraint on their ability to compete in international financial markets. Presumably in response to pressure from the banks, the tax reform introduced by the German government in 2001 drastically cut the capital gains tax and thus increased the incentives for banks and other corporations to sell off equity (often acquired at much lower prices than those that prevail today).

In sum, corporate finance in the social market economies has become securitized—stock and bond markets have become more important relative to bank lending—and also internationalized. The implication would seem to be that capital has become less "patient," potentially weakening trust-based relations among firms as well as between firms and their workers. Even when managers bargain in good faith, suppliers and unions must now ask themselves whether these particular managers will be around to honor their pledges.[7]

Several arguments may be advanced against this pessimistic assessment of the implications of changes in corporate finance for the social market model. To begin with, we must be wary of extrapolating from developments in the 1990s. Highly speculative in nature, the burst of the stock market bubble in the early 2000s and the subsequent realignments of the

Euro and the dollar have made European equity much less attractive to American investors. Furthermore, the developments sketched above pertain primarily to large multinational firms. Large sectors of the social market economies remain firmly embedded in domestic systems of bank-based finance. Also, it should be noted that proxy voting by banks provides German firms with stable governance even if the decline of cross-shareholding between firms continues. As I argued in chapter 2, the link between corporate finance and corporate governance is less straight-forward than commonly supposed. Patient capital does not necessarily equal bank finance.

The argument that globalization of financial markets undermines the social market model assumes that global investors invariably value American-style management over German-style management. It might be more reasonable to suppose, as David Soskice has suggested, that global investors assume ownership stakes in SME firms as part of a strategy to build a balanced investment portfolio, including firms with a variety of distinctive competencies. In other words, American pension funds do not buy stakes in German firms in order to turn them into American firms: rather, they buy such stakes precisely because German firms are different from American firms.[8] In the same spirit, one might well question whether the long-term commitments and cooperative relations characteristic of social market economies are really a function of patient capital. As we have seen, codetermination and employment protection in the social market economies are ultimately based on law. As for coordinated wage bargaining and vocational training, these features of the social market economies entail significant incentives for firms to behave as they do, and there is no reason to suppose that greater management responsiveness to shareholder interests alone alters this logic.

Related to the last point, it should be noted again that we observe a great deal of variation among social market economies in terms of the relative importance of equity markets in corporate finance and their exposure to international financial markets. The Dutch financial system has always been more equity-based and internationalized than the German system.[9] As shown in chapter 2, equity markets have also been relatively prominent in Sweden and Belgium, and the Nordic countries generally provide rather good protection for minority shareholders.

In sum, corporate finance and governance arrangements are changing in the social market economies, but the implications of these changes are far from certain. It is premature to conclude that organized capitalism is being displaced by American-style stock market capitalism. Moreover, some elements of the social market model would seem to be perfectly compatible with shareholder interests.

EQUALITY AND EFFICIENCY

As noted repeatedly in the preceding discussion, the mainstream econ-omist view posits a trade-off between equality and efficiency. The intuition that undergirds this view is that inequality of rewards is necessary to moti-vate individuals to make productive investments, to innovate, and to work hard. As one of my economist friends likes to put it, if a professor were to announce in advance that all students would get a B on the midterm regardless of their performance, no one would study for the exam. This is obviously true, but also, I think, rather trivial. Whether or not efficiency improvements presuppose some inequality of rewards is not the real question. Rather, the real question is whether or not more inequality always enhances efficiency, irrespective of initial levels of inequality (and holding all other factors that might affect efficiency constant). The conventional wisdom among mainstream economists, certainly among political advocates of market liberalism, seems to be that the efficiency gains associated with more inequality extend more or less indefinitely. Market liberals might be willing to concede that extreme levels of in-equality could be unproductive from the point of view of efficiency, but they surely would not concede that the United States might be a case of "excessive inequality." According to the conventional wisdom of our times, there should be efficiency gains to be realized along the entire continuum, from the least to the most inegalitarian of the advanced capitalist countries.

The evidence presented in figures 9.1 and 9.2 raises doubts about the trade-off between equality and efficiency. For the countries covered in this book on which we have the necessary data, figure 9.1 plots annual real growth rates of GDP per capita over the decade of the 1990s against levels of wage inequality at the beginning of the decade (measured as 90–10 ratios). Figure 9.2 in turn plots GDP per capita growth rates against levels of inequality measured in terms of the disposable income of working-age households for the early 1990s (Gini coefficients). With an annual growth rate of more than 6.5 percent, Ireland is a major outlier in both figures. In terms of wage inequality (before taxes) as well as disposable income inequality, Ireland is one of the most inegalitarian of the OECD coun-tries, but it seems clear from these figures that inequality alone cannot possibly explain the Irish miracle of the 1990s. Setting the Irish case aside, there is no association whatsoever between inequality and GDP per capita growth in figures 9.1 and 9.2. Egalitarianism apparently did not prevent the Norwegian economy from growing faster than the American economy over this period. And the Swedish and Canadian economies, at opposite ends of the spectrum as far as wage inequality is concerned, grew at roughly the same rate.

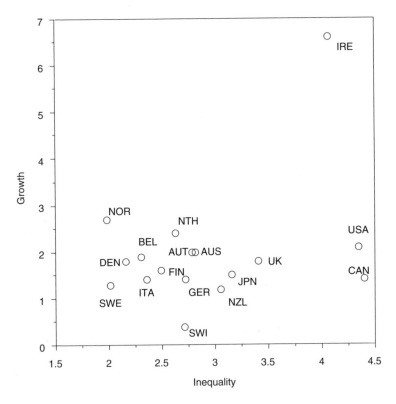

Sources: Tables 1.1 and 3.4.

Figure 9.1 Average annual growth of real GDP per capita 1989–2000 vs. wage inequality (90-10 ratios) circa 1990

    Should we infer from figures 9.1 and 9.2 that there really is no trade-off between equality and efficiency? Proponents of the trade-off thesis are bound to object that the data in figures 9.1 and 9.2 are too aggregate to capture the disincentive effects that egalitarianism entails or, alternatively, that we need to control for other factors that affect economic growth or efficiency in order to see the negative consequences of egalitarianism. The latter objection implies that more egalitarian countries would have grown more rapidly than they did in the 1990s had it not been for the egalitarian orientation of their wage bargaining, taxation, and social spending. By this counterfactual logic, the countries characterized by egalitarian institutions could have outperformed the countries with ine-galitarian institutions. While I readily admit that a more rigorous, multi-variate analysis is necessary to draw any definitive conclusions about the efficiency effects of egalitarianism, I cannot think of any comparative

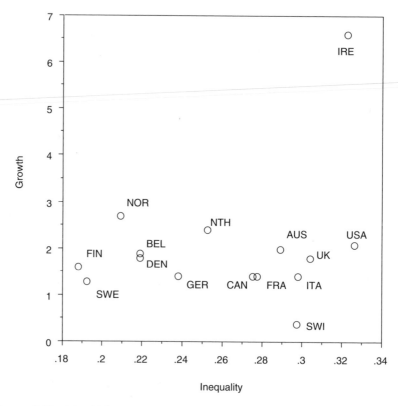

Sources: Tables 1.1 and 3.2.

Figure 9.2 Average annual growth of real GDP per capita 1989–2000 vs. inequality of disposable income among working-age households (Gini coefficients) circa 1990

advantage that this set of countries might be said to have squandered in the 1990s.

It is hardly necessary to point out that GDP per capita is not a direct measure of efficiency. As any standard economics textbook tells us, economic growth might result from increases in the amounts of labor and capital that are deployed for productive purposes or from more efficient use of these factors of production. Measuring GDP growth on a per capita basis controls for overall population growth, but it does not control for changes in the ratio of the employed to the total population or the average number of hours worked by each employed person. As we have seen, however, the liberal market economies clearly outperformed the social market economies in terms of employment growth in the 1990s and, as figures 9.1 and 9.2 again illustrate, the liberal market economies are also more inegalitarian than the social market economies. Hence there is no reason to believe that we would discover a trade-off between equality and efficiency if we were to "subtract" (control for) increases in employment from the growth data used to construct figures 9.1 and 9.2. On the contrary, all the circumstantial evidence suggests that this adjustment would tilt the comparison of efficiency improvements in favor of the more egalitarian countries. It should also be noted that the 1990s were, by historical standards, a relatively good decade for the liberal market economies and a relatively bad decade for the social market economies. If we could reproduce figures 9.1 and 9.2 for the 1960s or 1970s, we would almost certainly find a positive association between equality and economic growth.[10]

The lesson of figures 9.1 and 9.2 is not that monetary incentives for individuals are of no consequence for innovation and productivity. The point is rather that cross-national variation in broad measures of income inequality tells us rather little, perhaps nothing at all, about how different countries compare in terms of "getting the incentives right." All inequality is not productive, and we must guard against the simple-minded assumption that efficiency dictates the highly differentiated structure of rewards that exists in America today. The American economy is surely more efficient today than in the early 1970s, but the relevant yardstick is dynamic efficiency. Despite the sharp and sustained increase of wage inequality that has occurred over the last three decades, not to mention the more recent skyrocketing of executive compensation, productivity growth (however measured) has been sluggish by historical standards. The story of rising inequality in America involves discrimination, rent-seeking, and the exercise of political power and cannot be understood simply in terms of the unfolding logic of efficient markets.

There is every reason to believe that the way workers respond to any particular structure of monetary rewards is affected by considerations of fairness. Within companies and other organizations, extreme differentials or arbitrary allocation of rewards is likely to reduce employee commitment to the goals of the organization.[11] Of course, standards of fairness are embedded in a particular cultural context and will vary across countries and also over time. In other countries, employees often seem to compete intensely for status and for differences in annual pay increases that are tiny by American standards.

I do not wish to argue that it is altogether impossible to generalize about the incentive-effort nexus across cultures. In general, I am inclined to think that the incentives necessary to induce efficiency-enhancing investment and effort depend on the expectations of individuals and that individuals adjust their expectations to the existing structure of rewards. If Sweden's wage structure were suddenly imposed on the American labor force, labor productivity and economic growth would probably decline.

But Sweden did not acquire its egalitarian wage distribution (or its redistributive welfare state) overnight. Rather, Sweden's current wage structure is the cumulative product of a developmental process that dates back to the 1960s, if not earlier.

To sort out how inequality, incentives, effort, and efficiency relate to each other is clearly a complicated matter. Empirical research based on micro evidence, pertaining to the behavior of individuals in different societies, would be necessary to take the preceding discussion further. For now, suffice it to say that the available macro evidence indicates that the efficiency penalties associated with the egalitarianism of Europe's social market economies are not nearly as great as conventional American wisdom would have us believe, but this finding is based on cross-national differences that have persisted over long periods of time. From the point of view of progressive politics, my explanation for the absence of strong disincentive effects in the cross-national data—adaptation of reward expectations—amounts to a plea for a steadfast but moderate (gradualist) approach to redistribution.

REFORMING SOCIAL MARKET ECONOMIES

Human capital is critical to the ability of high-wage countries to compete and prosper in the new world economy. As suggested in chapter 6, public investment in primary and secondary education is particularly critical if we aspire to a more egalitarian society as well as to a prosperous society. Public support for families also matters crucially for this project and, under contemporary societal conditions, such policies must obviously be designed to accommodate the need and desire of mothers to work. As Gøsta Esping-Andersen argues most forcefully, families are the key to social inclusion as well as to a competitive knowledge-based economy. All welfare states ought to devote more resources to the pursuit of a "child-centered social investment strategy."[12] In this regard, the Nordic welfare states provide a model for liberal welfare states as well as for continental European welfare states. Even in the Nordic countries, however, public spending on children and families is under some threat of being squeezed out by the growth of spending on the elderly.

Population ageing poses a major challenge for all welfare states, but this challenge is most acute for social market economies because they provide more generous public pension benefits and have a more unfavorable demographic structure. One part of this statement needs to be qualified. As John Myles argues, the public and private costs of supporting the elderly population must be considered jointly: privatization of pensions, health care and other services for the elderly does not change the basic equation. Also, it does not matter, from this point of view, whether pensions are funded or financed on a pay-as-you-go basis. The value that pensioners will derive from funded schemes ultimately depends on the price that working-age individuals are willing (able) to pay for the assets accumulated through such schemes, just as the value of the pension benefits provided by pay-as-you-go schemes depends on the willingness (ability) of current workers to pay for those benefits. How, then, should the costs of the demographic shift be allocated between the elderly and the working population? Myles argues persuasively that the only politically viable solution to this problem is equal cost sharing: as costs rise, benefits should be adjusted downwards in proportion to increases in the taxes levied on current workers.[13]

Needless to say perhaps, the problem of sharing the costs of supporting the retired population becomes less severe as the working-age population increases or, more precisely, as the number of people in employment increases. Policies that promote female labor force participation reduce the pressures associated with population ageing. The Nordic countries have probably exhausted this solution, but the continental SMEs still have a significant untapped supply of female labor. The ability of governments to affect fertility rates is quite limited and, in any case, raising fertility rates only pays off over the long term. More immediately, the size of the working-age population can be increased either by raising the retirement age or through immigration. Clearly, there are many people over 65 who are both willing and able to work. As indicated earlier, however, there are also many people below the age of 65 who have already retired, particularly in the continental SMEs. As Myles points out, raising the mandatory retirement age in this context makes little sense: the immediate challenge is to reduce the incentives that firms and governments provide for people to retire early. Also, it must be recognized that the ability to continue to work beyond a certain age varies greatly across the social hierarchy. In Myles's words, reforms to raise the effective retirement age require "the bureaucratic and technical capacity to administer early retirement schemes for reasons of disability and labor market redundancy that are fair and perceived to be so by the larger community."[14]

"Early exit from work" became a common solution to the labor market problems generated by sluggish employment growth in many of the social market economies in the 1980s and 1990s. In the end, any solution to the problem of maintaining high standards of living for the retired population while investing in children and families depends on the capacity of the economy to generate jobs for the working-age population. As we have seen, employment growth constitutes the most obvious indicator by which the liberal market economies have more or less consistently outperformed Europe's social market economies over the last two decades. I argued in chapter 4 that the sluggishness of European employment growth in the 1980s and especially the 1990s can partly be seen as a macro-economic problem. For reasons having to do with the dynamics of European integration, the social market economies have generally pursued more restrictive fiscal and monetary policies than the liberal market economies. To address the employment problem, the SMEs have to reorient their approach to macro-economic management. Continued deepening of macro-economic coordination within the European Union may facilitate such a reorientation. However, it is surely too facile to conceive Europe's employment problem simply as a macro-economic problem, with no connection to the institutional and distributional features that distinguish social market economies from liberal market economies.

The preceding analysis brings out three factors that are relevant to the SME/LME distinction and also appear to be associated with cross-national differences in employment performance: wage compression, employment protection, and reliance on payroll taxes (possibly also consumption taxes) to finance government spending. Figures 4.5. 6.2, and 7.10 illustrate the negative effects of these SME characteristics for growth of total employment from 1990 to 2002. In each of these figures, there are important outliers, but the figures nonetheless do bring out problems that the social market economies need to address.

Looking at figures 4.5, 6.2, and 7.10 separately, one would conclude that social market economies might improve their employment performance by allowing wage differentials to rise, by relaxing employment protection legislation, and by cutting payroll taxes. The question immediately arises, however, whether or not the association between any one of these SME features and employment growth holds up when we control for the other features. To the extent that wage compression and employment protection, for example, are correlated with each other, the negative association between wage compression and employment growth shown in figure 4.5 might be spurious. It could be that the employment-inhibiting effects attributed to wage compression are actually effects of employment protection and that wage compression itself does not hamper employment growth. Sorting out this issue properly is almost impossible given the small number of observations available to us and the strong correlations that exist among wage compression, employment protection, and reliance on payroll taxes. Suffice to note here that multiple regression results reported by Lane Kenworthy suggest that all three factors have some negative effect on employment growth and that the effect of payroll taxes is largest and most consistent across different model specifications.[15]

Assuming that wage compression, employment protection, and payroll taxes all represent obstacles to employment growth, the crucial issue for progressive reform of social market economies becomes, which of these features might we be willing to relax or compromise in order to boost employment growth? Even if we could use multiple regression analysis to determine precisely the effects of each factor, we would surely not want to let such results alone determine reform priorities. The question of priorities depends not only on the employment-inhibiting effects of any one of these SME features but also on the social or redistributive purposes that they serve.

Of the SME features that seem to be associated with sluggish employment growth, wage compression strikes me as the most important to preserve. This is the area in which the trade-offs are most severe and where reform-minded progressives ought to tread carefully. As noted in chapter 3, egalitarian wage-setting norms, backed up by minimum wage legislation in countries (and sectors) where unions are weak, not only serve to redistribute income in favor of low-pay workers but also serve an important productive purpose by putting pressure on inefficient firms to rationalize production or to move into products with higher value added. In addition, egalitarian norms are an important component of orderly wage bargaining, facilitating the exercise of wage restraint by unions.

From the perspective of promoting productivity growth, the key is to minimize wage differentials that derive from differences in corporate profitability, as distinct from wage differentials based on differences in skill levels and the jobs that workers actually perform. It is probably the case that wage bargaining in Sweden went too far in the direction of generalized egalitarianism in the 1970s, but I do not believe that this holds for other social market economies, and Swedish wage-bargaining practices have become more decentralized and market-oriented since the early 1980s. Arguably, the welfare state could be used to offset the redistributive consequences of allowing wage inequality to rise. As we have seen, however, the redistributive properties of public welfare provision are already under a great deal of strain. In view of the growth of low-pay employment in most of the OECD countries over the last two decades, it would be counterproductive for unions to retreat from their traditional commitment to the idea that the wages of low-paid workers should rise at a faster rate than the wages of more highly paid workers or for governments to cut the real value of minimum wages. Shoring up coordinated wage bargaining constitutes the most obvious way to ensure that wage differentiation does not spiral out of control.

From a progressive point of view, the stakes involved in cutting payroll taxes are considerable if such cuts occur through a reduction of government spending on social programs. But greater reliance on income taxes provides an alternative way to achieve cuts in payroll taxes. As noted in chapter 6, there is no association between income taxation and employment growth on a cross-national basis. To the extent that employment growth can be boosted by shifting the tax burden from indirect to direct taxes, we do not face a trade-off between employment promotion and redistributive policy. Quite the contrary, greater reliance on income taxation as the source of government revenues would make tax systems more redistributive while removing some of the constraints on employment growth, especially on employment opportunities for unskilled workers. To clarify, I do not advocate selective reductions of payroll taxes for low-paid workers—an idea that has recently received a great deal of attention in Europe. Such a policy amounts to subsidizing low-paying employment. It would be more consistent with market principles as well as egalitarianism to reduce payroll taxes across the board.

Shifting the tax burden onto income taxes runs counter to the drift of tax policy in most OECD countries over the last two decades. While globalization may impose some constraints in this regard, the main reasons for the retreat from income taxation are surely political. To mobilize political support for visible tax increases, especially among middle-class voters at the center of the political spectrum, represents an obvious challenge for progressive parties. I cannot think of any simple recipe for success on this front. The one thing that we can say with some confidence, I think, is that meeting the challenge of legitimizing higher income taxes is politically incompatible with welfare state reforms that entail further targeting of government spending on the poor. Universalism remains the welfare state's best defense against tax fatigue.

Finally, I want to suggest that Social Democrats and other European progressives take another look at existing laws and regulations pertaining to employment protection and consider liberalizing measures in this area. There are minimum standards that need to be maintained in this area, and those standards certainly exceed current American standards. However, the costs of firing workers for employers could be significantly reduced without unduly compromising progressive social objectives provided that such reforms are accompanied by increased public income support to the unemployed and by an expansion of active labor market policies designed to improve the employability of unemployed workers. This reform strategy is the opposite of that pursued by most European governments, including Social Democratic governments, over the last ten to fifteen years. As we have seen, unemployment compensation has been cut quite sharply while employment protection has been maintained. Taken together, the elements of progressive reform sketched above might be conceived as a "new deal" with the business community. Crudely put, employers would be asked to participate in the maintenance of coordinated wage bargaining and the welfare state in return for lower payroll taxes and more liberal regulations governing employment.

The reform strategy suggested in the preceding section represents a return to the traditional orientation of Scandinavian Social Democracy. As noted in chapter 6, the principle guiding employment policies in Scandinavia, particularly Sweden, during the 1960s was that "employment security" should be conceived in terms of making workers more secure in the labor market and not in terms of "job security." The government should intervene to protect workers against the income losses associated with unemployment and to improve their ability to find new, better jobs, but it should not seek to guarantee that workers keep their current jobs. Again, the prominence that the idea of job security has come to assume in Europe over the last two decade owes more to the ideological legacy of continental Christian Democracy than to the ideological legacy of Scandinavian Social Democracy.

IMPLICATIONS FOR LIBERAL MARKET ECONOMIES

The tradition of comparative political economy that has inspired this book emphasizes complementarities among policies and institutional arrangements. Most scholars working in this tradition conceive varieties of capitalism in terms of internally coherent models for organizing advanced capitalism, each with its own distinctive logic and strengths and weaknesses.[16] Quite often, such scholars argue that coherent economies generally perform better than incoherent economies. The implication of this analytical perspective seems to be that there is very little that Americans and other "Anglo-Saxons" can learn from the experience of Europe's social market economies and that the notion of introducing elements of the social market model in piecemeal fashion is fundamentally misguided. There may be room for progressive, redistributive politics in liberal market economies, but the policies and institutional changes that progressive forces can and should pursue would be of a qualitatively different nature from the policies and institutional arrangements of the social market economies. In addressing issues pertaining to low-pay employment, for instance, American policy makers are better served by seeking to emulate the negative income-tax strategy pursued by successive Canadian governments and by Britain's current Labour government rather than seeking to emulate the German system of coordinated wage bargaining, vocational training, and social protection.

In my view, the notion that LMEs and SMEs constitute separate worlds with different internal dynamics should not be taken too far. As the preceding analysis indicates, the social and liberal market economies have many things in common. Market forces have been a source of rising inequality, while strong unions, institutionalized collective bargaining, and the public provision of social welfare based on universalistic principles have counteracted these forces in both sets of countries. Most importantly, I want to suggest that in discussing what liberal market economies might learn from social market economies we ought to distinguish between "social democratic policies" and "social market institutions." The former are more readily transferable than the latter and would appear to be perfectly consistent with economic conditions characterized by intensified international competition, capital mobility, and the emergence of services as the dominant source of employment.

Based primarily on the Scandinavian experience, the core components of the social democratic approach to economic and social policy might be summarized as follows: (1) wage solidarity as an instrument of industrial policy as well as of redistributive policy; (2) active labor market policies designed to promote labor mobility and more efficient allocation of labor; (3) public investment in education; (4) family policies designed to facilitate female labor force participation; and, finally, (5) universalism in the public provision of social welfare. The political mobilization of workers is obviously an important part of the story of how the Scandinavian countries came to adopt these policies. Also, one might well argue that the institutions characteristic of social market economies facilitated the implementation of social democratic policies. However, I do not see why (or how) one would argue that any of these policies are fundamentally inappropriate for liberal market economies.

In the liberal as well as the social market economies, union influence in the process of wage formation tends to be associated with some degree of wage equalization. To the extent that certain forms of wage equalization promote efficiency in social market economies, there is no obvious reason why this logic would not equally apply to liberal market economies. In a similar vein, I cannot see any reason to doubt that greater public resources devoted to the welfare of children and to the improvement of public education, especially in poorer neighborhoods or regions, would yield significant benefits for the American economy over the long run. The institutional infrastructure of the social market economies undoubtedly facilitates the implementation of active labor market policies designed to retrain unemployed workers and to facilitate their re-entry into employment, but there are quite a few examples of successful programs of this sort in liberal market economies. Finally, the most compelling reason why the work disincentive effects of generous unemployment compensation are greater in liberal market economies than in social market economies would seem to be that low-wage, dead-end jobs are more important to these economies. From a progressive point of view, this hardly constitutes a good reason to deny the unemployed adequate income support.

In short, the observation that liberal market economies are different from social market economies must not become an excuse to allow the market liberals to define the terms of economic and social policy debate. Clearly, the social problems associated with poverty and inequality in the United States have important economic ramifications. Any serious effort to address these problems would inevitably involve the introduction of social democratic elements into economic and social policy and may, over the long run, entail the buildup of institutional arrangements that resemble, in some respects, those of the social market economies. Germany's social market economy may be in deep trouble, but social democracy remains a coherent and viable alternative to market liberalism.

Notes

Chapter 1. Rethinking the Trade-off between Growth and Equality

1. Richard Freeman, "War of the Models: Which Labour Market Institutions for the 21st Century?" *Labour Economics* 5 (March 1998), 1–24.

2. Whether or not this logic explains variation in the extent of redistribution (or the size of the welfare state) over time and across countries has been a subject of debate among economists and political scientists in recent years. It is important not to confuse the median income with the income of the median voter: to the extent that low-income earners are less likely to vote than others, the income of the median voter will be closer to the mean income. For an introduction to some of these issues and references to relevant literature, see Lane Kenworthy and Jonas Pontusson, "Rising Inequality and the Politics of Redistribution in Affluent Countries" (forthcoming in *Perspectives on Politics*).

3. This book focuses on the economic and social consequences and, to some extent, the political dynamics of different political-economic arrangements. I will not address the question of why such arrangements differ across countries in any systematic way. For a very useful discussion of the reasons for American exceptionalism in the sphere of social policy, see Alessandro Alesina and Edward Glaeser, *Fighting Poverty in the U.S. and Europe* (Oxford: Oxford University Press, 2004).

4. My grouping and labeling of advanced capitalist political economies draw on previous literature, most notably Peter Hall and David Soskice, eds., *Varieties of Capitalism* (Oxford: Oxford University Press, 2000). See chapter 2 for further discussion.

5. Arthur M. Okun, *Equality and Efficiency: The Big Trade-Off* (Washington, DC: Brookings Institution, 1975), 2–4.

6. I use the term "market-liberal" in the way that "neo-liberal" is used in European political discourse. In the sphere of economic policy, American "neo-conservatives" subscribe to the same set of ideas.

7. The OECD collects, analyzes, and disseminates data on a wide range of social and economic indicators. Until recently, its membership consisted exclusively of "developed" countries (Japan, Western Europe, North America, and the Antipodes).

8. For consistency with tables in subsequent chapters, table 1.1 includes data on France, Italy, and Japan. These countries are not readily classified as either SMEs or LMEs, but they are of intrinsic interest. For now, however, my discussion will focus exclusively on differences between SMEs and LMEs.

9. Figures on the value of imports relative to GDP closely match those for exports. Note that Ireland stands out among LMEs as an exceptionally trade-dependent economy. On average, exports account for 30.0% of GDP in LMEs if we exclude Ireland, as compared to an SME average of 48.2%. Trade dependence is obviously related to the size of a country's domestic economy. Among the large economies included in table 1.1, Germany is the most trade-dependent while the United States and Japan are the least trade-dependent.

10. OECD, *Employment Outlook* (2001), 208, and OECD, *Main Economic Indicators* (September 2004), 16. The unemployment rates reported here are "standardized," which is to say that the figures for other countries roughly conform to the American definition of what it means to be unemployed. The EU figures are a weighted average, reflecting the relative size of different member states.

11. Like the other group averages reported in table 1.1 (and in contrast to the EU-wide figures cited previously in the text), these are "unweighted" averages, which is to say that they do not take account for size differences among the economies that make up each group. In other words, we are comparing average rates of unemployment for two groups of countries rather than comparing rates of unemployment in two groups of countries.

12. Stephen Nickell, "Unemployment and Labor Market Rigidities," *Journal of Economic Perspectives* 11, no. 3 (1997), 55.

13. See Nancy Bermeo, ed., *Unemployment in Southern Europe* (London: Frank Cass, 2000). Not included in table 1.1, Spain's unemployment rate averaged 11.1% from 2000 to 2003.

14. OECD, *Employment Outlook* (2001), 225. Implausibly, the most recent edition of the OECD's *Employment Outlook* (2004) presents a time series in which the average annual hours of work only increased slightly in the 1990s (from 1,829 in 1990 to 1,840 in 1999) and then declined sharply in the early 2000s (p. 312).

15. Note that these calculations are based on the most recent OECD estimates of average annual hours of work, which cast the American case in a more favorable light relative to other countries than previous estimates (see note 13). For a similar attempt to measure GDP per hour worked, see Nicholas Crafts, "East Asian Growth Before and After the Crisis, " *IMF Staff Papers* 46, no. 2 (June 1999), 139–66. In terms of country rankings, the picture conveyed by table 1.2 is broadly similar to that presented by Crafts, who also reports estimates on the growth of GDP per hour worked from 1973 to 1996.

Chapter 2. Varieties of Capitalism

1. Peter J. Katzenstein, *Small States in World Markets* (Ithaca: Cornell University Press, 1985).

2. Gøsta Esping-Andersen, *Three Worlds of Welfare Capitalism* (Princeton: Princeton University Press, 1990).

3. See Peter Hall and David Soskice, eds., *Varieties of Capitalism* (Oxford: Oxford University Press, 2001).

4. The most important statements of this approach to comparative political economy are Soskice, "Divergent Production Regimes" in *Continuity and Change in Contemporary Capitalism*, ed. Herbert Kitschelt, Peter Lange, Gary Marks, and John Stephens (New York: Cambridge University Press, 1999), 101–34, and Hall and Soskice's introduction to *Varieties of Capitalism*, 1–70.

5. The ambiguous status of France and Italy in the VofC literature should be noted here. VofC scholars commonly designated France and Italy as "hybrid" or "mixed" cases, but "non-market modes of coordination" have traditionally been very prominent in these countries. As I argue below, what distinguishes these cases from other European CMEs has to do with labor relations and the public provision of social welfare.

6. The classic statement on this remains J. J. Pempel and Keiichi Tsunekawa, "Corporatism without Labor?" in *Trends Towards Corporatist Interest Mediation*, ed. Philippe Schmitter and Gerhard Lehmbruch (Beverly Hills: Sage, 1979), 231–70. For a "revisionist"

account of labor's role in the Japanese political economy, see Ikuo Kume, *Disparaged Success* (Ithaca: Cornell University Press, 1998).

7. Soskice, "Wage Determination," *Oxford Review of Economic Policy* 6, no. 4 (1990), 26–61.

8. Wolfgang Streeck, "Lean Production in the German Automobile Industry," in *National Diversity and Global Capitalism*, ed. Suzanne Berger and Ronald Dore (Ithaca: Cornell University Press, 1996), 138–70.

9. For a more extended critique of the VofC approach, see Pontusson, "Varieties and Commonalities of Capitalism," in *Varieties of Capitalism, Varieties of Approaches*, ed. David Coates (London: Palgrave, 2005), 163–88.

10. John Zysman, *Governments, Markets, and Growth* (Ithaca: Cornell University Press, 1983) and Will Hutton, *The World We're In* (New York: Little Brown and Company, 2002). See also Michel Albert, *Capitalism vs. Capitalism* (New York: Four Walls Eight Windows, 1993) and Ronald Dore, *Stock Market Capitalism: Welfare Capitalism: Japan and Germany versus the Anglo-Saxons* (Oxford: Oxford University Press, 2000).

11. See Mary O'Sullivan, "What Drove the U.S. Stock Market in the Twentieth Century?" (INSEAD, 2004) and "Living with the U.S. Financial System: The Experiences of GE and Westinghouse in the Last Century" (INSEAD, 2004).

12. Jenny Corbett and Tim Jenkinson, "German Investment Financing," in *Competition and Convergence in Financial Markets*, ed. S. W. Black and M. Moersch (Amsterdam: Elsevier, 1998), 109–15. See also Mary O'Sullivan, *Contests for Corporate Control* (Oxford: Oxford University Press, 2000), ch. 7.

13. Reinhardt Schmidt and Marcel Tyrell, "Financial Systems, Corporate Finance, and Corporate Governance," *European Financial Management* 3, no. 3 (1997), 333–61.

14. Ekkehard Wenger and Christoph Kaserer, "The German System of Corporate Governance," in *Competition and Convergence in Financial Markets*, ed. Stanley Black and Mathias Moersch (Amsterdam: Elsevier, 1998), 61.

15. Richard Deeg, *Finance Capitalism Unveiled* (Ann Arbor: University of Michigan Press, 1999).

16. Such an argument is proposed in Mark Roe, *The Political Determinants of Corporate Governance* (Oxford: Oxford University Press, 2003). The question of employee representation on boards of directors, a distinctive feature of corporate governance in some SMEs, most notably Germany, will be discussed in chapter 6.

17. As measured by the OECD, collective bargaining coverage does not necessarily refer to wage bargaining: the remarkably high French figure probably has to do with collectively bargained provisions for holidays or workplace safety being extended by the government to firms and sectors without any real union presence.

18. Some of this discussion draws on Charles Ragin, *The Comparative Method* (Berkeley: University of California Press, 1987).

Chapter 3. *Income Distribution and Labor Markets*

1. See Margarita Estevez-Abe, Torben Iversen, and David Soskice, "Social Protection and the Formation of Skills," in *Varieties of Capitalism*, ed. Peter Hall and David Soskice (Oxford: Oxford University Press, 2001), 145–83. American exceptionalism is emphasized in Richard Freeman and Lawrence Katz, "Rising Wage Inequality," in *Working under Different Rules*, ed. Freeman (New York: Russell Sage Foundation, 1994) and also in Francine Blau and Lawrence Kahn, *At Home and Abroad: U.S. Labor Market Performance in International Perspective* (New York: Russell Sage Foundation, 2002).

2. See Lawrence Mishel, Jared Bernstein, and John Schmitt, *The State of Working America 1998–99* (Ithaca: Cornell University Press, 1999), 52.

3. Note that the previously presented U.S. figures on gross income do not include capital gains or "near-cash transfers" such as food stamps. There appears to be some cross-national

variability in the LIS database with regard to these items. Following conventional practice, LIS uses the square root of the number of persons in the household to derive estimates of "equivalent household income." The basic intuition behind this procedure is that the cost per household member of maintaining a certain standard of living declines with household size: a smaller household needs more income per household member to maintain the same standard of living as a larger household.

4. On the limitations of Gini coefficients and alternative measures of inequality, see Frank Cowell, *Measuring Inequality* (London: Harvester Wheatsheaf, 1995) and Anthony Atkinson, Lee Rainwater, and Timothy Smeeding, *Income Distribution in OECD Countries* (Paris: OECD, 1995).

5. The Gini coefficients for gross earnings among working-age households were computed by Lane Kenworthy as part of a collaborative project; Kenworthy reports the same figures in *Egalitarian Capitalism* (New York: Russell Sage Foundation, 2004), ch. 3.

6. Lawrence Mishel, Jared Bernstein, and Heather Boushey, *The State of Working America 2002/2003* (Ithaca: Cornell University Press, 2003), 67.

7. Ibid., 87.

8. According to Mishel, Bernstein, and Boushey's calculations, the upper fifth of American households received 81 percent, and the top 1 percent received 48 percent, of all income from capital in 1999. Ibid., 86.

9. See Gary Burtless, "Technological Change and International Trade," in *The Inequality Paradox*, ed. James Auerbach and Richard Belous (Washington DC: National Policy Association), 60–91.

10. Mishel, Bernstein, and Boushey, *The State of Working America 2002/2003*, 78–82.

11. Ibid., 172. By definition, the both-gender 90–10 ratio is a function of (a) the male ratio weighted by men's share of the full-time labor force, (b) the female ratio weighted by women's share of the full-time labor force, and (c) the ratio of the median male wage to the median female wage.

12. For cross-national data on the evolution of between-gender and between-industry wage differentials over the 1973–85 period, see Bob Rowthorn, "Corporatism and Labour Market Performance," in *Social Corporatism: A Superior Economic System?* ed. Jukka Pekkarinen, Matti Pohjola, and Bob Rowthorn (Oxford: Clarendon Press, 1992), 82–131.

13. The Canadian figures reported in table 3.4 appear to be inflated: for 1995 through 1999, the OECD's *Employment Outlook* (2004) records a both-gender 90-10 ratio of 3.65 for Canada, as opposed to 4.18 for 1994 in the earlier OECD dataset (p. 141). However, the change over time recorded for Canada in the earlier data appears quite plausible.

14. Blau and Kahn, *At Home and Abroad*, 63.

15. My discussion of this finding closely follows Pontusson and Kenworthy, "Rising Inequality and the Politics of Redistribution in Affluent Countries" (forthcoming). See also Kenworthy, *Egalitarian Capitalism*, 27–35.

16. Mishel, Bernstein, and Boushey, *The State of Working America 2002/2003*, 100.

17. Similar results are reported by Kenworthy, *Egalitarian Capitalism*, 30. Kenworthy includes measures of change in single-earner households and marital homogamy in some of his regressions. The signs of the coefficients for these variables are positive (meaning that they are associated with rising earnings inequality), but the coefficients are smaller than those for change in wage inequality and employment rate and rarely clear conventional criteria for statistical significance.

18. For more systematic evidence in support of some of the arguments developed in this section, see David Rueda and Jonas Pontusson, "Wage Inequality and Varieties of Capitalism," *World Politics* 52, no. 3 (April 2000), 350–83, and Pontusson, Rueda, and Way, "Comparative Political Economy of Wage Distribution," *British Journal of Political Science* 32 (2002), 281–308.

19. James Galbraith, *Created Unequal* (New York: Free Press, 1998), 145.

20. This line of argument is advanced most forcefully in Adrian Wood, *North-South Trade, Employment, and Inequality: Changing Fortunes in a Skill-Driven World* (Oxford: Clarendon Press,

1994). See also Dani Rodrik, *Has Globalization Gone Too Far?* (Washington, DC: Institute for International Economics, 1997), ch. 2, and Arthur Alderson and François Nielsen, "Globalization and the Great U-Turn," *American Journal of Sociology* 107 (2002), 1244–99.

21. Mishel, Bernstein, and Boushey, *The State of Working America 2002/2003*, 203.

22. Richard Freeman and Lawrence Katz, "Rising Wage Inequality," in *Working under Different Rules*, ed. Freeman (New York: Russell Sage Foundation, 1994), 50.

23. Germany was left out of figure 3.7 because the OECD data on educational attainment refer to unified Germany while the data on wage inequality are restricted to West Germany.

24. OECD, *Employment Outlook* (1998), 40–41.

25. Mishel, Bernstein, and Boushey, *The State of Working America 2002/2003*, 189–96.

26. Rueda and Pontusson, "Wage Inequality and Varieties of Capitalism."

27. See Pontusson, *The Limits of Social Democracy* (Ithaca: Cornell University Press, 1992), ch. 3.

28. On the economic effects of solidaristic wage bargaining, see Douglas Hibbs and Håkan Locking, "Wage Dispersion and Productive Efficiency," Working Paper, Trade Union Institute for Economic Research, Stockholm, 1995; on the employer offensive, see Peter Swenson and Jonas Pontusson, "The Swedish Employer Offensive against Centralized Bargaining," in *Unions, Employers, and Central Banks*, ed. Torben Iversen, Jonas Pontusson, and David Soskice (New York: Cambridge University Press, 2000), 77–106.

29. Blau and Kahn, *At Home and Abroad*, 60.

Chapter 4. Employment Performance

1. OECD, *Employment Outlook* (2003), 299.

2. Jelle Visser and Anton Hemerijck, *"A Dutch Miracle": Job Growth, Welfare Reform, and Corporatism in the Netherlands* (Amsterdam: Amsterdam University Press, 1997), 36.

3. The insider-outsider perspective is expounded most forcefully by Assar Lindbeck and Dennis Snower, *The Insider-Outsider Theory of Employment and Unemployment* (Cambridge, MA: MIT Press, 1988). For a less polemical application of this perspective to the politics of regulating labor markets, see David Rueda, "Insider-Outsider Politics in Industrialized Democracies," *American Political Science Review* (forthcoming).

4. Women, youth, and unskilled workers are, of course, included in the national rate of unemployment. If unemployment among unskilled workers was expressed as a ratio of unemployment among skilled workers, these figures would be higher than those reported in table 4.3. For further discussion of the structure of unemployment, as distinct from the level of unemployment, see Gøsta Esping-Andersen, "Who is Harmed by Labour Market Regulations?" in *Why Deregulate Labour Markets?* ed. Esping-Andersen and Regini (Oxford: Oxford University Press, 2000), 66–98.

5. Blau and Kahn, *At Home and Abroad: U.S. Labor Market Performance in International Perspective* (New York: Russell Sage Foundation, 2002), 161.

6. Western and Beckett, "How Unregulated is the U.S. Labor Market?" *American Journal of Sociology* 104 (1999), 1030–60. See also Richard Freeman, "The Limits of Wage Flexibility to Curing Unemployment," *Oxford Review of Economic Policy* 11 (1995), 63–72.

7. See Janet Gornick, Marcia Meyers, and Katherin Ross, "Supporting the Employment of Mothers," *Journal of European Social Policy* 7, no. 1 (1997), 45–70.

8. The figures in the second panel of table 4.5 are based on average hours worked per person as shown in the OECD's *Employment Outlook* (2004). According to this dataset, average hours worked in the United States increased only slightly from 1990 to 1999 and then declined from 2000 to 2003. By contrast, the data in the *Employment Outlook* (2001) show a substantial increase in average hours worked in the United States from 1990 to 2000. Using the latter data to calculate total employment from 1990 to 2000 in hours yields an average annual United States growth rate of 1.7%.

9. This argument is developed by Torben Iversen and Anne Wren, "Equality, Employment and Budgetary Restraint," *World Politics* 50 (July 1998), 507–46. See also Peter Hall, "Organized Market Economies and Unemployment in Europe," in *Unemployment in the New Europe*, ed. Nancy Bermeo (New York: Cambridge University Press, 2001), 52–86.

10. Ireland is an exceptional case in that through the first half of the 1990s it combined rapid growth of the working-age population with negative net migration (more out-migration than in-migration). Even without Ireland, the correlation coefficient for growth of working-age population from 1980 to 1999 and average annual net migration from 1980 to 1995 is only .395. For net migration data, see Fritz Scharpf and Vivien Schmidt, eds., *Welfare and Work in the Open Economy*, vol. 1 (Oxford: Oxford University Press, 2000), 352.

11. Measuring wage inequality by 90-10 ratios yields very similar findings to those reported below. The availability of observations of 50-10 wage ratios is the same as that for 90-10 ratios. See table 3.4.

12. Changes in wage inequality do correlate quite closely with growth of employment in private services, but wage inequality may be a result as well as a cause of employment growth. Figure 4.5 avoids the problem of "reverse causality" by plotting employment growth against initial levels of wage inequality.

13. See Kenworthy, *Egalitarian Capitalism* (New York: Russell Sage Foundation, 2004), ch. 5. Further cross-national evidence of a trade-off between wage inequality and employment growth is provided by Lawrence Kahn, "Wage Inequality, Collective Bargaining, and Relative Employment," *Review of Economics and Statistics* 69 (2000), 564–79.

14. The following discussion draws primarily on Visser and Hemerijck, "A Dutch Miracle," and Cees Gorter, "The Dutch Miracle?" in *Why Deregulate Labour Markets?* ed. Esping-Andersen and Regini, 181–210.

15. Visser and Hemerijck, "A Dutch Miracle," 27, 101.

16. Ibid., 28.

Chapter 5. Macro-Economic Management and Wage Bargaining

1. This perspective permeates the analysis and policy recommendations of the OECD's Jobs Study of 1994. See *The OECD Jobs Study* (1994), especially part I, ch. 2.

2. Soskice, "Macroeconomic Analysis and the Political Economy of Unemployment," in *Unions, Employers, and Central Banks*, ed. Torben Iversen, Jonas Pontusson, and David Soskice (New York: Cambridge University Press, 2000), 38–74.

3. On similar theoretical grounds, this method is also employed in Lars Calmfors and John Driffill, "Centralization of Wage Bargaining," *Economic Policy* 3, no. 1 (1988), 14–61.

4. The coverage rates reported in table 5.2 are rough estimates, described by the OECD as "lower bounds." More precise estimates for 1994 are reported in OECD, *Employment Outlook* (1997) 71.

5. Missing from the OECD data presented in table 4.1, Ireland is partly an exception to this rule as well. Jeremy Waddington and Reiner Hoffman report a coverage-rate estimate of 90% for Ireland in 1995. As for France (see footnote 7), there is reason to doubt that coverage refers to wage rates in the Irish case. See Waddington and Hoffman, *Trade Unions in Europe* (Brussels: European Trade Union Institute, 2000), 45.

6. It should be noted that collective bargaining coverage by itself does not tell us anything about the terms of the collective agreements whose coverage is being measured and that coverage in excess of unionization does not necessarily imply that collectively negotiated *wage rates* are extended to non-union workers. The nationwide extension of a single agreement on the length or scheduling of holidays alone could account for the fact that the French coverage rate is 95%, even though the unionization rate is only 9%. Certainly, the French coverage rate is due to government intervention rather than well-organized employees.

7. Mancur Olson, *The Rise and Decline of Nations* (New Haven: Yale University Press, 1982), esp. 48–53. See also Calmfors and Driffill, "Centralization of Wage Bargaining," and Soskice, "Wage Determination," *Oxford Review of Economic Policy* 6, no. 4 (1990), 36–61.

8. Miriam Golden, Michael Wallerstein, and Peter Lange, "Postwar Trade-Union Organization and Industrial Relations in Twelve Countries," in *Continuity and Change in Contemporary Capitalism*, ed. Herbert Kitschelt, Peter Lange, Gary Marks, and John D. Stephens (New York: Cambridge University Press, 1999), 212.

9. On German and Swedish wage bargaining, see Peter Swenson, *Fair Shares* (Ithaca: Cornell University Press, 1989) and Kathleen Thelen, *Union of Parts* (Ithaca: Cornell University Press, 1991).

10. OECD, *Employment Outlook* (2004), ch. 3. See also OECD, *Employment Outlook* (1997), ch. 3.

11. For example, see David Cameron, "Social Democracy, Corporatism, Labour Quiescence and the Representation of Economic Interest," in *Order and Conflict in Contemporary Capitalism*, ed. John Goldthorpe (Oxford: Clarendon Press, 1994), 143–78; Michael Alvarez, Geoffrey Garrett, and Peter Lange, "Government Partisanship, Labor Organization, and Macroeconomic Performance," *American Political Science Review* 85 (1991), 539–56; and Miriam Golden, "The Dynamics of Trade Unionism and National Economic Performance," *American Political Science Review* 87 (1993), 439–54.

12. See Wallerstein and Golden, "Postwar Wage Setting in the Nordic Countries," in *Unions, Employers, and Central Banks*, ed. Iversen, Pontusson, and Soskice, 107–37.

13. This argument is developed in Geoffrey Garrett and Christopher Way, "Public-Sector Unions, Corporatism, and Wage Determination" in ibid., 267–91.

14. See Peter Swenson and Jonas Pontusson, "The Swedish Employer Offensive against Centralized Bargaining" in ibid., 77–106.

15. Kathleen Thelen, "Why German Employers Cannot Bring Themselves to Dismantle the German Model" in ibid., 138–69.

16. See Harry Katz, "The Decentralization of Collective Bargaining," *Industrial and Labor Relations Review* 47 (1993), 3–22.

17. The association between RULC change and bargaining coverage remains statistically significant if we control for average unemployment rates in the 1990s. As standard economic arguments would lead us to expect, unemployment is strongly associated with falling RULCs. With or without controlling for unemployment and overall union density, the public sector's share of total union membership has no significant association with change in RULCs in the 1990s.

18. The most comprehensive statement of this line of argument is Alex Cukierman, *Central Bank Strategy, Credibility, and Independence* (Cambridge, MA: MIT Press, 1992).

19. Peter Hall and Robert Franzese, "Mixed Signals: Central Bank Independence, Coordinated Wage Bargaining, and European Monetary Union," *International Organization* 52, no. 3 (1998), 511. See also Torben Iversen, *Contested Economic Institutions* (New York: Cambridge University Press, 1999), chs. 2–3.

20. Hall and Franzese's classification of countries is based on their average scores on five commonly used indices of central bank independence and several indices of wage bargaining coordination. With the exception of Japan, the countries that they classify as coordinated bargaining systems are the same countries that I classify as social market economies.

21. Blau and Kahn, *At Home and Abroad: U.S. Labor Market Performance in International Perspective* (New York: Russell Sage Foundation, 2002), 92.

22. Wendy Carlin and David Soskice, "Shocks to the System: the German Political Economy under Stress," *National Institute Economic Review* 159 (1997), 57–76.

23. Dunn, "Why Won't the European Central Bank Ease?" *Challenge*, November–December 2004, 93.

24. See Peter Hall, "Central Bank Independence and Coordinated Wage Bargaining," *German Politics and Society* 30 (Autumn 1994), 1–23, and David Soskice and Torben Iversen,

"Multiple Wage-Bargaining Systems in the Single European Currency Area," *Oxford Review of Economic Policy* 14, no. 3 (1998), 110–24.

Chapter 6. Participation, Security, Mobility, and Skills

1. The literature on German codetermination is extensive. The following treatment draws primarily on Christel Lane, *Management and Labour in Europe* (Aldershot: Edward Elgar, 1989), ch. 9; Kathleen Thelen, *Unions of Parts* (Ithaca: Cornell University Press, 1991); and Lowell Turner, *Democracy at Work* (Ithaca: Cornell University Press, 1991). For a very useful comparative discussion, see Mary O'Sullivan, "Employees and Corporate Governance," in *Corporate Governance,* ed. Peter Cornelius and Bruce Kogut (Chichester: John Wiley and Sons, 2005).

2. O'Sullivan, "The Political Economy of Comparative Corporate Governance," *Review of International Political Economy* 10, no. 1 (2003), 50.

3. Martin Behrens, "Works Constitution Act Reform Adopted," *European Industrial Relations Observatory Online,* July 2001.

4. Göran Brulin, "Sweden: Joint Councils under Strong Unionism," in *Works Councils,* ed. Joel Rogers and Wolfgang Streeck (Chicago: University of Chicago Press, 1995).

5. Streeck, "Works Councils in Western Europe," in ibid., 344–45.

6. "German Business in Attack on Workers' Board Roles," *Financial Times,* November 10, 2004.

7. Italy scores 3.1 on the OECD's composite index for the late 1990s. For 2003, Greece scores 2.9, Portugal 3.5, and Spain 3.1.

8. The following summary is based on OECD, *Employment Outlook* (1999), 90–114, and *Employment Outlook* (2004), 110–16.

9. See Assar Lindbeck and Dennis Snower, *The Insider-Outsider Theory of Employment and Unemployment* (Cambridge, MA: MIT Press, 1988).

10. Streeck, "On the Institutional Conditions of Diversified Quality Production," in *Beyond Keynesianism,* ed. Egon Matzner and Streeck (Aldershot: Edward Elgar, 1991), 21–61. On trade-offs between different kinds of flexibility, see also Marino Regini, "The Dilemmas of Labour Market Regulation," in *Why Deregulate Labour Markets?* ed. Gøsta Esping-Andersen and Regini (Oxford: Oxford University Press, 2000), 11–29.

11. Estevez-Abe, Iversen, and Soskice, "Social Protection and the Formation of Skills," in *Varieties of Capitalism,* ed. Peter Hall and David Soskice (Oxford: Oxford University Press, 2001), 145–83.

12. OECD, *Employment Outlook* (1999), 71–88, and *Employment Outlook* (2004), 76–89. See also Esping-Andersen, "Who is Harmed by Labour Market Regulations?" in *Why Deregulate Labour Markets?* ed. Esping-Andersen and Regini, 84–90.

13. For a review of such evaluation studies, see John Martin, "What Works Among Active Labor Market Policies," Labour Market and Social Policy Occasional Papers No. 35, OECD, 1998.

14. Layard and Nickell, "Labor Market Institutions and Economic Performance," in *Handbook of Labor Economics,* ed. Orley Ashenfelter and David Card (Amsterdam: Elsevier, 1999), v. 3C, 3052–53.

15. Blau and Kahn, *At Home and Abroad* (New York: Russell Sage Foundation, 2002), 143–44.

16. The classic formulation of the skills problem is Gary Becker, *Human Capital,* 3rd ed. (Chicago: University of Chicago Press, 1993).

17. See Robert Reich, *The Work of Nations* (New York: Knopf, 1991) and David Finegold and David Soskice, "The Failure of Training in Britain," *Oxford Review of Economic Policy* 4, no. 3 (1988), 21–53.

18. Estevez-Abe, Iversen, and Soskice, "Social Protection and the Formation of Skills."

19. See Steven Reed, *Making Common Sense of Japan* (Pittsburgh: University of Pittsburgh Press), ch. 4, and Masanori Hashimoto, "Employment-based Training in Japanese Firms in Japan and the United States," in *Training and the Private Sector,* ed. Lisa Lynch (Chicago: University of Chicago, 1994). Also, see Kathleen Thelen, *How Institutions Evolve* (New York: Cambridge University Press, 2004) for an instructive historical account of different "skill formation regimes."

20. Streeck, "Lean Production in the German Automobile Industry," in *National Diversity and Global Capitalism,* ed. Suzanne Berger and Ronald Dore (Ithaca, NY: Cornell University Press, 1996).

21. Soskice, "Reconciling Markets and Institutions," in *Training and the Private Sector,* ed. Lisa Lynch (Chicago: University of Chicago Press, 1994), 25–60. See also Pepper Culpepper and David Finegold, eds., *The German Skills Machine* (New York: Berghahn, 1999).

22. Lane, *Management and Labour in Europe,* 45–53.

23. Lisa Lynch, "Payoffs to Alternative Training Strategies at Work," in *Working Under Different Rules,* ed. Richard Freeman (New York: Russell Sage Foundation, 1994), 74–75.

24. Evelyne Huber and John Stephens, *Development and Crisis of the Welfare State* (Chicago: University of Chicago Press, 2001), 95.

25. Francine Blau and Lawrence Kahn, "Do Cognitive Test Scores Explain Higher U.S. Wage Inequality?" National Bureau of Economic Research, Working Paper 8210, April 2001.

26. OECD, *Trends in International Migration* (2004), 307–8. Note that the cited figures for Belgium, Germany, and Switzerland refer to immigrants (noncitizens) rather than "foreign born."

Chapter 7. Welfare States, Redistribution, and Economic Growth

1. Tanzi and Schuknecht, *Public Spending in the Twentieth Century* (Cambridge: Cambridge University Press, 2000), 98.

2. Ibid., 60.

3. Tanzi and Schuknecht arrive at this conclusion by comparing average growth rates in the 1986–94 period for three groups of countries, organized according to the size of government. For individual countries, the data that they themselves provide (pp. 6–7, 78) yields an insignificant correlation between levels of spending and rates of growth (–.130).

4. Esping-Andersen, *The Three Worlds of Welfare Capitalism* (Princeton: Princeton University Press, 1990).

5. In addition to the work of Esping-Andersen, see Alexander Hicks, *Social Democracy and Welfare Capitalism* (Ithaca: Cornell University Press, 1999) and Evelyne Huber and John Stephens, *Development and Crisis of the Welfare State* (Chicago: University of Chicago Press, 2001). This literature is primarily concerned with explaining why welfare states differ. Again, my concerns in this chapter have to do with the consequences of the differences that we observe.

6. While transfers as a percentage of total social spending can be tracked through the 1990s, comprehensive data on public employment in welfare-related services are only available for the early 1980s. The same holds for the data presented in columns 4 and 5. For the sake of consistency, I decided to make 1980 the reference year for all the columns in table 7.2. The basic cross-national differences conveyed by table 7.2 appear to have been quite stable over the 1980s and 1990s. For example, the correlation between transfers in percent of total spending in 1980 and 1996 is .727.

7. Wilensky, *Rich Democracies* (Berkeley: University of California Press, 2002), 256–59.

8. Ibid., 321–30.

9. This point is developed by Walter Korpi and Joakim Palme, "The Strategy of Equality and the Paradox of Redistribution," *American Sociological Review* 63 (1998), 661–87.

10. See Hugh Heclo, *Modern Social Politics in Britain and Sweden* (New Haven: Yale University Press, 1974), ch. 5.

11. Esping-Andersen, *Three Worlds*, 202. On public policies pertaining to families and women's employment, see also Wilensky, *Rich Democracies*, ch. 7; Janet Gornick, Marcia Meyers, and Katherin Ross, "Supporting the Employment of Mothers," *Journal of European Social Policy* 7, no. 1 (1997), 45–70; and Mary Daly, "A Fine Balance," in *Welfare and Work in the Open Economy*, ed. Fritz Scharpf and Vivien Schmidt, vol. 2 (Oxford: Oxford University Press, 2000), 467–510.

12. The classic statement of this view is George Gilder, *Wealth and Poverty* (New York: Basic Books, 1980).

13. This hypothetical illustration is taken from Lane Kenworthy, "Do Social-Welfare Policies Reduce Poverty?" *Social Forces* 77, no. 3 (1999), 1119–39.

14. See Tanzi and Schuknecht, *Public Spending*, for a more elaborate exposition of these arguments and the *Economist*'s 1997 survey of the "Future of the State" (September 20, 1997) for the popularized version of the market-liberal critique of the welfare state.

15. See David Cameron, "The Expansion of the Public Economy: A Comparative Analysis," *American Political Science Review* 72 (1978); Peter Katzenstein, *Small States in World Markets* (Ithaca: Cornell University Press, 1985); Dani Rodrik, *Has Globalization Gone Too Far?* (Washington, DC: Institute for International Economics, 1997); and Geoffrey Garrett, *Partisan Politics in the Global Economy* (New York: Cambridge University Press, 1999).

16. Esping-Andersen, *Why We Need a New Welfare State* (Oxford: Oxford University Press, 2002), ch. 2.

17. George Akerlof and Janet Yellen, "The Fair Wage-Effort Hypothesis and Unemployment," *Quarterly Journal of Economics* 105, no. 2 (1990), 225–83.

18. Peter Lindert, "Does Social Spending Deter Economic Growth?" *Challenge* 39 (May–June 1996), 17–22.

19. Katzenstein, *Small States*.

20. Atkinson, *Economic Consequences of Rolling Back the Welfare State* (Cambridge, MA: MIT Press, 1999), ch. 2.

21. Outliers were identified by serially removing each country from the regression. By using initial levels of social spending rather than growth of social spending, this regression exercise at least partly avoids the problem of endogeneity (social spending as a percentage of GDP being, in part, a function of GDP growth).

22. With different control variables, Wilensky reports very similar findings (*Rich Democracies*, 459–60).

23. "Effects of Ageing Populations on Government Budgets," *OECD Economic Outlook* 57 (June 1995), 25.

24. John Myles and Paul Pierson, "The Comparative Political Economy of Pension Reform," in *The New Politics of the Welfare State*, ed. Pierson (Oxford: Oxford University Press, 2001), 309.

25. Kenworthy, "Do Social-Welfare Policies Reduce Poverty?"

26. Esping-Andersen, "Welfare States without Work," in *Welfare States in Transition*, ed. Esping-Andersen (London: Sage, 1996), 66–87.

27. Jelle Visser and Anton Hemerijck, "*A Dutch Miracle*": *Job Growth, Welfare Reform, and Corporatism in the Netherlands* (Amsterdam: Amsterdam University Press, 1997), 129, 138.

28. For further details, see Philip Manow and Eric Seils, "Adjusting Badly: The German Welfare State, Structural Change, and the Open Economy," in *Welfare and Work in the Open Economy*, ed. Scharpf and Schmidt, vol. 2, 279–84.

29. OECD, *Employment Outlook* (2000), 216, 219. On recent Dutch reforms, see Anton Hemerijck, Brigitte Unger, and Jelle Visser, "How Small Countries Negotiate Change," in *Welfare and Work in the Open Economy*, ed. Sharpf and Schmidt, vol. 2, 218–30; for a broader comparative discussion, see Bernhard Ebbinghaus, "Any Way Out of 'Exit from Work'?" in ibid., 511–53.

30. Manow and Seils, "Adjusting Badly," 294–95.

31. OECD, *Employment Outlook* (2001), 215.

32. Streeck, "High Equality, Low Activity: The Contribution of the Social Welfare System to the Stability of the German Collective Bargaining Regime," *Industrial and Labor Relations Review* 54 (2001), 698–706.

33. Switzerland (70.0%) and Norway (67.1%) do still better than Sweden on this score. OECD, *Employment Outlook* (2001), 213–14.

34. For example, Richard Layard and Stephen Nickell, "Labor Market Institutions and Economic Performance," in *Handbook of Labor Economics*, ed. Orley Ashenfelter and David Card (Amsterdam: Elsevier, 1999), vol. 3C, 3029–84.

35. Stephen Nickell, "Unemployment and Labor Market Rigidities: Europe versus North America," *Journal of Economic Perspectives* 11, no. 3 (1997), 55–74. Taken from a recent paper by James Allen and Lyle Scruggs, the income replacement rates used in figures 7.8 and 7.9 represent the average for two types of unemployment benefit recipients: a fully insured single worker earning the average production worker (APW) wage and a fully insured couple with a single APW and two children. While previous studies have relied on OECD data on gross replacement rates of unemployment insurance, these figures use post-tax income replacement (which is the more appropriate variable from a theoretical point of view). Plotting unemployment and employment rates against gross replacement rates yields essentially the same picture.

36. Ibid., 72.

37. Fritz Scharpf, "Economic Changes, Vulnerabilities, and Institutional Capabilities," in *Welfare and Work in the Open Economy*, ed. Scharpf and Schmidt, vol. 1, 75–82.

38. Ibid., 81–82.

39 See Wilensky, *Rich Democracies*, ch. 10.

Chapter 8. Welfare States in Retrenchment

1. The resilience thesis is argued most forcefully by Paul Pierson, "The New Politics of the Welfare State," *World Politics* 48, no. 2 (1996), 143–79. See also Pierson, *Dismantling the Welfare State?* (New York: Cambridge University Press, 1994); Evelyne Huber and John Stephens, *Development and Crisis of the Welfare State* (Chicago: University of Chicago Press, 2001), chs. 6-7; and Duane Swank, *Global Capital, Political Institutions, and Policy Change in Developed Welfare States* (New York: Cambridge University Press, 2002). For a critique of the resilience thesis, see Richard Clayton and Jonas Pontusson, "Welfare-State Retrenchment Revisited," *World Politics* 51, no. 1 (1998), 67–98. Recent anthologies on the comparative politics of reforming welfare states include Paul Pierson, ed., *The New Politics of the Welfare State* (New York: Oxford University Press, 2001) and Maurizio Ferrera and Martin Rhodes, eds., *Recasting European Welfare States* (London: Frank Cass, 2000).

2. Peter Flora, ed., *Growth to Limits* (Berlin: Walter de Gruyter, 1986).

3. Harold Wilensky, *Rich Democracies* (Berkeley: University of California Press, 2002), ch. 10.

4. This argument is articulated by Bo Rothstein, *Just Institutions Matter* (Cambridge: Cambridge University Press, 1998), ch. 6. On the politics of taxation, see also Sven Steinmo, *Taxation and Democracy* (New Haven: Yale University Press, 1993).

5. Amanda Hughes, "Employment in the Public and Private Sectors," *Employment Gazette* 495 (January 1995), 18; *Välfärd vid vägskäl* (Stockholm: SOU, 2000), 149.

6. See David Rueda and Jonas Pontusson, "Wage Inequality and Varieties of Capitalism," *World Politics* 52 (2000), 350–83, and Janet Gornick and Jerry Jacobs, "Gender, the Welfare State, and Public Employment," Luxembourg Income Study Working Paper no. 168 (1997).

7. See A. B. Atkinson and John Micklewright, "Turning the Screw: Benefits for the Unemployed 1979–88," in *The Economics of Social Security*, ed. Andrew Dilnot and Ian Walker (Oxford: Oxford University Press, 1989), 17–51.

8. Clayton and Pontusson, "Welfare-State Retrenchment Revisited," 91. On the reorientation of British housing policy, see John Hills, "Housing," in *The State of Welfare*, ed, Maria

Evandrou, Howard Glennerster, Hills, and Martin Evans, 2nd ed. (Oxford: Oxford University Press, 1998).

9. This argument is developed further by Lane Kenworthy and Jonas Pontusson, "Rising Inequality and the Politics of Compensatory Redistribution in Affluent Countries," forthcoming in *Perspectives on Politics.*

10. I owe this argument to Frank Castles, "When Politics Matter: Public Expenditure Development in an Era of Economic and Institutional Constraints," Research School of Social Sciences, Australian National University, n.d.

11. On the political implications of the distinction between insiders and outsiders, see David Rueda, "Government Partisanship and Economic Policy" (Ph.D. dissertation, Cornell University, 2001) and "Insider-Outsider Politics in Industrialized Democracies, *American Political Science Review* 99. no. 1 (2005), 61–74.

12. On cuts in minimum pensions compared to cuts in unemployment and sick pay benefits, see Walter Korpi and Joakim Palme, "New Politics and Class Politics in the Context of Austerity and Globalization," *American Political Science Review* 97, no. 3 (2003), 425–46. On pension reforms more broadly, see John Myles and Paul Pierson, "The Comparative Political Economy of Pension Reform," in *The New Politics of the Welfare State,* ed. Pierson, 305–33.

13. Swank, *Global Capital,* ch. 3.

14. This point applies equally to Huber and Stephens, *Development and Crisis,* and Geoffrey Garrett, *Partisan Politics in the Global Economy* (New York: Cambridge University Press, 1998).

15. Swank, *Global Capital,* 119.

16. The best single source on EU social policy and its implications for member states is Stephan Leibfried and Paul Pierson, "Social Policy," in *Policy-Making in the European Union,* ed. Helen Wallace and William Wallace (Oxford: Oxford University Press, 2000).

17. See Garrett, *Partisan Politics,* 60.

18. See Hyeok Yong Kwon, "Voting for Social Protection: The Political Economy of Voter Transition in Comparative Perspective" (Ph.D. dissertation, Cornell University, 2004).

Chapter 9. Directions for Progressive Reform

1. Peter Hall and David Soskice, eds., *Varieties of Capitalism* (Oxford: Oxford University Press, 2000) and Streeck, "Introduction," in *The Origins of Non-Liberal Capitalism,* ed. Streeck and Kozo Yamamura (Ithaca: Cornell University Press, 2001), 1–38.

2. For a convenient inventory of arguments on both sides of this debate, see Ross Levine, "Bank-based or Market-based Financial Systems: Which Is Better?" *Journal of Financial Intermediation* 11 (2002), 398–428.

3. See Soskice, "Divergent Production Regimes," in *Continuity and Change in Contemporary Capitalism,* ed. Herbert Kitschelt, Peter Lange, Gary Marks, and John Stephens (Cambridge: Cambridge University Press, 1999), 101–34.

4. The following summary of recent trends in corporate finance draws extensively on Joseph Foudy, "Shareholder Value and the German and Japanese Models" (Department of Government, Cornell University, 2001) and Mary O'Sullivan, "The Political Economy of Comparative Corporate Governance," *Review of International Political Economy* 10, no. 1 (2003), 23–72.

5. "Survey of European business," *Economist,* April 29, 2000, 8.

6. Ibid., 12.

7. This problem is explored further by Foudy, "Shareholder Value."

8. Soskice, "Divergent Production Regimes."

9. See Paulette Kurzer, *Business and Banking* (Ithaca: Cornell University Press, 1993).

10. For multiple regression results supporting this expectation, see Torsten Persson and Guido Tabellini, "Is Inequality Harmful for Growth?" *American Economic Review* 84, no. 3 (June 1994), 600–621.

11. See George Akerlof and Janet Yellen, "The Fair Wage-Effort Hypothesis and Unemployment," *Quarterly Journal of Economics* 105 (May 1990), 225–83.

12. Esping-Andersen, "A Child-Centred Social Investment Strategy," in *Why We Need a New Welfare State*, ed. Esping-Andersen, Duncan Gallie, Anton Hemerijck, and John Myles (Oxford: Oxford University Press, 2002), ch. 2.

13. Myles, "A New Social Contract for the Elderly?" in ibid., ch. 5.

14. Ibid., 158.

15. Kenworthy, *Egalitarian Capitalism* (New York: Russell Sage Foundation, 2004), ch. 5, and Kenworthy, "Do Affluent Countries Face an Incomes-Jobs Trade-off?" *Comparative Political Studies* 36, no. 10 (2003), 1180–1209.

16. For example, see Hall and Soskice's introduction to *Varieties of Capitalism*. See also Torben Iversen, "Decentralization, Monetarism, and the Social Democratic Welfare State," in *Unions, Employers, and Central Banks*, ed. Iversen, Pontusson, and Soskice (Cambridge: Cambridge University Press, 2000), 205–31.

Index

Ageing population. *See* Elderly and social spending

Akerlof, George, 164

Apprenticeships, 132, 133, 140

Atkinson, Tony, 167

Australia: collective bargaining in, 28; elderly population in, 170; employment growth in, 82; employment rates in, 80; female wage inequality in, 48; literacy rate in, 135, 137; part-time employment in, 49; public investment in education in, 135; public sector employment in, 191; redistribution of income in, 155, 195; social spending in, 184; unionization in, 100; wage inequality in, 45, 51, 55; welfare programs in, 144, 149. *See also* Liberal market economies (LMEs)

Austria: active labor market policy of, 126; egalitarian rating of, 6; employment growth in, 86; employment protection in, 122; employment rates in, 77; immigrant population in, 136; income inequality in, 38; sectoral bargaining in, 102; shareholder vs. stakeholder capitalism in, 22; social spending in, 184; unemployment in, 9, 67, 70; unionization rate in, 99, 100; union membership decline in, 103; wage inequality in, 47. *See also* Social market economies (SMEs)

Banks' role, 21–24, 107–8, 205

Beckett, Katherine, 76

Belgium: active labor market policy of, 126, 127; child poverty in, 161; employment growth in, 82; hours of work in, 11; immigrant population in, 136; literacy rate in, 135; minimum wage in, 60; poverty alleviation in, 157, 158; public sector employment in, 191; redistribution of income in, 155, 195; shareholder vs. stakeholder capitalism in, 21; social spending in, 184–85, 187; unemployment benefits cuts in, 191; unemployment in, 9, 67, 69, 70, 72, 76; unions in, 25, 103; vocational training in, 134; wage inequality in, 46, 47; welfare state of, 27. *See also* Social market economies (SMEs)

Benefits differentiation in welfare states, 150–51

Bernstein, Jared, 33, 35, 41, 42, 44, 54, 57

Blau, Francine, 65, 76, 110, 129, 136

Bond markets' role, 23

Boushey, Heather, 33, 35, 41, 42, 44, 54, 57

Bundesbank, 107, 110–11, 112

Business associations' role, 20, 102

Canada: economic growth in, 208; elderly population in, 170; employment growth in, 82; employment rates in, 81; higher education, growth in, 58; immigration trends in, 59; income inequality in, 38,

Canada (continued)
39; literacy rate in, 137; minimum wage in, 60; public investment in education in, 135; public sector employment in, 85; redistribution of income in, 155, 195; social spending in, 184; unemployment in, 69, 70, 72–73; unskilled workers' employment rates in, 89; wage inequality in, 45, 46, 47, 59; welfare programs in, 144. *See also* Liberal market economies (LMEs)

Capitalism: and economic growth, 2; and inequality, 2; non-liberal capitalism, 204; shareholder vs. stakeholder capitalism, 21–22, 204–5; and social market model, 207; southern European variant of, 28; varieties of, 15–31, 204, 217; and welfare spending, 143

Central banks and coordination of wage bargaining, 107–8

Chambers of commerce, 20, 132

Child poverty, 159, 161–62

Citizenship vs. social insurance in welfare programs, 149–50

CMEs. *See* Coordinated market economies

Codetermination, 114, 115–19

Codetermination Act of 1977 (Sweden), 117

Collective bargaining. *See* Wage bargaining

Collective bargaining agreements, scope of, 25–26, 99–100

Compensatory employment, 54

Continental variant of social market economies, 17; elderly and social spending in, 169; employment protection in, 114; employment rates in, 77; income inequality in, 38–39; industrial employment contractions in, 83; literacy rate in, 135; ownership rights in, 25; service employment growth in, 83; social spending in, 27, 198; unemployment in, 68, 73, 75, 76; unionization rate in, 99–100; union membership decline in, 103; unions in, 25; vocational training in, 115, 139; wage inequality in, 46; welfare programs in, 145, 146–48, 150; women's employment in, 78, 152

Coordinated market economies (CMEs), 18, 20

Coordinated wage bargaining. *See* Wage bargaining

Coordination of business, 20–25; and institutional arrangements, 18, 20

Corporate governance, 205, 207. *See also* Codetermination

Corporate mergers in European Union, 206

Cross-national comparison methods, 28–31

Cross-shareholding, 21, 24, 206

Deeg, Richard, 23

Denmark: active labor market policy of, 126, 127; apprentice programs in, 134; egalitarian rating of, 6; employment growth in, 82, 179; employment rates in, 54, 77, 78; immigrant population in, 136; income inequality in, 40, 54; part-time employment in, 49; redistribution of income in, 195; redistributive impact of welfare programs in, 156; shareholder vs. stakeholder capitalism in, 21; social spending in, 184, 187; unemployment benefits cuts in, 191; unemployment in, 9, 67, 69, 71, 75; unionization rates in, 103; unskilled workers' employment rates in, 89; wage inequality in, 45, 46; welfare programs in, 144. *See also* Social market economies (SMEs)

Deunionization, effect of, 61, 103

Deutsche Gewerkschaftsbund (DGB), 101

Disability insurance, 171–73

Dismissal rights of employees, 119–20

Dunn, Robert, 111

Early retirement, 171, 173–74, 213

East Asian model of capitalism, 28

Economic growth: and capitalist policies, 2; and egalitarian policies, 208; and social spending, 199; stagnation of, 1; in welfare states, 162–71

Economist: on cross-shareholding, 206; on unemployment in United States vs. Europe, 8

Education. *See* Training and education

Efficiency. *See* Equality and efficiency

Elderly and social spending, 168–70, 198, 212–13

Employee participation in corporate decision-making. *See* Codetermination

Employment access, 48–55

Employment growth, 67–94; and ceiling effect, 80; and early retirement, 213; and employment protection, 124, 140; versus equality, 88–91; and high school dropouts, 89; and job creation, 81, 90; in Netherlands, 92–94; rates, 68, 76–81; in services vs. industry, 83–84; in social

market economies, 10, 12, 68, 82, 86, 214; and taxation, 178; and wage inequality, 89–91; in welfare states, 171–79. *See also* Unemployment
Employment security and protection, 119–25; and employment growth, 124, 140; in Japan, 19; reform of, 13, 216; in social market economies, 27, 114, 214
Equality and efficiency, 2, 208–12; effect of institutional arrangements on, 16; and GDP measurement, 11, 210; trade-off between, 4, 13, 208, 209. *See also* Wage inequality
Esping-Andersen, Gøsta, 16, 17, 27, 146, 150, 164, 171, 212
Estevez-Abe, Margarita, 122, 131
Euro, effect of, 96, 109, 110, 200
Europe: causes of unemployment in, 95; economic and monetary union (EMU) in, 110–12; pro-market forces in, 1. *See also specific countries*
European Central Bank (ECB), 111
European Economic Community, formation of, 3
European Union: corporate mergers in, 206; distinguished from "Social Europe," 3; Single Market Program, 206; social policy standards in, 200; unemployment in, 9–10; and works councils, 118

Fairness issues, 211
Family ownership, 24
Family policy: importance of, 212, 218; in welfare states, 151–53
Finland: active labor market policy of, 126, 127; elderly population in, 170; employment growth in, 82, 85; employment rates in, 54, 78; female wage inequality in, 48; immigrant population in, 136; income inequality in, 38, 54; redistribution of income in, 195; social spending in, 183–84; Soviet trade, effect of loss of, 69; training and education in, 27–28; unemployment in, 9, 67, 69–70, 72, 75; unions in, 103; vocational training in, 134; wage inequality in, 45, 47. *See also* Social market economies (SMEs)
Flora, Peter, 186
France: active labor market policy of, 127; categorization of, 17, 28; child poverty in, 161; employment growth in, 82; employment protection in, 119, 125;

employment rates in, 77, 78; health care privatization in, 187; higher education, growth in, 58; hours of work in, 11; income equality in, 38; minimum wage in, 60; redistribution of income in, 195; redistributive impact of welfare programs in, 156; shareholder vs. stakeholder capitalism in, 204–5; social spending in, 184; unemployment in, 9, 69, 70, 72, 75, 76; unions in, 25, 28; women's employment in, 152
Franzese, Robert, 107–8
Freeman, Richard, 57–58
Full employment as public policy goal, 68

Galbraith, James, 56
GDP per capita, comparison of OECD countries, 6, 11, 167, 174, 184, 210
Gender differences. *See* Women
Germany: active labor market policy of, 126, 127; codetermination in, 115–16; coordination of business in, 18; corporate governance in, 207; early retirement in, 173–74; economic difficulties of, 1–2; employment growth in, 82; employment protection in, 19, 119–22; employment rates in, 78; female wage inequality in, 48; higher education, growth in, 58; immigrant population in, 137, 138; immigration trends in, 59; income inequality in, 39, 54; literacy rate in, 135; pattern bargaining in, 111; poverty alleviation in, 158; public sector employment in, 191; redistribution of income in, 155, 195; sectoral bargaining in, 102; shareholder vs. stakeholder capitalism in, 23–24; social spending in, 184; taxation in, 197; temporary employment in, 121; training of skilled workers in, 19, 131, 132, 133, 140, 141; unemployment in, 9, 67, 70–71, 72, 76, 173; unfair dismissal in, 120–21; unification, impact of, 9–10, 71, 96, 110–11, 173, 197; unionization rate in, 99, 100, 101, 105; union membership decline in, 103; wage inequality in, 47, 59; women's employment in, 153; works councils in, 116–19, 120; youth unemployment in, 75–76. *See also* Social market economies (SMEs)
Global Capital, Political Institutions, and Policy Change in Developed Welfare States (Swank), 198

Globalization: of stock ownership, 207; and welfare states, 182, 198–200, 202
Government employees. *See* Public sector employment

Hall, Peter, 107–8
Health care, privatization of, 187–88
Hemerijck, Anton, 73
Higher education, growth rates of, 58–59
Higher-paid and skilled workers: and monopoly power, 56; and wage inequality trends, 58
Hours of work: and employment growth, 82; and GDP per hour, 11, 94; by low-income workers, 54
Household income distribution, 33–43
Huber, Evelyne, 135–36
Hutton, Will, 21

Immigration. *See* Migration trends
Income distribution, 32–66; of household income, 33–43; and wage compression, 8, 63–64. *See also* Wage inequality; *specific countries*
Income taxes, 179, 216
Industry: relative unit labor costs (RULCs) in, 106–7. *See also* Services vs. industry
Inequality. *See* Income distribution; Wage inequality
Inflation and misery index, 108–9
International Adult Literacy Survey, 135, 137
Ireland: active labor market policy of, 127, 129; elderly population in, 170; employment growth in, 82; employment rates in, 77, 78, 81; hours of work in, 11; income equality in, 38, 208; part-time employment in, 49; poverty in, 170; unemployment benefits cuts in, 191; unemployment in, 69, 73, 75, 127; unskilled workers' employment rates in, 89; wage inequality in, 208; welfare programs in, 145, 146, 165, 183, 185; women's employment in, 152. *See also* Liberal market economies (LMEs)
Italy: active labor market policy of, 127; categorization of, 17, 28; employment growth in, 82; employment protection in, 119, 125; employment rates in, 77, 78, 81; health care privatization in, 187; hours of work in, 11; income equality in, 38; public sector employment in, 191; redistributive impact of welfare programs in, 156, 195; shareholders vs.

stakeholders in, 204–5; social spending in, 184; unemployment in, 9, 69, 70, 72, 75, 76; wage inequality in, 46, 57; women's employment in, 152
Iversen, Torben, 122, 131

Japan: categorization of, 17, 18–19; coordination of business in, 18; in East Asian model of capitalism, 28; economic difficulties of, 1–2; employment growth in, 86, 174; employment protection in, 19; employment rates in, 77, 78; female wage inequality in, 48; minimum wage in, 60; shareholder vs. stakeholder capitalism in, 204–5; social spending in, 184; training of skilled workers in, 19, 131; unemployment in, 70; unskilled workers' employment rates in, 89; wage inequality in, 45, 46, 47; welfare programs in, 144, 145

Kahn, Lawrence, 65, 76, 110, 129, 136
Katz, Lawrence, 57–58
Katzenstein, Peter, 16, 17, 165, 198
Kenworthy, Lane, 91, 170, 214

Labor market policies, 114, 125–30. *See also* Training and education
Labor movement. *See* Unions
Landsorganisationen (LO), 63
Lane, Christel, 132
La Porta, Rafael, 24
Layard, Richard, 129
Liberal market economies (LMEs): active labor market policy of, 127, 218; child poverty in, 161; compared to coordinated market economies, 18, 20; compared to social market economies, 3; economic performance of, 4–7; employee participation in, 114; employment growth in, 10, 68, 82, 86–87; employment rates in, 77; hours of work and GDP per hour in, 11; literacy rate in, 135; means-testing, reliance on, 148–49; poverty alleviation in, 157; public investment in education in, 135; public sector employment in, 85; recommendations for, 217–19; service employment growth in, 83; and service sector, 140; shareholder vs. stakeholder capitalism in, 21, 205; unemployment in, 9, 67–68, 70–71, 73, 97, 110; and unionization rate, 99; union membership decline in, 103; wage

bargaining in, 105; wage inequality in, 46, 91; welfare programs in, 150; women's employment in, 78
Literacy skills, 135–38
LMEs. *See* Liberal market economies
Long-term unemployment, 71–73, 76
Lopez-de-Silanes, Florencio, 24
Low-income families: decline in real income of, 1; hours worked and number of working members in, 54
Luxembourg Income Study (LIS), 6, 35–39, 154, 156, 170
Lynch, Lisa, 132–33

Macro-economic issues, 95–113, 214; of coordinated wage bargaining, 113; and social market economies, 13, 212; of unemployment, 96–98
Market-liberal view, 4, 182, 201, 208, 218
Means-tested social assistance, 148–49, 187, 194
Meidner, Rudolf, 63, 64
Metalworkers' Union (IG Metall), 101
Micro-economics and social market economies' weak employment performance, 13
Migration trends, 59, 87; and literacy skills, 136–37
Minimum wage, 4, 59, 215
Misery index, 109
Mishel, Lawrence, 33, 35, 41, 42, 44, 54, 57
Monetary policy and wage bargaining, 107–9
Myles, John, 212, 213

Netherlands: active labor market policy of, 126, 127; collective bargaining approach in, 105; corporate finance in, 207; disability insurance in, 171–73; elderly population in, 170; employment growth in, 10, 48, 49, 54, 82, 92–94, 179; employment protection in, 122; employment rates in, 77, 78, 81; health care privatization in, 187; higher education, growth in, 58; immigrant population in, 137; income inequality in, 38, 39, 41, 54; literacy rate in, 135; minimum wage in, 59; part-time employment in, 49, 92; poverty alleviation in, 158; redistribution of income in, 155, 194, 195; shareholder vs. stakeholder capitalism in, 21; social spending in, 184–85, 187, 195;

unemployment benefits cuts in, 191; unemployment in, 9, 67, 69, 71, 73, 75, 93, 127, 172; unionization rate in, 99, 100; union membership decline in, 103; unions' role in, 92–93, 105; wage inequality in, 45, 47, 48, 51, 57, 93; wage restraint in, 92; welfare programs in, 27, 144, 146–47, 183. *See also* Social market economies (SMEs)
New Zealand: elderly population in, 170; employment growth in, 82, 86; employment rates in, 78, 81; literacy rate in, 135, 137; minimum wage in, 60; poorest of liberal market economies, 6–7; restructuring of welfare state in, 202; social spending in, 184–85; unemployment benefits cuts in, 191; unemployment in, 72, 75; wage inequality in, 47, 57; welfare programs in, 149, 165. *See also* Liberal market economies (LMEs)
Nickell, Stephen, 9, 129, 177, 178
Non-liberal capitalism, 204
Nonprofit organizations' role, 148
Nordic variant of social market economies, 17; apprentice programs in, 133; employment growth in, 82, 85, 86; employment protection in, 114; employment rates in, 77, 79, 80; health care privatization in, 187; immigrant population in, 136; income inequality in, 38–39, 40; literacy rate in, 135; ownership rights in, 24, 25; public investment in education in, 115, 134–35, 139, 140; redistribution of income in, 155; social welfare expenditures of, 27, 202; unemployment in, 69, 178; unionization in, 25, 100, 112–13; and wage compression, 63; wage inequality correlated with employment rates, 89; wage inequality in, 46, 48, 51; welfare programs in, 145, 146–48, 150, 212; white-collar vs. blue-collar unions in, 103–4; women's employment in, 152, 153
Norway: active labor market policy of, 126, 127; economic growth in, 208; employment growth in, 10; employment protection in, 122; employment rates in, 78; hours of work in, 11; income inequality in, 54; part-time employment in, 49; redistribution of income in, 194–95; social spending in, 184; training and education in, 27–28; unemployment

Norway (continued)
in, 9, 67, 69–70, 71, 72, 73, 75;
unionization rates in, 103; vocational
training in, 134; wage inequality in, 47;
wealth of, 6; welfare programs in, 165.
See also Social market economies
(SMEs)
Notification prior to dismissal, 119–20

OECD: dataset on wage distribution,
43–55, 56–57; *Historical Statistics,*
discontinuation of, 84–85, 189; *Labour
Force Statistics,* 189
Okun, Arthur, 4
Olson, Mancur, 100
Overlapping directorships, effect of, 21

Part-time employment, 49–51, 65, 79, 92
Payroll taxes, 178–79, 215–16
Pensions, 151, 168–69, 198, 212–13
Political economy, defined, 15
Poverty alleviation, 156–61, 170–71. *See
also* Welfare states
Prison population and male
unemployment, 76
Privatization of health care, 187–88
Progressive reform. *See* Reform
Public employment services, 125
Public sector employment, 62, 78, 85, 104,
189–91
Public Spending in the Twentieth Century
(Tanzi & Schuknecht), 143

Recession of 1990s: and deceleration of
social spending, 197; and
unemployment rates, 69
Redistributive impact of welfare states,
143–44, 153–62, 194–97
Reform of social market economies,
212–17; reduction of employment
protection, 13, 216; tax reform, 13, 93,
215–16
Rehn, Gùsta, 63, 64
Rehn-Meidner model, 63–64
Relocation subsidies to workers, 125
Retirement. *See* Early retirement; Pensions
Retrenchment of welfare states, 182–203;
indicators of, 187–94; pressures and
politics of, 197–202; redistribution,
consequences for, 194–97

Scharpf, Fritz, 178–79
Schmidt, Reinhard, 23
Schuknecht, Ludger, 143, 162, 167, 181

Services vs. industry: employment growth
in, 83–84; and training, 140, 141; and
union membership, 103
Severance pay, 120
Shareholders: globalization of, 207; legal
rights of, 24; vs. stakeholder capitalism,
21–22, 204–5
Shleifer, Andrei, 24
Siaroff, Alan, 152, 161
Skilled labor and wage inequality, 57
SMEs. *See* Social market economies
Social insurance model, 149–50, 164. *See
also* Welfare states
Social market economies (SMEs): active
labor market policy of, 126–27, 130; and
American style stock market capitalism,
207; child poverty in, 161; compared to
liberal market economies, 3; continental
variant, 17; and coordinated market
economies, 17–20; corporate finance in,
206, 207; distinguishing features of, 17;
economic performance of, 4–7, 12;
education in, 140; employment growth
in, 10, 12, 68, 82, 86, 214; employment
security in, 27, 114, 214; hours of work
and GDP per hour in, 11; means-testing,
reliance on, 148–49; public investment
in education in, 135, 140; public sector
employment in, 85; reform of, 212–17;
sectoral bargaining in, 102; social
spending in, 198; unemployment in, 9,
12, 67, 73, 74, 97, 110; and
unionization rate, 99; wage inequality in,
91; and wage restraint, 8. *See also*
Continental variant of social market
economies; Nordic variant of social
market economies
Social protection, 27
Social spending trends across welfare
states, 183–87
Soskice, David, 16, 17, 18–20, 96–97, 122,
131, 132, 207
Spain: employment protection in, 125;
unemployment in, 9
State of Working America 2002/2003, The
(Mishel, Bernstein, & Boushey), 33
Stephens, John, 135–36
Streeck, Wolfgang, 117–18, 121–22, 131,
174, 204
Swank, Duane, 198, 199
Sweden: active labor market policy of,
125–26, 127; codetermination in,
117–18; collective bargaining in, 102;
decentralization of unions in, 105;

economic growth of, 208; elderly population in, 170; employment growth in, 82, 85; employment rates in, 54, 77; immigrant population in, 136; income inequality in, 38; older workers in, 174; part-time employment in, 49; pension reform in, 151; public sector employment in, 191; redistribution of income in, 155, 195; redistributive impact of welfare programs in, 156; shareholder vs. stakeholder capitalism in, 21; social spending in, 184, 187; training and education in, 27–28; unemployment benefits cuts in, 191; unemployment in, 67, 69–70, 75; unions in, 25, 63, 64, 103; unskilled workers' employment rates in, 89; vocational training in, 134; and wage compression, 63; wage inequality in, 45, 47, 51, 54, 57, 215; welfare programs in, 144, 146–47, 203; women's employment in, 153. *See also* Social market economies (SMEs)

Switzerland: active labor market policy of, 126; egalitarian rating of, 6; employment growth in, 82; employment protection in, 27; employment rates in, 77; immigration trends in, 59; income equality in, 38; income inequality in, 54; literacy rate in, 135, 137; redistribution of income in, 155, 195; redistributive impact of welfare programs in, 156; social spending in, 184; unemployment in, 9, 67, 70, 97; unionization rate in, 100; union membership decline in, 103; unskilled workers' employment rates in, 89; wage inequality in, 46, 47, 59; welfare programs in, 144, 146, 185. *See also* Social market economies (SMEs)

Tanzi, Vito, 143, 162, 167, 181

Taxation: consumption taxes and employment rates, 178–79; payroll taxes, 178–79, 215–16; and redistribution of income, 155–56; in welfare states, 144, 163, 197. *See also* Tax reform

Tax reform: compensating workers for wage restraint through, 93; shifting from payroll taxes to income taxes to finance public welfare programs, 179, 216; in social market economies, 13

Temporary employment, 121

Thatcher, Margaret, 1, 193

Three Worlds of Welfare Capitalism, The (Esping-Andersen), 146

Trade associations' role, 20

Trades Union Congress (TUC), 101

Training and education, 8, 130–40; Japanese and German approach to, 19, 131, 132, 133; literacy skills, 135–37; and "low-skills trap," 131; public investment in, 115, 132, 134–35, 139, 140, 141, 144, 212, 218; in Rehn-Meidner model, 64; retraining in Sweden, 125; vocational training in Europe, 75–76

Transfer payments, 27, 146–48

Tyrell, Marcel, 23

Unemployment, 69–76; among women, youth, and unskilled workers, 74–75; benefits contingent on job search, 178; benefits cuts from 1985 to 1999, 191–93, 216; and disability insurance or early retirement, 171–73; effect on social market economies, 12, 67; European Union vs. U.S., 8–9; and generosity of benefits, 175–77; income support for, effect of, 54; and labor market policy, 128; long-term, 71–73, 76; macro-economic dimension of, 96–98; and misery index, 109; and part-time employees, 52; political repercussions of, 110; in social vs. liberal market economies, 67; Soskice's approach to, 96–97; subtracting current account balances from actual rates of, 97; and wage inequality, 56–57

Unions: and apprenticeships, 132; centralization in, 102, 104; employer associations bargaining with, 20, 102; public sector, 104; sectoral bargaining, 102; and wage compression, 60–61, 63–64, 85; and wage restraint, 3, 59, 98–103, 215; and welfare states, 25–28. *See also* Wage bargaining

United Kingdom: child poverty in, 161; corporate ownership in, 24; elderly population in, 170; employment growth in, 10, 86; employment rates in, 78; health care privatization in, 188; household earnings inequality in, 55; income inequality in, 38, 39; public sector employment in, 85, 190–91; redistribution of income in, 155; restructuring of welfare state in, 202; social spending in, 27, 28, 184;

United Kingdom (continued)
unemployment compensation cuts in, 192–93; unemployment in, 75; unionization rate in, 101; wage inequality in, 45, 46, 57. *See also* Liberal market economies (LMEs)
United States: egalitarian rating of, 6; elderly population in, 170; employment growth in, 82, 87; employment protection in, 119; employment rates in, 77, 78; government employees, decline in, 62; higher education, decline in, 58; hours of work in, 11; household earnings inequality in, 55; immigrant population in, 136; inequality in household income in, 33–35, 38, 41; inequality vs. efficiency in, 208, 211; literacy rate in, 135; minimum wage in, 59; part-time employment in, 49; poverty rate in, 156–57, 170; public investment in education in, 134–35; recommendations for, 217; redistribution of income in, 155, 195; redistributive impact of welfare programs in, 156; severance pay in, 120; shareholder vs. stakeholder capitalism in, 21, 22, 23; social spending in, 184–85; social welfare provision comparison, 3; unemployment benefits cuts in, 191; unemployment in, 9, 69, 71, 72, 73, 75, 76, 97; unions in, 25, 59, 61–62; unskilled workers' employment rates in, 89; wage inequality in, 45, 46, 47, 57, 61; welfare programs in, 144, 145, 165; women's employment in, 153. *See also* Liberal market economies (LMEs)
Unskilled workers: demand for, 88–89; and employment protection, 123; high school dropouts' employment rate, 89; literacy rate among, 135; and unemployment, 74–75, 93

Varieties of Capitalism School, 17–20, 204. *See also* Soskice, David
Vishny, Robert, 24
Visser, Jelle, 73
Vocational training. *See* Training and education

Wage bargaining, 95–113; coordinated bargaining, 96, 103–7, 111, 113; decentralization of, 104–5; and egalitarian distribution of wages, 2,

215;and monetary policy, 107–9. *See also* Unions
Wage compression, 8, 63–64, 82, 85, 164, 214, 215
Wage inequality, 43–48; and literacy rate, 135; part-time vs. full-time employees, 49–51; trade off with employment rates, 89–91; trends in, 32–33, 55–64, 65, 215. *See also* Minimum wage; *specific countries*
Wage restraint: and Dutch jobs miracle, 92; and social market economies, 8, 95–96; and tax reform, 93; and unions, 3, 59, 98–103, 215. *See also* Wage bargaining
Welfare states, 142–81; benefits differentiation in, 150–51; citizenship vs. social insurance in, 149–50; comparison with United States, 3; and economic growth, 162–71; elderly and social spending in, 168–70; and employment, 171–79; family policy in, 151–53; and globalization, 182, 198–200, 202; means-tested programs, 148–49, 187, 194; pressures and politics of retrenchment, 197–202; redistributive impact of, 143–44, 153–62, 194–97; regimes of, 146–53; retrenchment of, 182–203; size of, 144–46; social spending trends, 144–46, 183–87; and taxation, 144, 163, 197; transfers vs. services in, 27, 146–48; and unemployment, 110; and unions, 25–28; universalism of social welfare, 218; women's employment in, 151–53
Western, Bruce, 76
Wilensky, Harold, 148
Women: in Dutch jobs miracle, 93; employment in welfare states, 151–53; employment rates of, 77, 78–79; entry into workforce, effect of, 57, 93, 212, 218; part-time employment of, 79; and unemployment, 74–75; wage ratios by gender, 44, 47–48, 65
Worker participation schemes, effect of, 8
Works Constitution Act of 1972 (Germany), 116
Works councils, 115–19; and apprentice programs, 132; and employment security, 120

Yellen, Janet, 164
Youth: entry into labor force, 79; and unemployment, 74–75

Zysman, John, 20–21